A significant contribution to the history of religion in the United States, this book traces fully and critically an important aspect of American Protestantism. In celebration of the 200th anniversary of the Church of Christ in Yale, Professor Gabriel examines religion, the liberal arts, and student life as the College and University have known them from 1757 to 1957—pursuing their interrelationships and setting them against American social and literary history.

He recalls vividly the many conflicts and crises that are part of his story and the long roster of students, professors, chaplains, and presidents that figure in it. Beyond these, however, he has set forth Yale's role in the history of religion in the United States and religion's role in the history of the liberal arts program at Yale. Illustrated.

Mr. Gabriel, Sterling Professor of History at Yale, has been a member of his department since 1915. Formerly general editor of the Pageant of America series, he is the author of *Course of American Democratic Thought*. For the past five years he has served as president of the New Haven Colony Historical Association.

Religion and Learning at Yale

*The Church of Christ in the
College and University, 1757–1957*

RELIGION AND LEARNING AT YALE

The Church of Christ in the College and University, 1757-1957

BY RALPH HENRY GABRIEL

New Haven, *Yale University Press, 1958*

To *R.T.G.*, *J.C.G.*, and *S.G.C.*
For each of whom the chapel has special memories.

Preface

This book began at a lunch at Mory's. A committee of the University Church asked me to join them. Charles Seymour, Liston Pope, and my classmate Sidney Lovett explained the desire of the Church that a history be written. They pointed out that, from the beginning, the Church of Christ in Yale University had been a unique organization in that it was and is a parish church set in the midst of an institution of higher learning. Moreover, in 1957 the Church would enter its third century. But I undertook the assignment with the understanding that the study would be wider than a mere presentation of ecclesiastical annals. Hence the title *Religion and Learning at Yale*.

President Thomas Clap created the Church in a time of religious controversy. Ezra Stiles led it through the years when the influence of the rationalism of the eighteenth-century Enlightenment was at its height. At the turn of the nineteenth century President Timothy Dwight led what has been called the Second Great Awakening in Connecticut. Though theology changed and new religious outlooks appeared, the College Church remained for a century after the death of Dwight a significant center of American Protestantism. In this book I have looked upon the changes in religion as expressed in the Yale chapel as an important aspect of the larger history of Protestantism in the United States. In all the chapters I have used the words of the chief figures in the story and with the original spelling and punctuation in order that the twentieth-century reader may be helped to come into immediate contact with their thoughts and moods.

I have not attempted to write a history of the Yale Divinity School. Roland Bainton has told that story. I have, however, insofar as the evidence permitted, attempted to assess the impact of the religion of the Church upon the life of the Yale community. This task has made necessary some account of changing undergraduate life.

The chief peculiarity that sets off the Yale institution from a normal parish church has been its presence from the beginning in an institution of higher learning and, in particular, in a liberal arts college. If religion changed through the centuries, an understanding of the nature and an appreciation of the importance of the liberal arts has grown also. The long record of religion and learning at Yale is the story of the unfolding of two distinct yet related credos. The chapel has taught faith in God. A humanistic faith has supported and inspired the protagonists of the liberal arts—the faith that the cultivation of the disciplines in that area of learning enlarges and enriches the life of the individual. The history of religion and learning at Yale includes also the narrative of two separate yet related ethical codes. Thomas Clap in the spirit of the Middle Ages made theology the queen of the arts and sciences and attempted to subordinate learning to the purposes of religion. He gave a narrow and sectarian interpretation to the injunction: seek ye first the Kingdom of God. The liberal arts, however, rest on scholarship; and scholarship, in turn, depends upon an ethical code that brooks no violation. The code includes freedom to pursue truth wherever the inquiry may lead, honesty on the part of the investigator in reporting his discoveries, and responsible cooperation with his fellow workers in what is, in effect, the social process of acquiring new knowledge. The code of religion comes to focus in worship; that of scholarship is powered by the conviction that knowledge is an end in itself. The history of Christianity in the West contains a long record of collisions between ecclesiastics defending what they interpreted as the interest of religion and scholars whose labors were inspired by the faith and disciplined by the code of their calling. The story of religion and learning at Yale has its own examples of collision and conflict. It contains also a long record of partnership among men who have believed that the good life can only be achieved when the two complement and supplement one another.

Through more than two and a half centuries Yale has contributed significantly to an evolving American civilization. From the beginning of this narrative I have attempted to deal with the College and the University against the background of American culture and as an institution in a larger society.

In the spring of 1932 the Corporation appointed the Rev. Sidney Lovett chaplain of the University. He was still chaplain when this book was written. Because a friendship continuing through more than forty years must color any attempt on my part to appraise his pastorate, I have concluded the detailed narrative of this book with the year in which he took office, and have dealt only in general terms with religion and learning in those years after 1932 in which the University and the Church, carrying on in its midst, both achieved maturity.

I record gratefully my indebtedness to many persons. Mrs. John Schroeder gave her full time for a year as assistant in research. Through her diligence, care, and perceptiveness she has contributed fundamentally to the volume. Sydney Ahlstrom, Liston Pope, Charles Seymour, and Frederick W. Hilles have read critically the entire manuscript and have given much aid. Edmund S. Morgan contributed much to the chapters through the administration of Ezra Stiles. Miss Jane W. Hill and Hollon A. Farr of the Yale Memorabilia Room never flagged in giving help and suggestions. Marshall Bartholomew generously gave of his great knowledge of the history of music at Yale. Gordon Kenefick of Sterling Library permitted me to transport a scandalous number of books for use in England. My son-in-law and daughter, Keith and Susan Cunliffe gave me during a sabbatical a place to work in their home at Bury

St. Edmunds. Clarence W. Mendell, Henry Knox Sherrill, and Morgan P. Noyes have granted permission to quote from important letters they wrote to President Angell. For assistance of many kinds and for continuous support of the project my profound thanks go to C.D.G. Finally it is a pleasure to acknowledge the help received from those two volumes in which George Wilson Pierson has narrated with charm and full detail the story of Yale College and its faculty from the inauguration of President Porter to the retirement of President Angell.

R.H.G.

Trumbull College
June 1957

Contents

Chapter I. 1757

On July 3, 1757, a Sabbath quiet lay over the small but growing town of New Haven beside Long Island Sound. The weekday clatter that arose from moving goods and ships' stores on the long wharf had ceased. Owners had closed the doors of the warehouses at the head of the harbor and of the shops near by. No travelers either for business or pleasure journeyed on the unpaved highways leading out into the country. Citizens esteemed travel on the Sabbath a sin; the authorities of the college west of the common had disciplined an undergraduate who, returning from home, had traveled with a pack on his back from Wallingford to New Haven on Sunday. The Puritan Sabbath was a community ritual, the most important symbol of the Calvinist faith, reminding men, women, and children of the duties of obedience and worship they owed to their Creator.

When the church bells rang, people came out of their houses, mostly near the water front but some scattered sparsely in the neighborhood of the common land called the Green. Leading citizens were dressed in the formal wigs and short clothes of the eighteenth century, the common people more simply. Children, subdued not only by much washing and brushing but by the solemnity of the day, accompanied their parents. On July 3, many families, but not all, walked across the Green to the weather-beaten and poorly provided meeting house of the First Ecclesiastical Society that stood in the center of the common beside a burying ground. The building lacked distinction and its furnishings recalled the poverty of the town at the time when it was erected. Early in the next century it would be replaced by a Georgian church that through subsequent decades would be treasured as one of the most beautiful buildings of old America.

To the meeting house on that first Sunday in July walked the minister, the Reverend Joseph Noyes, now advanced in years. More than age, however, gave him dignity. As a minister of the established church of the colony and so a member of the "standing order," he ranked with the greatest in the town. In addition he had long sat with that small company of Congregational clergymen which had been constituted by the law of Connecticut the Corporation of Yale College. Perhaps on this particular Sabbath the Reverend Mr. Noyes remembered the troubles of the recent past that had split his parish and had brought a new church society into being. During the years of his ministry Joseph Noyes had moved perceptibly away from the hard doctrines of an uncompromising Calvinism. When conservatives in his flock had expressed their dissatisfaction, he had stood fast, refusing to change his convictions for any man. So a schism had occurred. From the steps of the meeting house of the First Church the minister could look northward to the bold, red cliffs of East Rock rising in the distance above farm land and salt meadows. Perhaps the prospect gave him strength as the hills of another land had once given fortitude to the Psalmist. On this July Sunday, Joseph Noyes needed strength.

Activities running through more than three years had preceded the events of July 3. President Thomas Clap of Yale had grown dissatisfied with the preaching of Mr. Noyes. The minister had directed his sermons—simple, moralistic, and dull —primarily to the instruction of his flock in man's duties to his brothers. Almost never did the pastor of the First Church expound those robust doctrines of original sin and of the majesty and justice of God that had so long given power to Calvinism. The congregation seldom got a glimpse into the fiery pit. The President, listening in his pew, had come to consider the spiritual sustenance provided by Mr. Noyes to be a watery porridge, inadequate for the needs of the spirited young men

whom parents had put in the charge of the College. Moreover,
the function of the College was to train ministers. Should Yale
send out from its halls preachers trained only in the platitudes
of Mr. Noyes? In September 1755 the Corporation, urged by
the President, had invited the Reverend Naphtali Daggett, then
preaching at Smithtown, Long Island, to come to New Haven
for conference and trial. A few months later the Corporation
had appointed him Professor of Divinity, the first professorship
in the history of the institution. Because the College community
was part of the parish of the First Church, Mr. Daggett had
shared its pulpit with Mr. Noyes. But the arrangement had
proved unsatisfactory. Three tutors of the College, a resident
graduate, and eight members of the student body had drawn
up, signed, and presented to the Corporation a petition that
set forth their desire "to attend the ordinance of the Lord's
Supper under the administration of the Rev. Professor and to
walk together in stated Christian communion." On June 29,
1757, the Corporation had granted the request.

As the aging pastor of the First Church on that last Sunday
in June looked down on the seats once occupied by undergraduates, he knew the young men would never come back.
For a second time within his parish schism had occurred. Perhaps, as Joseph Noyes preached that day, he saw dark looks on
the faces of some of his congregation. Subsequent events were
to demonstrate that there were Puritans not only in New Haven
but beyond its borders who would not stand idly by at a time
when, as they thought, Yale College challenged the rights and
the authority of a venerable church whose history ran back
one hundred twenty-nine years.

On a summer Thursday, June 30, 1757, the ringing of the bell
called undergraduates and tutors to the large hall of the building that stood at the corner of the yard made by the intersection
of College and Chapel streets. This original building, called
Yale College, was a pretentious wooden structure, long, high,
and narrow. It looked awkward and ungainly as it stood be-

side the new brick edifice of the Georgian style recently completed and called Connecticut Hall. The large room where the
members of the College assembled served as a dining hall
and for academic exercises. Its windows looked out upon
the broad village common and upon Joseph Noyes' church.
Connecticut Hall, considered by some at the time to be the
finest building in the province, heralded better days. Perhaps,
however, the college authorities, even as they took satisfaction
in the new dormitory, recognized a certain appropriateness in
a bare room as a place in which to found a church. They held
an austere faith. The tradition in which they lived rejected
icons and the conventions of formal ritual. They believed that
men, endowed with immortal souls, deal face to face with God.
They read literally the text: "Where two or three are gathered
in my name, there am I in the midst of them." In this faith
they called into being the first college church in America.

The undergraduates trooped into the College Hall and took
their places behind the tutors and the President. The Professor
of Divinity pronounced a sermon from a text in St. Matthew:
"Ye are the light of the world. A city that is set on a hill cannot
be hid." When the preacher had finished, President Clap rose
to make an official pronouncement.

Thomas Clap had the dignity that comes from learning and
from authority. As president of Yale he was one of the first
men of the colony. He had carefully prepared what he was
about to say, weighing each word with the solicitude of a
lawyer writing a brief. The statement disclosed a man of im-
perious will who drove without deviation to his objective. He
well knew that in Connecticut, in conformity with a practice
established in 1708 and set down in what was called the Saybrook Platform, regional consociations of ministers governed
the affairs of the established church. The President had not seen
fit to lay his proposed action before the consociation in whose
jurisdiction it would properly fall. In his opinion the peculiar
character of Yale College gave him authority enough. As the

colleges of Oxford and Cambridge had in the beginning been religious establishments, so Yale had been founded as a religious institution by a group of Connecticut clergymen. These founders had created it as a seminary to preserve and to propagate the faith brought to America by Winthrop, Cotton, Hooker, and Davenport. Thomas Clap labored earnestly in that tradition.

Naphtali Daggett faced the President. The young men gathered in the College Hall watched with interest what they understood to be an historic occasion. "Reverend Sir," said the President addressing the Professor of Divinity, "You having been formally ordained a Minister of our Lord Jesus Christ, with Power to administer all the Ordinances of the Gospel, and having been since introduced into a special, sacred Office-Relation to this Ecclesiastical Society:—and there now appearing a sufficient Number of qualified Subjects, desirous to have the Sacred Ordinances administered to them in this place; We, the President and Fellows of this College, being a Number of Ministers especially delegated to have the oversight and Government of this sacred School, do approve your administering all the Ordinances of the Gospel, to the Members of this Society, who are Subjects qualified for them; depending upon it, that you will do it with the utmost care and Fidelity, according to the Institution of our Lord Jesus Christ." In the establishment of the College Church the President and Fellows had replaced the consociation.

Thomas Clap turned and addressed the tutors and the young men who had drawn up and signed the petition. These were the first members of the College Church. "We approve of your Confederation . . . and your acting as the Brethren of a particular Church, under the Administration of the Rev'd Professor of Divinity, and the Inspection of this venerable Corporation. . . . And as you make a distinguishing Profession of Religion beyond others, so let your Lives and Conversation be in a peculiar Manner holy and exemplary;—your light ought to shine with a peculiar Lustre in this Fountain of Light and Knowledge, that others, beholding your good Conversation, may glorify your Father which is in Heaven. And let all the Members of this Society of Religion and Learning, by having the Ordinances brought near to them, be put in a serious Frame of mind, to search their Hearts, and examine into the State of their Souls, and earnestly endeavor after those Qualifications, which are necessary to your enjoying Communion with God, both in this World, and that which is to come."[1]

The young men tramped out of the hall. On Sunday, July 3, Naphtali Daggett administered for the first time to the Yale church the sacrament of the Lord's Supper.

The world which Daggett in his first sermon in the College Church exhorted the undergraduates to illuminate stirred in 1757 with momentous events. News of these, however, came somewhat tardily to the cloistered academic community set on the eastern margin of a vast continent that was still, for the most part, wilderness. But communication with life beyond the college yard had been improved two years before by the establishment of the first post office in New Haven. As President Clap spoke in the College Hall on that June Sunday, scarcely two hundred miles to the northwest an army struggled southward through the forest beside Lake Champlain. General Montcalm with some regiments of French regulars and a band of Indian braves was advancing from Montreal with the purpose of pushing back the frontier of British North America. Barely more than a month after the founding of the College Church a tale of tragedy came out of the north woods. The French had struck and captured Fort William Henry at the north end of Lake George. Ineptitude in the British high command had left the outpost undermanned. When the British prisoners of war had moved out under French escort to retire to Fort Edward on the Hudson, Montcalm's Indians had fallen on the column and had killed or taken captive hundreds of the luckless, defeated soldiers. Throughout New England the news deepened the old bitterness toward the Catholic French of the St. Lawrence valley and spread dismay at British fumbling. But in this very year of disaster the tide turned when the king recalled William Pitt to be prime minister and to take over direction of the war.

The year, 1757, was a time of transition. New outlooks contending with old habits brought both life and, sometimes, confusion to the colony of Connecticut disturbed by new trends in religious thinking. President Clap established the College Church to implement and further a sectarian position. Even as the President achieved his goal, Benjamin Franklin sailed for England to be agent at the imperial capital for the disgruntled colony of Pennsylvania. Three years before the first citizen of Philadelphia undertook this—his first—diplomatic mission, Yale, honoring learning, had bestowed on him the degree of Master of Arts in recognition of his contributions to scientific knowledge through his work in electricity. In that same year, 1754, Jonathan Edwards, graduate of Yale, laboring in virtual exile in a frontier mission station at Stockbridge, Massachusetts, published *Freedom of the Will*. The essay not only revived powerfully the vitality of a flagging Calvinism but established its author as a philosopher and theologian of the first order. On September 26, 1757, seven weeks after Naphtali Daggett preached the first sermon in the College Church, the College of New Jersey, recently removed to Princeton, elected Edwards its president. A few months later he died of an inoculation for smallpox.

Across the Atlantic, civilization in England in 1757 enjoyed a brilliant flowering. It was the age of Johnson and Garrick, of Hume, Smollett, and Hogarth. In this England in the summer of 1757 a fourteen year old lad was completing at the grammar school at Giggleswick, Yorkshire, his preparation for the university. His father was master of the school. In 1758 the boy went up to Cambridge, the university of Isaac Newton and John Milton. He became a member of Christ College, where he made a brilliant record. The young man's name was William Paley. In the nineteenth century more than fifty Yale classes were to struggle through his formidable opus in preparation for their meetings with their instructors.

Chapter 2. An Embattled Puritan

In November 1739, eighteen years before the founding of the College Church, two men rode on horseback out of New Haven, taking a road that led into the interior of the colony. Occasional splotches of late autumn color decorated the wood-lots standing between the fields of snug farms. The party crossed the broad Connecticut River by ferry. Their journey ended, on November 12, at Thomas Clap's house in Wind-ham. The minister, aged thirty-seven, met them. He played the host alone, for his wife had recently died, an event that had sadly shaken him. Before the open fire that kept out the November chill he listened to the message of the visitors. They told him that the rector of the Collegiate School at New Haven had resigned. The nine ministers who held the office of trustees, meeting on October 31, had chosen him as rector. Would he accept? After hearing the account of the condition of the school given by the committee and of the opportunities for service it offered, the Reverend Mr. Clap made up his mind. He would accept if the consociation of ministers within whose jurisdiction Windham fell would release him from his local responsibility.

Windham was a country parish of some eight hundred souls. Its life typified that throughout most of the colony. John Greenleaf Whittier was later to draw in *Snowbound* a romantic picture of the New England farm family. Thomas Clap, hard-working pastor, knew the other side of the coin. In Windham, where virtually every man knew personally the whole com-munity and where families lived neighbor to one another to the second and third generation, the old Adam in human nature was sufficiently exposed to provide the town with its most interesting topics of conversation. Mr. Clap dealt professionally and single-handed with original sin. He spoke, however, with authority. As a Congregational clergyman he represented in his parish an established church. The laws of the colony supported this church and provided for the financial support of its clergy. These came to be called "the standing order," whose influence and power in Connecticut was second only to that of government itself.

Learning, as well as official position, however, set the Puritan minister of the seventeenth and early eighteenth centuries apart from the mass of his people. Clap had graduated from Harvard in 1722 at the age of nineteen, two years after the brilliant Edwards had finished his course in the Collegiate School at New Haven. Two postgraduate years in the study of divinity completed Clap's preparation for his life's work. In these years he had mastered the tough and uncompromising doctrines of John Calvin, delineating the indubitable picture of that supernatural world of such infinite consequence for the souls of men. In Windham, Clap earnestly taught the people the essentials of old truth. At a time when Puritanism was tending to fall into a cold formalism Clap was not numbered among the considerable company of unprofitable shepherds. He exchanged views by correspondence with dynamic colleagues as far away as Boston and Northampton. In the latter town in the 1730's the preaching of Jonathan Edwards had ignited a conflagration, called the Great Awakening, that swept through the Connecticut valley. Clap cautiously welcomed the quickening of religious interest that followed Edwards' work. The Windham pastor did not permit the dull routine and the narrow horizons of a country town to stifle the intellectual activities begun at Harvard.

News reached New Haven that the Windham preacher was not only a defender of the strictest Calvinism but also that, when occasion required, he could deal vigorously with the unrepentant sinner in his flock. When the report of such virtues came to the ears of the trustees of the Collegiate School they ended their search for a new rector. As soon as he could after the Trustees' committee had returned to the Quinnipiac valley, Thomas Clap, with the approval of the consocation, wound up his parish affairs. In due time he rode to New Haven. Without ceremony or fanfare he took over the direction of the Collegiate School.

No doubt when Clap and the undergraduates faced one another for the first time in the College Hall, each party eyed the other for clues as to what the future might bring forth. In one sense the rector was the school itself. With the assistance of two or three tutors chosen from recent graduates he carried the burden of instruction. He, with his young assistants, undertook to maintain order and decorum in the institution. The rector assumed a responsibility not to be lightly undertaken. Perhaps Thomas Clap, as he looked into the faces of the assembled young American colonials, did not comprehend at first that they also thought of themselves as the school. Most of them came from the farms and villages of Connecticut but some had ridden to New Haven from beyond the boundaries of the province. In costume and in mental outlook they reflected the eighteenth century, though with a style peculiar to Connecticut. They took monarchy for granted and were loyal to a king few of them ever expected to see. But they lived in a little republic whose legislature and governor were elected and whose surprisingly liberal charter was a virtual constitution. Perhaps half of them planned to become ministers in an age when the clergy stood first in prestige among the members of professions. The ministers held their high place because religion was important in Connecticut life. Moreover, no young man aspired to the status and responsibility of a clergyman without a genuine faith, for ambition without faith was blasphemy. The vigorous life of a thriving colony stirred in the little company of boys and young men who assembled in the College Hall to see and hear the new rector. If they were to learn that

Thomas Clap intended to govern with a firm hand, he also was one day to discover that undergraduates had ideas of their own and a will to take a hand in shaping their own destinies.

Yale had entered its fortieth year when Clapp took over its management. He found the Collegiate School, though supported by the General Assembly, inadequately developed. As soon as he had settled into his new routine, he prepared with meticulous care in 1742 the first catalogue of the 2,600 volumes in the college library, an excellent collection. In the preface of the published catalogue that appeared in the following year he set down his ideas regarding a proper curriculum. "In the First Year to study principally the Tongues, Arithmetic, and Algebra; the Second Logic, Rhetoric, and Geometry; the Third, Mathematics and Natural Philosophy; and the Fourth Ethics and Divinity." At Harvard Clap had discovered an interest in mathematics that never left him. In 1751 he introduced Declamations into the course of study. The final sentence of the preface, however, set forth the goal that for Clap transcended all others: "Above all have an Eye to the great End of all your Studies, which is to obtain the Clearest Conceptions of Divine things and to lead you to a Saving Knowledge of God in his Son Jesus Christ." Perhaps the new rector felt the warning to be of particular importance at the time he made it. Even as he took up his duties in New Haven he sensed that a trying period in the history of the colony had opened. In 1740 when he first entered the building called Yale College to take up his duties as rector, danger of the most serious kind threatened the established churches of Connecticut.

To understand the problems facing Rector Clap in 1740 it is necessary to recall an age in which knowledge of science, elementary at best, had significance only for the small minority of educated men. The mass of the subjects of the king in Connecticut, though many rendered no more than lip service to religion, still thought in terms of two worlds: the mundane cycle of birth, marriage, and death, and that supernatural world of spirits and angels, good and bad, and of Heaven and Hell.

It was a late phase of that Age of Faith that had its climax in the Middle Ages.

A closer look at the lives of the Connecticut people of the 1730's and 1740's reveals a situation hard for a twentieth-century person to visualize. Most of the families lived on farms or in small country villages, their geographical horizons those of the township, for only seldom did the husbandman or villager venture any great distance abroad. They had their corn huskings and occasional other frolics, but Puritanism sanctified work and discountenanced frivolity. No newspapers enabled the men and women to follow the drama of events in a broader world. They had no music beyond untutored psalm singing in the meeting house and remembered ballads and folk songs from England and Scotland. No developed sports, either individual or organized, gave them the thrill of friendly competition. For most of them no literature of novel or drama enriched the imagination or stirred the emotions. For the Puritan the Bible provided literature enough. Magnificent though its varied resources are, it did not and could not provide fully for the needs of a vigorous people bred of a sound stock. The conditions of their lives starved their imaginations and constricted their emotions. The preacher's expositions of theology on Sunday provided them with their chief intellectual sustenance. Divisions in matters of belief or of the management of the affairs of the churches led to the most important diversities and to the most acrimonious party differences. The little company of instructors and students at the Collegiate School, though they ventured farther than most of their contemporaries in the world of thought, were confined within the limitations of the place and time. In such a world at Northampton in Massachusetts Jonathan Edwards in the 1730's unwittingly touched off an explosion in the Connecticut valley. It marked the beginning in New England of the Great Awakening.

A mystical experience while he was still an undergraduate at Yale conditioned ever afterward Edwards' Calvinism. As he walked one day in a beautiful countryside he felt, as he had never done before, the overpowering majesty, beauty, and goodness of the infinite God. He experienced an ineffable joy in surrendering his being and submerging it in the Divine Spirit. So for Edwards, one of the most brilliant minds of the eighteenth century, Calvinism became, first and foremost, a religion of the heart, a heart transformed by Divine Grace. In Edwards' thought that old word "conversion," which had come to mean little more than formal acceptance of Christian teaching, became charged with emotion. When in the 1730's Edwards tried to communicate from the pulpit his feelings as well as his thoughts to men and women whose lives were narrow and bleak, he loosed an emotional upsurge that spread through the Connecticut valley as a fire runs through a dry forest. The preacher deplored the hysterical excesses that appeared in the revival. He turned to the intellectual task of renovating, developing, and reinvigorating in the light of new knowledge and new experience that old system of theology he had studied as a boy in dry-as-dust Wollebius at Yale. But Edwards only reinterpreted, he did not deny, the divine determinism taught by Calvin. He found no place for the concept of the freedom of the will.

In 1740 Thomas Clap, busy at Yale with teaching and administrative duties, learned that George Whitefield, powerful evangelist who had come northward from Georgia, had entered Connecticut. Whitefield, a product of the great Wesley revival movement in England, brought to New England the second phase of the Great Awakening. In Connecticut crowds flocked to hear him whenever he preached. His meetings were exciting, made so by that emotionalism called at the time "enthusiasm." Whitefield preached a conservative theology. He called upon his hearers to repent and to pray for that experience of conversion without which they could not be saved. He preached in New Haven and visited Yale.

Thomas Clap had not yet established his position at the Collegiate School when he found himself in a midst of a hurricane. The undergraduates had seized ardently upon the new doctrines of freedom and emotional conversion taught not only by Whitefield but soon by itinerant imitators of the evangelist. These sometimes turned out to be uneducated men who preached a militant anti-intellectualism that affirmed the supremacy of emotion and jeered at the pretensions of those who insisted that only through learning and the vigorous logic of a trained mind could men hope to understand the mysteries of God. In 1745 in a published letter to a friend in Boston, Clap described the conditions he had been facing for nearly half a decade at Yale: "it is notorious to the world," he wrote, "that Mr. *Whitefield* and other *itinerants* did endeavor to persuade People, that the generality of the Ministers were *unconverted,* Pharisee Teachers, &c. and that all *unconverted* persons were *half Beasts* and *half Devils,* and could no more be the *Means* of any Man's conversion, than *a dead man could beget a living child;* from whence it necessarily followed, that People ought to *discard* them, as accordingly they did, in a short Time, in a multitude of places in the *Country,* especially in Connecticut." It requires little imagination to visualize the kind of neighborhood fights that such preaching stirred up in isolated country communities. Friends separated. Members of families quarreled. Churches split. The General Assembly rose to the support of the established church by enacting legislation that made "separate" meetings unlawful, in effect required itinerant preachers to have a license.

Clap's letter of 1745 reflected the deep concern felt not only by himself but by the great majority of his clerical colleagues. Since 1708 religious peace had prevailed in the colony and its people had moved forward and prospered. In that year at Saybrook the Congregational clergy had agreed upon a platform that had prescribed the ecclesiastical organization of the established church and had accepted the Westminster Confession as containing the true expression of Christian doctrine. The framers of the Saybrook Platform had been moderate men who drew back from doctrinal extremes. After 1740 their spiritual successors in the pulpit suddenly found themselves old-fash-

ioned. The revivalists of the Great Awakening, beginning with
Edwards, had brought a new light—a more rigorous Calvinism
together with emphasis on the vital importance of experienced
conversion. Whitefield preached the New Light doctrine. Edwards became its theologian. Clap, though he followed a
stricter Calvinism than many of his party, found himself an
Old Light. But he agreed wholeheartedly with the party in
its opposition to enthusiasm. The clergymen who comprised
the Corporation, with one exception, agreed with the Rector.

Within two years after his inauguration Rector Clap faced
and rode out a storm. The New Light contagion infected the
Collegiate School. Undergraduates, imitating the ideas and the
manners of the itinerant preachers became critical of their
superiors. On one occasion some of them interrupted classroom work to go about the town of New Haven preaching in
the manner of Whitefield. Clap and his tutors expelled David
Brainerd for saying to a friend that Tutor Whittelsey "had no
more grace than this chair." The circumstances were peculiar.
Brainerd, a quiet and sincere young man, had made his remark
in a private conversation with a friend. A freshman had over-
heard it and had repeated the defamation to a lady in the town.
She had tattled to the Rector. Brainerd, it may be noted, had
also attended a meeting of separatists. Clap's action in the
Brainerd case revealed not only a narrow outlook but a determination to commit the school to a sectarian position. Three
years later, in 1744, Clap expelled John and Ebenezer Cleaveland. At home in Canterbury, Connecticut, on vacation between terms the brothers had attended with their parents a
"separate" meeting. They later attended a meeting conducted
by a lay exhorter. Rector Clap adjudged that by such devia-
tions the students had broken the law of both the school and
the colony. The General Assembly ignored a petition for re-
instatement forwarded by the Cleavelands. Later Yale gave
the Cleavelands their degrees, and they both lived useful lives
as respected ministers. Brainerd died while serving as a missionary to the Indians.

Inevitably the expulsions raised a storm of criticism. Clap and the tutors answered the attacks of critics in a pamphlet.[1] The Rector took the position that the colony could hardly expect the Collegiate School which it supported to permit students to be taught to break the law enacted by the General Assembly. Ten years later the Rector published his position on the issue of the liberty of conscience. "The great Design of Founding this School," he said, "was to educate Ministers in our *own* Way." Other founders might establish in accordance with their consciences different institutions so long as the law permitted them. The student who came to Yale must abide by the rules of the institution. Actually, Episcopalians were numbered in the student body. After 1754 they were allowed to attend on Sunday the Episcopalian Trinity Church in town. Clap might have pointed out that at this time dissenters were not permitted to enroll in either Oxford or Cambridge. In Connecticut, however, the Rector's action raised up bitter enemies of the institution.

As soon as he was inaugurated Thomas Clap began to build up the school. Using as models the disciplinary regulations of Harvard and of Oxford and Cambridge, the Rector drew up and printed an elaborate code of rules (with appropriate punishments) for governing student life. As in English universities, fines bulked large in the list of sanctions. Dissatisfied with a certain vagueness and with manifest inadequacies in the charter granted the Collegiate School, Clap with infinite care prepared a revised charter which, in 1745, the General Assembly approved and the Governor agreed to. The Rector's crusade against the New Lights in the school doubtless made a favorable impression on the Old Light majority in the Legislature. The instrument created Yale a college, autonomous and vested with powers and authority appropriate to an institution of higher learning. The indeterminate post of rector became the powerful office of president. The new charter evidenced the constitutionalism natural to a man steeped in Calvinist thought, an attitude of mind that would be important again in Clap's administration. The changes enhanced the prestige of the institution and of the man who directed it.

In this college twelve years after the granting of the new charter the Church of Christ in Yale College appeared, a peculiar institution existing in the school yet not including in its membership all of the Yale community. The college law, however, required all students to attend the services of the Church. To understand the origin of the Church and the normal activities of the faculty and the students who comprised its members, it is necessary to look more closely into the life of the College in the seaport at the mouth of the Quinnipiac.

The College grew in numbers under the new head. In twenty years after Clap's coming it counted around one hundred seventy undergraduates. The old Yale College and the new Connecticut Hall could not house them all. Some found quarters in the town.

Undergraduate life in the rooms and entries of these two structures and in the yard and town about them proceeded with the unhurried tempo of the age. A junior, who came to Yale after Connecticut Hall had been built, set down in his diary the routine of his day. "The method in which I divide my time is as follows nearly: Go to bed at nine o'clock; rise about perhaps (5½) [the figures are uncertain; that was the usual time for the College to start the day]; prayers and recitation which last to about 7½; go to breakfast, and, if the weather is good, commonly take a small walk. This carries it to 8 or 8¼. Commonly from this time till 11 pursue my studies, unless something special; then attend recitation, which lasts to 12; then go to dinner; after, walk or follow some other exercise till (3?); then pursue my studies again till near six, when I attend prayers; after prayers go to supper and spend the remainder of the evening commonly in conversation." The age knew no organized sports. Inevitably, on occasion, the young man, after the summer had passed, got his exercise chopping wood at the

AN EMBATTLED PURITAN 19

pile on the margin of the yard and carrying the sticks to his room. Undergraduate opinion at the time deemed it effeminate to hire this work done. Open fires provided the only heat for studies and classrooms. Candles gave the only light after sundown. The meeting house of the First Church where the students long went for Sunday service had no heat whatsoever. John Cleaveland, a freshman, noted in his diary for the Sabbath, January 17, 1742, the consequences of a cold snap. "Heard Mr. Noice [Noyes] all day." He set down the texts of the morning and of the afternoon sermon. "It was so cold that many students left before the sermon was over." Cleaveland's entry for the following Sunday suggests a little more fully the Sabbath regime in the College of the liberal arts. He noted that during the day he had listened to sermons by Mr. Noyes and by Tutor Whittelsey. "At night Mr. Clap prayed above an hour, as I judge; and I was as stupid as stupidity itself, all the while he prayed."[2] To have been sparkling after a day like that would have been a miracle.

Puritanism confined but did not subdue the Yale animal of the 1750's. Clandestine ringing at unscheduled hours of the college bell evidenced normality, as did the punishment meted out to a hapless freshman named Miner, who was caught in the act. The faculty record that dealt with the crime concluded: "It is therefore considered and determined by the president, with the advice of the tutors, that the said Miner, shall have his ears boxed by the president." Grumbling at the fare offered in the compulsory commons suggests no originality. One of the protesters, however, who remained unknown, showed an aptitude for novelty in pointing up his complaint. The most reasonable reading of the evidence suggests that he provided the ignorant Acadian–French cook with a substance that "physicked" half the college. Occasional wine parties in their rooms helped the students to forget the food which, in spite of complaints, seems normally to have been reasonably good. In Puritan New England drink inevitably appeared at social functions, even those associated with the meeting house. The school butler sold, among other things, beer, metheglin (a fermented honey solution flavored with hops), and cider in the buttery on the first floor of Connecticut Hall. Overindulgence in the commodities provided by the butler and normal explosions of exuberance contributed to the occasional small riot.

English school tradition found a reflection in the custom that required freshmen to fag for sophomores and to submit to their "instruction" in college ways. The same custom subordinated the sophomores to the watchful seniors. From Oxford and Cambridge came originally the law that required undergraduates, when outside their rooms to wear their gowns, and hats or caps or wigs. Rolls that arranged the members of a class in order of their supposed social rank recalled the tradition of a rigidly stratified society that was already fading in America. In the days of President Clap, undergraduates—most of whom, in all probability, came from the provincial aristocracy or the level just below it—took their standings sufficiently seriously to make the faculty action of "degradation" a punishment keenly felt. A large fraction of the young men aimed at the ministry at a time when ministers of the established Puritan church were numbered among the aristocracy of Connecticut. The Puritan ethos lay behind the fines, of three shillings each, levied on one occasion on the actors in a play put on in successive evenings in the house of a tavern keeper on State Street and of eight pence each on the students who attended. First and last these included most of the undergraduate body. When Rector Clap in 1740 in the College Hall first looked into the faces of his hopeful charges, he had only a dim idea of the possibilities open to Satan in the cultivation of that vineyard.

The clergymen who founded the Collegiate School in the second year of the eighteenth century defined learning in terms of knowledge of the ancient languages, Hebrew, Greek, and Latin. Latin was a tool, for many of the books in science, mathematics, and theology that had to be read were written

in that tongue. Learning also included some knowledge of
nature together with a mastery of the essential propositions of
the Calvinist system of theology. When Thomas Clap took
over the leadership of Yale, Hebrew had declined in importance in the curriculum, yet an undergraduate of the day, Ezra
Stiles became, after getting his degree, one of the most distinguished Hebrew scholars in America. Greek and Latin continued, though the decline of Hebrew did not mean that they
enjoyed a compensating increase in attention. All students read
the Greek New Testament and Virgil. Some pushed on into
wider explorations of the great classics of antiquity.

By the middle of the eighteenth century the impetus that
Newton had given to mathematical and astronomical science
had made itself felt in the colonies. Deeply interested in the
Newtonian system, President Clap and Tutor Whittelsey con-
structed an orrery in which not only were the planets shown
but wires marked the orbits of comets. When compared with
the masterpiece of clockwork built by David Rittenhouse at
Philadelphia, the Yale machine was crude, but perhaps it served
better the purposes of instruction, for calculations by the students had to be made before the planets could be moved by
hand to their proper positions. The President took an active
interest in the observation of comets and other celestial phenomena that came within the powers of the small college telescope. After Whittelsey left to take a parish, Tutor Ezra Stiles
carried the responsibility of teaching the astronomy and mathematics offered to the undergraduates. On one occasion, Clap
offered instruction in the calculus.

The Newtonian system made possible the almanac, which,
even in the eighteenth century was an important American
institution. In 1761 an undergraduate, J. Huntington, prepared
and published a college almanac. In the edition of the following
year he placed beside the calculations for each month doggerel
verses that, in effect, repeated the lessons in astronomy he had
learned in class. For July he wrote:

He [Newton] traced the motions to their head
And found the laws by which the spheres are led.
His boundless genius led him to explore
The comet's mysteries unknown before,
Nor yet to vague hypothesis restrained
Bright demonstration all its parts explained.

The standard pattern of a polite education and the need for training the future pulpit orator lay behind the instruction in logic and rhetoric. To what he found when he came to New Haven, Clap added exercises in public disputation—delivered in Latin. The undergraduates organized in 1753 their own literary and debating society, which they called Linonia. A second organization, Brothers in Unity, appeared in 1768. In a day when meager resources limited the growth of the college library the two societies met a keenly felt need by building up collections of their own. The societies evinced a determination on the part of the young men of the school to have a share in the direction of their common life. Thomas Clap was one day to learn how strong that determination could be.

But with all the development in the arts and sciences, theology remained the capstone of a Yale education still oriented to the training of ministers. In Clap's day the basic theological text remained a little book by John Wollebius, the seventeenth-century professor of Divinity at Basle. One may picture an undergraduate sitting before his hearth fire of an evening struggling by the light of a candle with an English translation of Wollebius' *Abridgement of Christian Divinity,* published in London in 1660. By fiat of the Corporation he had to recite from it next day. Nothing gives better the flavor of Yale's instruction in religion than sentences from this gnarled little book.

God's word at first was unwritten, before Moses his time; but after Moses it was written, when God in his most wise counsel would have it to be sealed and confirmed by Prophets and Apostles. . . . God is a spirit, existent eternally in himself; one in Essense, Three in Persons, Father, Sonne, and Holy Ghost. God is known in himself, and in his works. . . . That sin which is derived from the first

AN EMBATTLED PURITAN   23

or primitive Sin, is either original or actual; original sin is that
native corruption derived into the whole man and into the whole
race of man naturally descending from Adam, whereby man having
utterly lost his freedom to good, becomes prone to evil.

Wollebius most probably had never seen Michelangelo's Last
Judgment in the Sistine Chapel. After all, the Vatican was the
seat of the Anti-Christ. But the prose of the Professor of
Theology still conjures up images as vivid as those of the great
artist.

Hitherto of sin; now of the misery that follows upon sin: This
misery is either temporal or eternal, both which is either corporal
or spiritual. . . . *But the chief evil* [that sinners must suffer] *shall be a
communion forever with the Devil and his Angels. . . . The place appointed for the damned is Hell. . . . But where Hell is we are not to search
or enquire. 'Tis sufficient that in* Scripture *it is named* Gehenna, *a
Fiery Furnace, the* place of torment, *a* Prison, bottomless pit, *the*
lake of fire, burning with fire and brimstone. . . . It is most certaine,
that Christ shall returne to Judgement. . . . The Judgement itself is
that most glorious act, whereby Christ shall judge the whole
Wor[l]d. . . . The infidelity and impiety of the wicked, shall be so
laid open before their eyes in their own conscience, that they shall
not be able to deny or gain-say anything. . . . Although the Elect
shall remember their sins, they shall be so filled with the joy of the
Spirit, that the remembrance thereof shall not sad them. . . . The
execution of the Judgement will presently follow upon the pro-
nouncing of sentence: So that the wicked in the presence of the
godly shall be carried away to Hell; and the godly being caught up
to meet Christ, shall with him enter into life eternal. . .

J. Huntington in his almanac scrambled on one occasion Wollebius and Newton. Speaking of the Last Judgment he wrote:

> Then may Yalensia's Sons with glad surprise
> Hear the dread Trumpet sound, "Awake, arise!
> Your clay-cold Beds forsake, forget the Tomb.
> Bid lower Worlds adieu; with Seraphs roam
> Through trackless Fields of Aether [Newton] on your way,
> To Worlds of Pleasure and immortal Day."

Huntington's couplets might appropriately have been set under the rubric "Yale Self-assurance."

One can imagine a classroom in the gaunt and drafty original building of the College. A fire in the fireplace combats the chill of a cold morning. The instructor—perhaps a tutor, perhaps the President—hears the class on Wollebius. "And what is the Covenant of Grace?" A few hours earlier the conscientious members had learned the answer. No doubt the teacher worked hard to pound it into the heads of the delinquents, for covenant theology was important in early New England. "In the Covenant of grace," said the Basle professor,

we must consider both the offering of it and the confirming or sealing of it: the offering of the Covenant of Grace, is that whereby God promiseth to the elect to be their Father in Christ if they perform filial obedience. . . . *By the name of Covenant we understand not that general, which God made with all creatures: nor the covenant of works made with our first parents, but that which after the fall, God of his meer mercy hath made with us. . . . Therefore the covenant of Grace is called a Testament or Disposition, because by this, God hath appointed to his sons an heavenly inheritance, to be obtained by the mediation of his own Sons death.*

The boys—that is, those who had studied their lessons—had also learned about the enemies who faced the church. They had found that Wollebius pulled no punches. "The Churches Enemies are either open or secret," said the Swiss savant. "Her open foes are Heathenes, Jews, and Mahumetans. . . . The hid or counterfeit enemies are either False Christs, or Antichrists. . . . The great Antichrist, is he, who under the name of Christs Vicar, persecutes him . . ."[3]

Perhaps some of the more religious among the young men of the College as they rose at five-thirty for prayers and a recitation before breakfast found reinforcement for the spirit in another passage in old Wollebius. "Neer to Sobriety is Vigilance, when we abstain from untimely and too much sleep, that we may serve God with Chearfulness, and follow the

works of our vocations. . . . To Vigilance is opposite Sleepiness,
and Monkish superstitious Watchings."

Wollebius spoke for seventeenth-century Calvinism. Thomas
Clap found him still useful in eighteenth-century Yale. But
the President came to the conviction that Wollebius in the
classroom was not enough. Having brought about the eleva-
tion of the Collegiate School to the status of a college in 1745
and having built Connecticut Hall in 1750, Clap pushed on to
his next goal, the establishment of the College Church.

Here the absence of full records makes impossible the re-
covery of some significant details. The President fell out with
Joseph Noyes, member of the Corporation and Old Light
pastor of the First Church. Clap decided to bring the religious
instruction of the students wholly within the walls of the College. To effect the change Yale would have to appoint a Professor of Divinity, secede from the First Church, and establish
a church society within the College. The political scene in the
Province had shifted. A rough equality between Old Lights
and New Lights had appeared in the General Assembly. Among
the latter, moreover, the enthusiasm of the 1740's had faded.
The New Lights of the 1750's differed from the opposite party
chiefly in their affirmation of a rigorous Calvinism derived
from Edwards. But party animosities continued. These developments provided the background for Thomas Clap's about-
face.

The Rector-President who in the 1740's had ridden herd on
the New Lights among the undergraduates emerged in the
1750's, to use the language of his adversaries, as a "political
New Light." Perhaps his motive was the desire for personal
power. Perhaps his purpose was to implement and complete
the autonomy of the College operating under the new charter.
Perhaps he wished to strengthen and to perpetuate the bond
that tied the College to a particular expression of religion. It
must be remembered that the President had always been nearer

to the New Light theology than most of his former Old Light
confrères. Whatever the explanation for his shift, the consequence of the President's act was to plunge Yale into the midst
of the controversies of ecclesiastical and secular politics. The
existence of an established church made it inevitable that the
two should be intermingled.

Philip Livingston, a great landowner of New York who had
sent four sons to Yale, had donated to the College a considerable
gift. At the time, the Corporation had earmarked it for a professorship of Divinity. The General Assembly had favored the
project. By 1754 sufficient funds had accumulated to make
possible the call to Naphtali Daggett. Preaching on Long
Island, Daggett had no immediate contact with Connecticut
politics. In theology he took the New Light position.

Before the call a significant event had occurred. In 1753 the
Corporation reaffimred and strengthened an earlier ordinance
that dealt with orthodoxy but which in the struggling Collegiate School had not been of great importance. The new
statute required "that every person who shall hereafter be
chosen a President, Fellow, Professor of Divinity, or Tutor of
this College, shall before he enters upon the execution of his
Office, publicly give his consent to the [Westminster] Cate-
chism of Faith as containing a just summary of the Christian
Religion, as before expressed, and renounce all Doctrines or
Principles contrary thereunto and shall pass through such an
examination as the Corporation shall think proper, in order to
their being fully satisfied that he shall do it truly without any
evasion or equivocation." In addition any candidate for the
professorship of Divinity must write a paper setting forth in
his own words his beliefs and understandings. After Daggett,
as candidate for the professorship, had written out a declaration of faith running to thousands of words, the Corporation
spent an entire day plying him with questions. The testing of
Daggett in 1754 makes the twentieth-century doctor's examination look by comparison but little better than a ten-minute
paper. Nor did the requirements for appointment complete the

test of orthodoxy. Any officer who, after entering upon his duties, should be suspected of falling away from the true faith (the twentieth-century word is "deviation") might be hailed before the Corporation for questioning and possible dismissal.

President Clap left no one in doubt about the significance in his mind of this test for orthodoxy. "Religion," he said in 1754, "is a matter of so great Consequence, and Importance; that the Knowledge of the Arts, and Sciences, how excellent soever, in themselves, are comparatively worth but little, without it." For the President theology was clearly still queen of the sciences and the arts.

In 1757, consequently, President Clap, ignoring the ministerial council that had jurisdiction over the churches of the New Haven area, used the powers granted by its charter to the College to establish a fully developed parish church within it. Clap, moreover, considered the College Church to have a higher status than its contemporaries in the communities of Connecticut. "Colleges," he remarked in 1754, "are *Religious Societies* of a Superior nature to all others. For whereas Parishes, are Societies, for training up the *Common People;* Colleges are Societies of Ministers for training up persons for the work of the *Ministry* and therefore *all their Religious Instructions, Worship, and Ordinances, are carried on within their own jurisdiction, by their own Officers, and under their own Regulation."* Clap cited in support of his contention as to the nature of colleges "the Statutes of the University of Oxford at large."4 Reading these words, all parties to religious controversy in Connecticut came to understand the full meaning of the autonomy granted to Yale.

Clap created the professorship of Divinity and established the independent College Church while the religious contentions touched off by Whitefield continued not only to disturb the colony but to swirl through and about the College itself. Opposition to the President in the student body expressed itself in the fact that only eight undergraduates signed the petition that provided the technical reason for setting up the Church. At the time, the enrollment of the College numbered around a hundred, roughly half of whom ultimately went into the ministry.

Clap's establishment of the College Church roused an angry buzz of criticism of the President and the College. Enemies accused the man who had expelled the Cleavelands for attending a "separate" meeting of himself establishing such a meeting. Clap added further provocation when he attempted to hail before his fellow members of the Corporation the aging Noyes for investigation of his theological positions. The President invoked the Corporation's ordinance of 1753 that dealt with orthodoxy. Noyes refused to be coerced and had sufficient public support to make good his defiance. Perhaps at the time of his own troubles, however, he regretted that some years before he had not raised his voice when the Old Light majority of the Corporation had summoned before it its single New Light member. Rather than face the inquisition that member had resigned.

The storm of opposition to the College continued without abatement after the Church had been established. Pamphleteers attacked the institution and were answered by other pamphleteers. Finally in 1763 the opposition, with the aid of distinguished legal talent, memorialized the General Assembly. The petitioners affirmed that at the common law the Legislature by the act of granting the charter made itself founder of the institution. They prayed that the General Assembly pass an act authorizing an appeal to the Governor and Council of the Colony from every sentence given by the authorities of the College and requested further that the Assembly appoint visitors to look into and, if necessary, put in order the alleged confusion and demoralization at Yale. In his answering brief the President marshaled impressive precedents from England to confute the argument of the memorialists concerning the common law. He reminded the General Assembly, moreover, that Magdalen College in Oxford had successfully defied an attempt of James I to send visitors. The memorial failed. The College remained autonomous. The memorialists had appealed to the political state in the interest of a larger measure of religious liberty in the College. Clap's victory meant that his policy of furthering a conservative theology and maintaining sectarian purity would continue. Clap kept the College independent of the state; but Yale was ultimately to pay a high price for its autonomy.

Two years before, 1761, Thomas Clap led a procession into Yale's first chapel, built of brick and standing just south of Connecticut Hall. Clap's energy and sound financial management had produced both buildings. Its main door opened on the town, whose citizens had contributed the steeple. The Chapel had the dignity and the charm of an eighteenth-century New England meeting house. On the second floor the books of the growing library stood on their shelves. President Clap had achieved his final objective, a sanctuary for the College Church. Here, morning and evening, the members of the College assembled for prayers. Here, twice on the Sabbath, Naphtali Daggett preached. But though all the students were required to attend the daily and the Sunday services the membership of the College Church remained small. Smoldering opposition to the President forecast the flames of revolt soon to break out.

In the North American world outside the College events moved to a climax. The year 1763 was one of those of momentous and irrevocable decision that mark off great periods in history. The struggle between England and France for mastery in North America that had produced four wars in seventy-four years had ended. Quebec, that seemingly impregnable fortress of the hated Catholic enemy in the St. Lawrence valley, had fallen in 1759 and now by the Treaty of Paris in 1763 had become a docile market town in the British Empire. The tension that New Englanders had known for

nearly three-quarters of a century relaxed. There would be no
more Deerfield raids or massacres like that at Fort William
Henry. The American subjects of the young George III looked
with new eyes upon the prospects of the Western World from
which the power of France had vanished.

The undergraduates at Yale, now grown to some one hundred and seventy, sensed the feeling of release and freedom in
the air. But as the years passed, they found no new liberty
within the bounds of the College yard. Perhaps some of them
noticed the lines of age in the face of the President when they
met him on the walk in front of Connecticut Hall. But he still
ruled. He enforced a strict discipline with many fines. The students knew him to be a sectarian but they probably did not
know that religious bias had extended on one occasion in the
1760's to the library. He refused a proffered gift of books for
the library because they included the works of an English
divine whose unorthodox views bordered on deism. Former
tutor Ezra Stiles, now a minister in Newport, Rhode Island,
knew of the offer because it was made by a citizen of Newport.
Stiles wrote a letter of protest to his former president and
teacher in which he pointed out that the way to meet deism
was to face it in open and honorable argument.

On the other hand the students most certainly knew that in
1765 Clap had dismissed two tutors who had accepted the
beliefs of a tiny sect called Sandemanians, whose doctrine of
salvation differed greatly from that of Calvinism. The President
had used the powers granted under the law of 1753. Even before this event discipline had deteriorated. One Sunday evening
in 1764 in the new chapel, as the aging President offered
prayer, a student, in the words of the faculty minute, "stood
up and profanely mimicked him." At commencement in 1765,
the year in which the tutors were dismissed, a mob of students
and townspeople attacked the home of the President, broke
his windows, and slightly injured Clap himself. In the summer
of 1766 a petition signed by most of the members of the upper
classes laid before the Corporation a variety of charges against

all of their instructors and asked that they be dismissed. Thomas Clap had come to the end of the trail. The college authorities dispersed the undergraduates to their homes. The dormitories and yard fell silent. The seniors studied with the local clergy. In September the President officiated at his last commencement. When the ceremony ended, he resigned.

Four months later Thomas Clap died, aged sixty-three. To the end he remained faithful to the truth as he saw it. On January 8, 1765, Naphtali Daggett, the first incumbent of the first professorship in the College and who had been chosen President *pro tempore* of the College, preached the sermon in the Chapel. "Having been long favored with a close connexion, and intimate acquaintance with him," said the Professor of Divinity, "I may be allowed to bear testimony to the deep, habitual sense of eternal things, which he appeared to maintain upon his mind, and the steady regard he paid to the great concerns of Religion. And as he lived, so he died. . . . when it was observed to him, that he was looked upon to be very dangerously sick, he made a little exception to the propriety of the expression: that the situation could not be properly called *dangerous,* in which he was advanced so near to the end of his trials and labors and so nigh to the Haven of eternal rest."[5]

Chapter 3. The Chapel in a Revolutionary Age

In September 1770 the Corporation, faculty, students, parents, and friends assembled at the meeting house of the First Church for the commencement exercises. Naphtali Daggett presided. Four years had passed since that autumn after Clap's resignation when as president *pro tempore* the Professor of Divinity had reassembled the dispersed undergraduates at the beginning of a new term. The life of the College had then dropped back into the familiar routine. Rebellion had ended. The clergymen who comprised the Corporation had taken pains to give Daggett the support of three able tutors. These young men had won the respect of the students for their handling of the established subjects and stirred the enthusiasm of some of them by encouraging the reading of modern English literature. One of the products of the new regime, John Trumbull, delivered an address at the exercises in 1770. Its tone and subject matter evidenced new interests in the College.

John Trumbull, cousin of Governor Jonathan Trumbull, came from the aristocracy of the province. He had achieved a brilliant B.A. in 1767. Awarded a Berkeley Scholarship, he had stayed on at Yale for three more years, continuing to read in the classics but steeping himself in the essays, novels, and poetry of seventeenth- and eighteenth-century England. In 1770, when he received his master's degree, he spoke on a theme that later generations would call nationalism. The young colonial, bred in a Puritan colony whose cultural ties did not extend much beyond Massachusetts, talked about America as one country, a "Nation" moving toward a noble destiny. His thoughts ran beyond politics and his speech closed with some vigorous lines.

> For pleasing Arts behold her matchless charms
> The first in letters as the first in arms.
> See bolder genius quit the narrow shore,
> And realms of science, yet untraced, explore,
> Hiding in brightness of superior day,
> The fainting gleam of Europe's setting ray.

Nathan Hale completed his freshman year with the commencement of 1770. Perhaps he heard the Trumbull address. In all probability Timothy Dwight also listened to the sentiments so much at variance with traditional ideas of colonial subordination. Dwight, the grandson of Jonathan Edwards, had graduated in 1769 and had stayed on in New Haven as rector of the Hopkins Grammar School. These three, Trumbull, Hale, and Dwight, were only part of an extraordinary company of young nationalists who came out of Yale College in the 1760's and 1770's. Others included David Humphreys, soldier, diplomat, and man of letters; Joel Barlow, champion of human rights and author of *The Vision of Columbus;* Noah Webster, postwar advocate of a strong central government and lexicographer of American English; and Manasseh Cutler, colonizer and author of the Ordinance of 1787. Of this list four graduated during the administration of Naphtali Daggett and two, Barlow and Webster, the year after he resigned from the presidency and while he still remained Professor of Divinity.

President Daggett may have been surprised at the extent of Trumbull's departure from tradition in his address at commencement, but he could not have been displeased. Long before that ceremonial occasion Daggett had become aware not only of a threat to the political rights of American colonials but of a particular danger that seemed to him and to his colleagues of the Standing Order to threaten the very foundations of their authority in the province.

At the commencement of 1767, Daggett's first, an unusual number of out-of-town persons filled the hostelries or were guests in private homes in New Haven. Dr. Samuel Johnson, alumnus of Yale and first president of King's College in New

York, was in town to attend another conference. He had abandoned Puritanism and had taken orders in the Church of England. In a letter to the Archbishop of Canterbury, Johnson commented on the meeting in the little seaport "of Delegates from the Presbyterians southward and the Congregationalists this way, in further pursuance of their grand design of co-alescing or union . . ." "It is said," added the writer, "there was much disputation, and therefore we suspected they did not all agree."[1] Johnson, experienced in the ways of ecclesiastics, expressed no surprise. Intelligence that leaked out later disclosed that this and some seven conferences held in following years had as one of their main objectives the concerting of measures to prevent the establishment of an Anglican bishop or bishops in the colonies. Connecticut Congregational ministers understood that Episcopalians were persuaded that the only valid ordination was by that spiritual authority which had come down through the historic episcopate. A pamphlet written by one of the Standing Order expressed the fears of the day. "We are as fully persuaded," said Dr. Charles Chauncey, "as if they had openly said it that they [the Episcopalians] have in view nothing short of a COMPLETE HIERARCHY after the pattern of that at home, with like officers in all their degrees of dignity, with like revenue for their support, and with the allowance of no other privilege to dissenters but that of bare toleration."[2]

Naphtali Daggett undoubtedly attended one or more of the Presbyterian–Congregational conferences that discussed ways of averting the danger of the appointment of an American bishop. His contemporaries knew him to be more interested in political activities than in managing the domestic affairs of the College. Along with the laymen of Connecticut he resented those assertions of imperial authority to be found in the Stamp Act of 1765 and Townshend Acts of 1767, his first year as president. But the specter of the possible disestablishment of Congregationalism in Connecticut raised in his mind visions of a catastrophe not only for the Standing Order but for the

College. Inevitably Daggett opposed the extension of imperial authority and quite naturally, with the unfolding of events, opposition to Parliament grew into outright nationalism.

The College Church had been born in ecclesiastical controversy. After the death of Clap, its pastor, for both secular and ecclesiastical reasons, moved into a larger conflict. Morning and evening the undergraduates assembled for prayers in the Chapel that stood at the end of Connecticut Hall. Twice on Sunday they listened to preaching. The prayers, the psalms that were sung without accompaniment, the Scripture reading, and the Christian message from the pulpit remained constant. But the mood outside the Chapel changed as events moved swiftly forward. In late December 1773 students coming out of Sunday morning service talked of the violence in Boston that the Patriots called a tea party. In the following year they denounced the punitive measures which the British government directed against the Massachusetts sea port. Then in April 1775 news of Lexington and Concord brought the excitement of war.

Through these changing years Naphtali Daggett managed the College and served as pastor. He was not a great preacher, but he presented competently the old truths as these truths were understood by the followers of the New England theology. On the first Sunday in the month the Pastor presided at the communion service. The choice of the first Sunday had been made originally in a conscious effort to carry on in America what the founders of the Church understood to be the practice in the chapels of the colleges of Oxford and Cambridge. Though this bit of tradition continued unimpaired as part of the custom of the College in New Haven, other ties with what colonials still called "home" grew steadily weaker. Undergraduates, tutors, and members of the congregation knew that the Pastor and President belonged to that large company of divines in New England who stood unwaveringly for American rights. Daggett led his flock to the day when on one Sunday in 1777 the Chapel door did not open. War had compelled him as president to disperse the students and faculty to communities in the interior.

President Daggett's support of the humanities equaled his devotion to religion. Young John Trumbull in 1770 had suggested that the liberal arts had implications of importance for the emerging spirit of nationalism. In 1771 Daggett appointed Trumbull tutor. At the same time the President added to his staff the brilliant and energetic Timothy Dwight. The tutors, Dwight and Trumbull, determined to start their country on the road to that cultural eminence that the latter had envisioned. New life stirred in the College as they added, not without some jeering from the traditional-minded, the reading of contemporary "polite" literature to the standard course. They determined also to do as well as to teach. A Boston and later a New Haven newspaper published their first sprightly essays. These led to more ambitious undertakings. Trumbull turned out *The Progress of Dullness,* a gay satire in verse on the older Yale curriculum and on the manners of the time. It enjoyed a long popularity in spite of the fact that some persons in a generation whose reading was limited largely to polemical pamphlets could not take the chaffing and solemnly attacked the author in the public prints. Solemnity marked young Dwight's larger work, nothing less ambitious than an epic, *The Conquest of Canaan.* Greece and Rome had had their epics. So had Puritan England in Milton's *Paradise Lost.* America, Dwight thought, must not be a voiceless laggard. Each week the tutor spent many hours grinding out the lines of what ultimately became almost an interminable poem. Trumbull and Dwight, also, founded the group known as the Connecticut Wits, which made the first significant attempts in America to create *belles-lettres.*

Trumbull left Yale after a year to prepare for the law and to continue his writing. Dwight carried on in charge of student discipline, teaching the regular courses together with the new work in English literature, and inserting transparent allusions to American persons and scenes in his narrative of Canaan's conquest. He overworked. His health broke. He found himself in 1774 not only threatened with blindness but uncomfortably near to the grave so much emphasized in Puritan preaching. As he discovered his old vigor ebbing, his grandfather's New Divinity took on a personal meaning for him. He experienced that conversion which marked the beginning of a new and deeper life. In 1774, before his father had come down from Northampton to take him home, Timothy Dwight in the Chapel was admitted to the fellowship of the little company that comprised the College Church. Sadly his students saw him quit his room and ride away from the College yard.

Months of sensible living back home restored his health, save for permanently weakened eyes. Joining the warm discussions in Northampton that followed Lexington and Concord, he found himself, though among staunch defenders of colonial rights, the only person willing to advocate independence and the treason it implied. Meanwhile, the students living in Connecticut Hall and in what was now called the "Old College" formed a military company. It escorted General Washington through the town on his way to assume command at Cambridge. Later some of them marched off to war. Timothy Dwight returned to his tutorial duties and, on his own, to the study of divinity.

In 1776 fighting in the war shifted from Boston to New York. British warships controlled Long Island Sound. After a succession of troubles and alarms in New Haven, the College was dispersed in March 1777, the separate classes to reassemble each under a member of the faculty in designated inland towns. Tutor Dwight took charge of the seniors at Wethersfield. In that month Naphtali Daggett resigned the office of President, for which he had neither inclination nor aptitude. He remained, however, Professor of Divinity and, as such, pastor of a scattered Church. Timothy Dwight carried the seniors through to the end of the academic year in September.

He had finished his studies in divinity and had been approbated to preach. At Wethersfield he gave the graduating class a spirited patriotic address and resigned his tutorship to become a chaplain in Washington's army. The fortunes of the College stood at lowest ebb.

On September 11, 1777, the harrassed Corporation elected Ezra Stiles president and sent off their invitation to Portsmouth, New Hampshire, where he was preaching. The desperate need of the College seems to have won over some who had suspicions as to the orthodoxy of the tutor who had served under President Clap. Doubtless the Corporation knew that during his tutorship young Stiles had gone through a period of doubt. But September 1777 was not the time to indulge in theological hairsplitting. Burgoyne, invading from Canada by Montcalm's old route, stood at Saratoga. Howe, on the very day of Stiles' election, drove Washington from his positions on the banks of Brandywine Creek and opened the way for the British occupation of Philadelphia.

Stiles took six months to make his decision. For two decades he had served as pastor of a church in Newport. His post had given him an opportunity he valued highly to pursue learning in many fields. But the British occupation of the town had driven him out, for he was notorious among the local Tories as an ardent and active Whig. His new church at Portsmouth wished him to stay. At the same time the exigencies of the war had forced the General Assembly to cancel its annual subvention to Yale College. The institution, moreover, had enemies in the state whose hostility dated from the intransigent policies of President Clap. And the war clouded every prospect with uncertainty. Only a brave man would undertake the management of a disorganized and demoralized college under such circumstances.

Yet Stiles found the Corporation's invitation challenging. He approached the Assembly to learn if that body would approve of him as president. He drew up a plan for a university —the first man in America to do so. He proposed that to Yale College be added three postgraduate schools in the major branches of learning—medicine, law, and theology. He borrowed the plan from Europe, where universities were already centuries old. But he sought to adapt European experience to American needs. He sent the plan to the Corporation and to the General Assembly in the full knowledge that universities do not spring into being in the midst of a desperate war. He accepted the invitation.

In June 1778 Ezra Stiles with his family drove to New Haven in a caravan sent to Portsmouth by the Corporation. On July 8 he took the oath of loyalty to the independent state of Connecticut. His predecessors had sworn to support the king. The new president made an affirmation concerning religion: "I, Ezra Stiles, being chosen President of Yale College, do hereby declare my free assent to the Confession of Faith & Rules of Ecclesiastical Discipline agreed upon by the Churches in the State of Connecticut, A.D. 1708, and established by the Laws of this Government: and do promise to teach and instruct the pupils under my care accordingly."[3] Significantly, Stiles omitted specific mention of the Westminster Confession. He made no renunciations. He believed in a broad, less rigorous Calvinism. He disliked oaths to support religious creeds. Yet he was a man of deep faith. There was conscious symbolism in his first public act as president. On June 23 he attended evening prayers in the Chapel.

On July 8 undoubtedly most of the 115 undergraduates in residence occupied, along with visitors, the pews of the Chapel. With the curiosity inevitable on such an occasion the audience eyed the stranger on the rostrum who was being inaugurated as president. They saw a small man, short, well proportioned, but of delicate build. A penetrating glance came from his dark eyes. Naphtali Daggett opened the ceremony with an invocation. The Senior Fellow of the Corporation in a Latin address committed to Stiles the instruction and government of the in-

stitution. A Senior Bachelor pronounced in Latin a congratu-
latory address. In the same language and with vigor and anima-
tion Stiles gave his inaugural oration. Perhaps to some of those
present he seemed too frail a man to meet the stern demands of
the time. Ten days before, Washington, at Monmouth, New
Jersey, had fought Clinton but had failed to prevent the retirement of the British army from Philadelphia to New York.
Other news suggested an even greater menace. Only eight
days previous to the inauguration Admiral Howe had brought
the British fleet from Philadelphia to New York. New Haven,
some eighty miles to the eastward of the mouth of the Hudson
lay exposed to any sea-borne attack.

   Timothy Dwight, an army chaplain when Stiles was inaugurated, later described the environment of the College at a
time when it struggled to survive in a location dangerously
close to the center of the military and naval strength of the
enemy. "On our part," said Dwight in 1801,

the war was prosecuted with vast difficulty, and with various successes and disasters. . . . Our towns were burned, our fields wasted,
our houses plundered, and our soldiers in great numbers perished
by sickness, by the sword, and by the hard-handed oppression,
famine, and disease of prisons and prison ships. Our country was
impoverished, and the surviving inhabitants were harrassed by continual alarms, driven from their dwellings by invasion, and distressed by anxiety and suspense to a degree which experience only
can comprehend. At the same time a great part of our country was
wasted by disease little less effective than the pestilence. A depre-
ciating currency, also, sundering the bonds of amity between man
and man, destroying confidence in dealing, perplexing the sense
and relaxing the ties of justice, and infusing in all human intercourse
apprehension and distrust, harrassed the peace of society, and
threatened with no small probability its utter ruin . . .[4]

   The diary of President Stiles provides specific details to
point up Dwight's generalized description. No funds came from
the state. The Old College fell into decay. Some young men
came to the College to enjoy the exemption from military

service accorded to students. Inadequate housing accommo-
dations compelled the undergraduates to seek rooms in town.
More than once the College broke up for a period because the
steward could not "support the commons," either because of
the depreciation of the currency or the hard fact that Jonathan
Trumbull, indefatigable war governor of Connecticut, had
swept up all the available supplies of provisions for the use of
Washington's army. More than once the President noted in
his diary that he had released an undergraduate to study in the
home of a private teacher because his family could not meet
the Treasurer's bills. Intermittent news of the movements of
British warships on Long Island Sound alarmed alike the College and the citizens of the town. Invasion came in July 1779,
when British and Loyalist troops occupied New Haven. The
small library and the primitive scientific apparatus of the College had, however, been removed to places of safety. Ex-
President Daggett, along with many students, joined the impromptu home guard that marched out of the town to stop
the invaders. Taken, gun in hand, Daggett suffered from his
captors injuries from which he never recovered.

On Sunday, July 4, 1779, the British fleet was less than a
day's sail from New Haven harbor, outside which on the next
day the commanding officer put his attacking force ashore.
On that third anniversary of the Declaration of Independence
Stiles made a note for the record in his diary:

Ldsdy—After Sermon, Cook a Senior Sophister was admitted into
full Communion, according to the following formula draughted
by President Clap: Chh. Covenant. "You do in the presence of God
and before this Assembly, declare your Belief of the Holy Scriptures
as being given by Divine Inspiration, and of all the Doctrines
therein contained as professed in our Chhs: and do accordingly
avouch the Ld Jehovah, the only true and living Gd to be your God;
and do give yourself up to Gd the Father as your Creator, to Gd
the Son as your Redeemer, and to Gd the Holy Ghost as your
Sanctifier, and do promise by the Help and Assistance of divine
Grace to walk in a holy Obedience & Subjection to all the Laws

and Commandments of X; and to attend upon and be subject to all the ordinances and Institutions of the Gospel, and particularly in this Church."

"You do thus profess and promise."

"We then receive you into our Christian Communion and Fellowship and will endeavor by the Help of Divine Grace to conduct towards you as a member of this Chh. according to the Rules of the Gospel."5

In November 1780 Naphtali Daggett died. The College mourned a man who had served well both church and state. While the Fellows of the Corporation cast about for a successor, the President, aided sometimes by visiting ministers, filled the pulpit. As the year 1781 opened, the war in the North was quiescent. Clinton continued to occupy New York. Washington's encircling army held him in the city. Cornwallis campaigned in the South.

On Sunday, January 7, a collection was received in the Chapel. By custom contributions were given on the first Sabbath in January and in July. On this first Sunday in the new year Stiles occupied the pulpit. A narrative he set down in his diary at the end of the day permits a glimpse into the Chapel when the College Church carried on in the midst of war:

After Sermon in the Forenoon, I ordered the whole Congreg-n to stay and descended from the Pulpit to the Communion Table, and administered the Lord's Supper to the Chh. before the whole Congregation. This was the first time it was ever done in this manner, it being my own judgment. I hope hereby others may be impressed by the solemnity of this holy Ordinance. The two Senior or fore seats were evacuated & the Communicants took their place there. We have no Deacons of the College Church it is so changeable; and therefore the oldest Graduate present or Undergraduate carries round the Elements of Bread and Wine. Sir Nott carried them today. Previous to the administration I publickly notified that any Communicant of other Chhs. occasionally present might freely partake with us. Upon which the two Deacons of Mr. Mather's Chh. (he being absent) & others removed and took their seats with the Communicants. I then observed to the Chh. that I shd take their silence for consent that they shd be admitted to Commune with us. Then I proceeded to consecrate the Elements & having administered the supper as usual, and sung an hymn I dismissed the Chh. and Congregation with a Blessing. A decent Solemnity appeared in the Congregation as well as the Chh. and I cant but hope that we had the presence of Jesus with us in this Holy Ordinance.[6]

In the following year Tutor Ely presented to the Church in the name of nineteen communicants two new silver cups for use in celebrating the sacrament of the Lord's Supper.

The spring and summer of 1781 were quiet. The President lectured, heard recitations, and supervised the daily life of the College. In September fears rose again with the rumor that a British fleet was standing down Long Island Sound. This time New Haven escaped. Some weeks later Stiles noted sadly in his diary that on a Sunday in the autumn a special contribution had been received in the Chapel. The money went to the citizens of New London whose shops and homes had been burned by a raiding party led by that former New Haven apothecary Benedict Arnold.

Yale College faced other hazards than those that stemmed from war. On May 4, 1780, Stiles set down a note: "Foster applied for Dismission to Dr. Dwight's school—it is said he expects 30 from the Jun. and Soph. classes in the College."[7] Timothy Dwight, the tutor whose students had once suggested to the Corporation that he be made Daggett's successor, was now out of the army and had founded a school at Northampton. No prospective student could overlook the inland location, far removed from the threats of the British fleet and British raiding parties. Two years later a friend of Stiles reported to the President a conversation with Dwight. The former tutor was unhappy in Northampton in spite of the fact that his school was worth "200 pounds a year Silver." Some friends of the former tutor, the informant added, talked of a subscription for a professorship at Yale and of a recommendation to the Corporation that Dwight fill it. The news filled Ezra Stiles with anger. "He [Dwight]," wrote the President in his diary, "is chagrinned and mortified—does not intend to spend his life in his Northampton School—determined against settling in the Ministry tho' he preaches constantly for 5 doll. old wat Sabbath—He is waiting for the meditated stroke upon Yale College . . . and nothing but great things will serve him —& everything that comes in the way of his preferment must fall before him. Aut Caesar, aut Nullus."8 Actually Dwight was doing well at Northampton. Besides his school he ran two large farms. Going into politics, he got himself elected to the Legislature of Massachusetts.

But in 1783 Timothy Dwight accepted a pastorate at Greenfield Hill in Connecticut. Here again he established a school, and he began to play politics in Connecticut. The dislike of Yale that had been roused by President Clap had never died down. A note in the diary in the spring following Dwight's removal to Greenfield Hill suggests the troubles that beset the President. "Much talk about Four Memorials prepared to be presented to the Assembly against or about Yale College signed by numbers in all counties—one signed by Mr. Dwight praying for a Board of Civilians to correct etc. otherwise to build a new College; this said to be generally rejected as abounding with Accusations and Aspersions & injurious Reflexions upon the College."9

Dwight's school at Greenfield Hill prospered. But it did not supersede or swallow up Yale College. In 1785 Timothy Dwight finally brought *The Conquest of Canaan* to publication. It made him a man of letters and in that day brought him fame.

Ezra Stiles carried on in the face of difficulties and uncertainties through the war years and through the critical times that followed the peace. He strengthened the College and worked diligently to overcome the opposition to it in the General Assembly. In the early 1790's Stiles won a signal triumph when, with the aid of Treasurer James Hillhouse, he effected a *rapprochement* with the state and brought about a change in the charter. Under the new arrangement the governor, lieutenant-governor, and six senior members of the state

Senate became members, along with the seven clergymen of the Yale Corporation. Then the state provided the funds for a new dormitory that, when completed, was known as South College. The re-establishment of the desperately needed aid from the state was Stiles' last important achievement. He had not created the University of which he had dreamed in 1778. But he had preserved and firmly established the College about which a university could later rise.

Ezra Stiles was a scholar, reputed in his day the greatest in America, though he made no contribution to thought comparable to that of Franklin in electricity or of Edwards in theology and philosophy. Stiles' mind ranged over all the fields of learning of the time. Oriental languages and particularly Hebrew never ceased to interest him. Throughout the war he taught Hebrew in the College so that prospective ministers could read the Old Testament in the original tongue. Vanity, no doubt, colored his preparations for his first public commencement, held in 1781, when the war was nearing its end. In the forenoon the President contributed to the exercises what Theodore Woolsey later described as "an oration in Hebrew, Chaldaic and Arabic." The record does not reveal how many in the audience understood the morning discourse. No doubt his hearers were impressed, for it was an age in which mastery of ancient languages was a symbol of erudition. In the afternoon Stiles delivered an address in the more familiar Latin. The President had displayed the College as a seat of learning.

Tutor Stiles had taught mathematics and astronomy; the President never ceased to be fascinated by astronomical phenomena, in particular the aurora borealis, the height of which on one occasion he tried to measure. He lectured on astronomy when the Professor of Mathematics was unable to fulfill his duties. While preaching at Newport Stiles had become deeply interested in the culture of the ancient Jews. He had long and close relations with a learned rabbi of that town and had discussed with him the question of the coming of the Messiah. As a teacher of Hebrew after he became President, Stiles initiated what was to be a permanent emphasis at Yale on oriental studies and Hebrew culture. At his own request the Corporation appointed him Professor of Ecclesiastical History. Throughout his long term he lectured faithfully in this field. He also heard the juniors and seniors recite in philosophy. On Saturday afternoons he held his "private or chamber lecture on theology."

An insatiable curiosity took him into every subject. He drew back from no labor in acquiring a new language or mastering a new science. He took pains to preserve the information he gathered from his investigations in memoranda or in his diary. Stiles corresponded with many learned men in America and across the Atlantic. He listened attentively to his many distinguished visitors, setting down in his diary after their departure the geographical, economic, political, or military information they had imparted. One can picture him in the late 1780's in his study listening with rapt attention to Manasseh Cutler, back from the frontier and pausing for a visit at his old college, as Cutler described the great mounds, built in antiquity by unknown men, that the first settlers had found at the confluence of the Muskingum and Ohio rivers. Stiles accumulated knowledge as an Australian bowerbird her hoard. He packed his lectures with facts. But he did not have the philosophical turn of mind to draw from his researches those new insights that push out the boundaries of understanding.

Ezra Stiles worked in the tradition of the Renaissance. He honored learning and loved it. He sought also to make learning serve the interests of society; his work with the silkworm gave him a place among the founders of the silk industry in the United States. He believed in the free mind. Before the change in the composition of the Corporation, he modified the oath that professors and tutors were required to take so that any Christian could subscribe. An undated manuscript in the Sterling Library contains an affirmation that Thomas Jefferson might have written. "There are some Rights," said Stiles, "inherent in Human Nature, never supposed to be given up, or can't be given up, if supposed to be because absolutely inalienable—such among other things is religion."

Stiles kept abreast of the shifts in thought in the second half of the eighteenth century. He introduced into the curriculum the reading of Montesquieu's *The Spirit of Laws*. The rationalism and humanism of the Enlightenment had caused that skepticism and doubt through which he had struggled when he was a tutor. He looked upon deism as a philosophy to be examined and understood. After the French alliance brought Rochambeau with an army to the United States, French thought became increasingly influential in America. Stiles was only one among many of his countrymen who exchanged views with officers of the allied force. A letter of Stiles to a chaplain in the French army disclosed the attitude of the scholar carried into the province of religious belief. The President told his correspondent that he "had acquired much knowledge from the great and learned men of all sects of Christians, nay, from Deists, from Mohametans, and even from disciples of the Bonzes and Brahams; that time has, or ought to have arrived, when religious disputes should be contemned, so far as, either by inimical or inquisitorial influences, they prevent a philosophical urbanity, and a most ample progress of the Sciences."[10]

In the story of religion and learning at Yale, Ezra Stiles has a special place. In his thought he held two credos in balance—the Christian gospel and the humanistic faith that the cultivation of the liberal arts enlarges the life and enriches the spirit of the individual. Thomas Clap had respected learning and had strengthened the liberal arts within the College. But Clap with what was in effect a test oath had subordinated learning to sectarian doctrine. Stiles, though in his historical researches he was often uncritical and credulous of fanciful tales, nevertheless brought to eighteenth-century Yale the essentials of the scholar's code of ethics. He saw learning as an end in itself. If the circumstances of a turbulent and unhappy time did not permit him to build the University he had outlined when offered the presidency, he brought to the College what was more important than expansion—an emphasis on the open-minded search for truth in the concerns of both this world and the next. In his administration, in which religion and learning were equally respected, the later University was born in spirit.

After the war the rationalism of the Enlightenment profoundly affected American thought. Older men found in the new humanism inspiration to push forward in that hopeful and creative age when Americans who had just made good their independence wrote the Constitution and made it the supreme law of the Republic. Young men, following enthusiastically the new fashions in thinking, turned their backs on the preachers of the old theology. After the fall of the Bastille in 1789 many of them added to their largely American list of heroes the champions of liberty in France.

In such an age Stiles saw no reason to abandon the attitude of the open and inquiring mind. If deism was to be opposed, it had to be with reason and fairness, putting a better system beside an inferior one. Above all, if religion had to do battle with deism, let narrow creedalism and the spirit of party be put aside. In 1788 the President wrote in his diary his thoughts on reading a current poem that attacked what its author thought was the influence of Voltaire in America:

Read Dr. Dwight's Triumph of Infidelity. It contains some fine poetry and beautiful Satyre. But I have two objections against it. He brings in the Roman Catholics & a number of protestant erroneous Divines as subserving the Cause of Deism. This spoils the whole; he should have confined himself to Deists. Romanists think all Protestants subserve the cause of Infidelity: and the Protestants think the Romanists do the same. Calvinists think Arminians, Arians & Socians subserve Deism. Arians and Socians think Calvinists, Presid Ed & New Divinity all subserve Deism. The Chh of Engl think Dissenters and Dissenters the Chh of Engl &c. This is not a candid nor fair Satyre. . . . His poem is filled with a degree of ill

Nature, Acrimony & Malevolence, which ought never to enter into the mind of a Christian, and especially of a Xtian minister.[11]

Stiles was not alone in his opinion of the poem. Dwight had hidden behind anonymity. When publicly charged with writing the piece, he never acknowledged it. If, however, this foray against infidelity failed, Dwight was to have the opportunity for a second campaign.

Stiles, the scholar, lived and worked also in the tradition of the Reformation. The great doctrines of historical Christianity illumined his life. His study of ecclesiastical history and his interest in all learning gave him a breadth of religious outlook in which narrow creedal formulations had no place.

He was as remarkable for his kindliness as for his learning. Kindness was almost a weakness and often left him defenseless before an erring student armed with a plausible excuse. One recalls John Trumbull's portrait of the resourceful undergraduate in *The Progress of Dullness*.

> His sickness puts on every name,
> Its cause and uses still the same;
> 'Tis tooth-ache, cholic, gout or stone,
> With phases various as the moon;
> But though through all the body spread,
> Still makes its cap'tal seat the head.
> In all diseases, 'tis expected,
> The weakest parts be most infected.

But perhaps gentleness triumphed in the end, for his long administration, though much of it fell in turbulent times, saw no serious disorders. Yet the President had a temper, and on one occasion, when an old man, he broke his cane on the chapel stage in quelling a bit of student rowdyism that had developed before he entered the building.

Misfortune added to Stiles' burdens in supervising the religious life of the College. Samuel Wales, the distinguished pulpit orator, who succeeded to the professorship of Divinity after the death of Naphtali Daggett in 1780, had scarcely gotten well started on his work at Yale when he fell victim to a tragic nervous disorder. At first the trouble merely impaired his usefulness, but in the end, when he had completely lost touch with reality, he had to be removed from New Haven. The President assumed the duties that Wales could no longer perform. Again Stiles preached in Chapel and again guest ministers were called from the outside.

Stiles watched over the spiritual life of the College with unflagging solicitude. Meticulously he recorded in his diary the number of communicants at the sacrament of the Lord's Supper—nine, seven, sixteen, and, after the beginning of the French Revolution, three, four. From its organization the membership of the Church had been only a small minority of the student body. But the rules of the institution required all undergraduates to attend daily prayers and services on Sunday. An entry in the President's diary at the end of a long day in August 1780 gives a picture of a Sabbath in the College in a year when defeats in the South spread gloom throughout the nation. "I have been five hours this day in Chapel," wrote the weary Stiles. "One hour of Morning Prayers; longer than usual as I expounded the 2nd Chapter of Matthew: we sing at Chapel Ldsday morn-g prayers; two hours divine service Forenoon and Afternoon each at w-c we sing five times [from Watts' version of the Psalms]; an hour Even-g prayers at w-c one of the Students read a Sermon of Dr. Evans on the Xtian Temper."

The singing was without instrumental accompaniment. Stiles would have no organ—let worship be by the voices of men, not by machines. In 1784 the President for the first time admitted "a Flute in Chapel with vocal music." Four years later the junior class elected six of their number to lead the hymns in Chapel during the following year.

On December 10, 1781, Stiles wrote a paragraph that revealed the inner fears and hopes of a man who combined the roles of administrator, scholar, teacher, and, at two different periods, pastor. He set it down in a notebook in which for years on each birthday he had appraised himself on the completion of another year of his pilgrimage:

The College has been studious, orderly, & to an agreeable degree religious in the year past. We have had no Tumults in the College. I am continually praying Heaven that my Presidency may be with Tranquility and Peace. I take great pains to look carefully into the interior state of the College & to convert the students privately both Scientifically and Religiously. As the College Chapel has devolved upon me the year past, I have endeavored to preach the unsearchable Riches of Xt & Salvation by the Cross and holiness as consisting of the Supreme Love of God for the Innate Excellencies, Holiness & Glory of his Nature and Character. I have advised and Sincerely Importuned the Youth of this University to devote themselves to that Divine Jesus who hath loved them to the Death. And . . . I have reason to hope the blessed Spt. hath wrot effectually on the hearts of Sundry who have, I think, been brot home to God, & experienced what flesh and blood cannot impart to the human mind. . . . . I am Principally concerned lest I should instill former mistakes and Errors into the numerous Youth: For by the admission of Ninety Freshmen at June Commencement we have a College of 224 Undergraduates. The good Lord give me grace to go in and out before them in such manner as shall be most for his Glory.[12]

One day in 1790 a box of books for the library arrived in New Haven from Philadelphia. It came from Benjamin Franklin. Relations between Stiles and Franklin ran back as far as 1766, when Stiles from Newport had appealed to Franklin, then colonial agent in England, to defend him before the imperial authorities against the calumnies of the Newport loyalists angered by Stiles' vigorous opposition to the Stamp Act, and even earlier still when Tutor Stiles had corresponded with the Philadelphia scientist concerning some electrical apparatus he had given to Yale. Later Franklin had persuaded the University of Edinburgh to award Stiles an honorary degree. The

box of books in 1790 gave to the Yale president an excuse to
look into the face of deism as it found expression in the life and
thought of a man whom the people of the day considered one
of the two greatest living Americans. Stiles sent a letter of
thanks to the donor of the books, then aged eighty-four. He
begged for a portrait that might be hung near the shelves on
which the books stood. Then he added: "You know, Sir, I am
a Christian; and would to Heaven, all others were as I am, except my imperfections and Deficiencies of Moral Character.
As much as I know of Dr. Franklin I have not an idea of his
religious Sentiments. I wish to know the Opinion of my
venerable Friend concerning Jesus of Nazareth."

Franklin replied in such a way as to manifest his respect for
the President of Yale, only eleven years his junior:

You desire to know something of my religion . . . I do not take your
curiosity amiss & shall endeavor in a few words to gratify it. Here
is my creed. I believe in one God, Creator of the Universe; That he
governs the World by his Providence. That he ought to be wor-
shipped. That the most acceptable Service we can render to him is
doing good to his other Children. That the soul of Man is immortal,
and will be treated with Justice in another Life, respect^g its Conduct
in this. These I take to be fundamental Principles of all sound Religion, and I regard them, as you do, in what ever sect I meet with
them. As to *Jesus of Nazareth* . . . I think the *System of Morals & his
Religion as he has left them to us, the best the World ever saw,* or is
likely to see; but I apprehend it has received various corrupting
changes; and I have, with most of the present Dissenters in England,
some doubts as to his Divinity: tho' it is a question I do not dogma-
tize upon, hav^g never studied it & think it needless to busy myself
with it now, when I expect soon an Opport^y of know^g the Truth
with less trouble.[13]

Ezra Stiles, still the seeker after new truth, carefully copied
the letter in his diary. If his own religion differed from that of
the philosopher–statesman, the President respected a faith so
candidly declared. Stiles was still able to gain benefits from
deism. Nationalist, scholar, and Christian, he attempted in his

thought and in his life to bring the Renaissance and the Reformation into unity. In a dynamic and creative age Stiles tried
to make that unity the fundamental characteristic of the life
of Yale.

Chapter 4. Timothy Dwight

Spring in 1795 had brought out the leaves on the trees in New Haven when a sudden and swift illness brought death to Ezra Stiles. At the commencement in the following September, Josiah Meigs, Professor of Mathematics and Natural Philosophy, pronounced a eulogy. In June the Corporation had elected Timothy Dwight, Master of Greenfield Hill School, President of the College. At the same time the governing body had chosen the Rev. David Parsons of Amherst, Massachusetts, to be Professor of Divinity. But Parsons declined. So Dwight, at the request of the Fellows of the Corporation, supplied the pulpit of the College Church in addition to his duties as President. In 1805 the arrangement became permanent when Dwight himself accepted the title of Professor of Divinity. In Dwight's case the double assignment seemed almost inevitable. To foster education and to further religion had long been his primary interests.

The new President was a doer, a practical man interested in results. To Dwight the liberal arts college had a purpose that was crystal clear. He saw the institution as a company of teachers, and he understood the purpose of teaching to be to train the mind of the student. But training the mind without implanting morals ran the danger of magnifying evil. In Dwight's thinking the function of religion was to establish character. Christianity provided the only foundation for public and private morals. For Dwight religion took a central place in the liberal arts.

Dwight's practicality had value for the College. At the same time the new President displayed some of the limitations of the practical man. Unlike Stiles, Dwight had no interest in

learning for itself. The world of ideas interested him only as
it provided ammunition that he could use to win specific and
immediate campaigns. In a baccalaureate sermon repeated to
three different graduating classes Dwight expressed his opinion
of the scholar who was uninterested in the practical utilities of
learning. Dwight described the man who

> *sits down soberly to the engrossing attainments of science.* To be learned
> is the great object of his ambition. . . . In his study he dwells: in his
> books he passes his life. *To think* appears to him the only proper end
> of human existence: while *to do* is not even entered upon the register
> of his duties. . . . He has not discovered that science is a means, and
> not an end. . . . He mistrusts not that the clown, who faithfully
> follows the plough, or wields the hoe and the spade, is a better
> member of society than himself: nor dreams, that the two mites
> of such a man will be accepted as a gift to God, while his own
> abundance will be slighted and forgotten.[1]

Obviously the teachers whom the President might select would
be well advised to be diligent at their trade. But Josiah Meigs
soon discovered that diligence could, in Dwight's opinion, be
misdirected. Meigs spoke up, near the end of the century, for
the principles of Thomas Jefferson. Not long thereafter the
Professor of Mathematics and Natural Philosophy found it ex-
pedient to accept the presidency of the University of Georgia,
an institution of somewhat nebulous existence at that moment.
Dwight in fact joined in his thought anti-intellectualism and
intolerance. The union is a common one. For Dwight, as for
Clap, religion took precedence over learning.

Nevertheless the new President showed wisdom in his work
of building up the College. To replace Meigs he appointed a
young man, Jeremiah Day; he chose another young man,
James L. Kingsley, to be Professor of Languages; and a third,
Benjamin Silliman, to be Professor of Chemistry and Mineralogy. The appointment of Silliman revealed not only the wise
administrator but a basic belief of the President. He picked his
man and then let the man learn his subject. Silliman had plans

for the law when Dwight made to him the astonishing proposal that he abandon his intentions and prepare for a career in a science little developed in America. President Dwight made it possible for young Silliman to master what Americans had to teach and later to go to Britain for extended study. If Dwight felt sure of his professor, he also had no fears of the science of Newton and Boyle. He believed that the more deeply the scientists penetrated the mysteries of nature, the more vividly they would disclose the wonderful works of the Creator. The laboratory as well as the chapel would proclaim the glory of God. The three young men selected by Dwight who began their duties as the century opened worked in team as the core of Yale College until near the middle of the century. Their appointment was one of his most important contributions to Yale. Silliman after Dwight's death was to make Yale the leading center of science in the United States in the first half of the nineteenth century.

Dwight, before he died in 1817, had made it famous as a center of religion. His religion revealed to his generation the power of Calvinism, modified by Jonathan Edwards into the New England Theology and altered still further by Dwight himself to meet the needs of revivalist preaching. It also expressed the ideas of the Standing Order as to proper relations between church and state, relations which were to be profoundly altered by events in Connecticut in the very year in which Dwight died.

In 1791 Thomas Jefferson, Secretary of State, proclaimed the ratification of the First Amendment by the states and its inclusion in the Constitution. It opens with the restrictive ordinance: "Congress shall make no law respecting an establishment of religion, or prohibiting the free exercise thereof . . ." Timothy Dwight, at the time, was preaching and managing his flourishing school at Greenfield Hill. One wonders whether it occurred to him that the principle embodied in the amendment might one day be written into the constitution of Connecticut.

Around 1810 the President of Yale College expressed himself with considerable vigor on the question of the proper relation between church and state. He had made one of his many
journeys to parts of America far from New Haven, a practice
that gave him a wide and firsthand knowledge of the country.
This time he had explored New Hampshire on the northern
frontier. He learned that New Hampshire in adopting a constitution in 1792 had included in its Bill of Rights the provision
that "no person of any particular religious denomination shall
be compelled to pay toward the support of a teacher who is of
a different one." He found, moreover, that the Legislature had
levied no tax for the support of the clergy. Dwight noted in
his travel journal his opinion of certain religious denominations
that had obviously been active in New Hampshire. He doubtless knew also that in Virginia in the 1780's Baptists had strongly
supported Jefferson in his victorious fight to bring religious
liberty to that state. "Of all religious sects," wrote Dwight,

those which owe their existence to the reluctance, felt by every
avaricious man, to support the public worship of God, are the
worst in their character and the most hopeless of reformation. . . .
To preserve his self, the man [who belongs to a sect opposing public
support of religion] belies his conscience and insults his Maker. To
appease the one, and soothe the other, and at the same time preserve
some appearance of character among his neighbors he endeavors to
make up in a shew of zeal what he so evidently lacks of common
honesty. Hence he becomes enthusiastic, bigoted, censorious, impervious to conviction, a wanderer after every straggling exhorter,
and every bewildered tenet. . . . This conduct is often challenged
as a mere exercise of the rights of conscience; but conscience is
equally stranger to the conduct and the man.[2]

With all his gifts, Dwight never rose above the fighting parti-
san. He never transcended the Federalist's contemptuous attitude toward the common man.

Dwight, the Connecticut aristocrat, failed to appreciate the
significance of the spirit of freedom and equality that prevailed

in frontier settlements. He never fully comprehended that Christianity, which through the centuries had adapted itself to such varying social scenes as the Roman Empire, Byzantium, and feudal Europe, was compelled on the swiftly advancing American frontier of the early nineteenth century to adjust itself to a simple, fluid, and isolated society. It was Protestant Christianity, moreover, that moved with the settlements. No Spanish-style mission stations, guarded by presidios, existed in Tennessee, Kentucky, Ohio, or northern New England. In the forest clearing Protestantism, perforce, came down out of the high pulpit. The swift beat of camp-meeting hymns accompanied by clapping hands and stamping feet stirred the emotions. The words of the songs brought to dull and restricted lives a romantic vision of pearly gates and golden streets. A Protestantism brought down to the level of untutored cabin dwellers not only gave comfort and hope to the suffering and bereaved but did much to tame the lawlessness of the back country.

Dwight had neither understanding of nor sympathy for the simplified and often primitive Protestantism of the frontier. He saw only straggling exhorters, "bewildered" tenets, and men who wanted an excuse for not paying taxes for the support of public worship. Yet the religion of the frontier made on one occasion a direct impact on Timothy Dwight's Yale.

The President looked upon the support of religion as a matter of the utmost concern. He developed his ideas one day in a classroom that probably on this occasion was the Chapel which at the time served multiple purposes. It occurred in the midst of the War of 1812, a conflict, incidentally, which his Federalism compelled him to criticize. He had listened to a routine disputation by the senior class. The question had been: "Ought the clergy to be supported by law?" Dwight's hold on the undergraduates is demonstrated by the fact that a student took down in shorthand the President's "decision" as one of a complete record for the academic year, 1813–14. Dwight answered in the affirmative the question about clerical support.

"Where will you get your ministers," asked the instructor, "if you do not support them by law? You will get them from the pettifoggers of religion; the separatical preachers; those who pretend to differ from everybody, and know little or nothing of what they talk about. Such men are a disgrace to religion." Clearly sectarians still plagued the Standing Order. Dwight pushed on to an exposition of the basic tenet of his social philosophy. "From the intimate and inseparable connection between morality and religion," he said, "arises a most manifest necessity of religion for a nation. No free government has ever existed without religion . . . for in it is the great preventative of crimes of all sorts, and the foundation of morality, we must ever remember, is religion. On the grounds of public happiness and public security, then, even those who do not wish to avail themselves personally of the direct benefits of religion, might as well plead an exemption from the support of roads, bridges . . . because they do not use them, as excuse themselves from the support of the public preaching of the Gospel."[3] One wonders what the seniors said to one another as they picked up their papers and hurried out into the college yard. Connecticut politics at the time made the issue a live one. The undergraduates were likely to be found in the vanguard of change. Some five years later the state, unmoved by Dwight's long and stubborn campaign, would decide to take the risk to morals involved in the abolition of religious taxes.

The debate and decision in the classroom must be set beside the services in the Chapel. The routine of the eighteenth-century college continued into the nineteenth, its order of events unchanged from that which John Trumbull had once described:

> In the same round condemn'd each day
> To study, read, recite and pray.

A graduate of the Class of 1817, writing in a time of greater comfort, recalled with feeling the start of the college day—the

undergraduates "routed from their beds at six o'clock a.m. in
the months of winter, with the thermometer at ten degrees, to
go to morning prayers in a Chapel which had never dreamed
of a stove . . . the officiating tutors . . . as glad when the thing
was over, as were the glum and shivering students." The same
alumnus left a picture of the President. "He was accustomed
to attend and conduct the evening worship of the college, and
his image is vividly before me . . . as he entered the door, with
stately tread, grasping with both hands his broad-brimmed
beaver over his breast, and bowing alternately to the right and
left, as he passed up the aisle through the ranks of students, as
they stood and made reverent answering obeisance."[4]

During practically all of his presidency Dwight served as
pastor of the College Church. The Corporation tried four
times to fill the post of Professor of Divinity but, as in Stiles'
day, had found the clergymen whom they desired to appoint
reluctant to undertake the assignment. Both Corporation and
students, however, were more than happy when the President
agreed to assume the extra burden. Dwight had power as a
preacher. He never lost his hold on the undergraduates.

Often the Chapel contained distinguished visitors. New
Haven shared with Hartford the distinction of being a capital city. When the General Assembly met or the High Court
sat in the statehouse on the Green, notables of the state frequently occupied the hard pews of the Chapel during Sunday service. Occasionally, out-of-state celebrities, passing
through New Haven, paused to hear the man known as the
leading preacher of Connecticut. The Church of Christ in
Yale College occupied a position unsurpassed by any church
in the nation.

There were times when both preaching and listening required
in themselves a generous measure of that character that the
pastor worked so hard to foster. More than one observer described a service on a frigid winter day—the President in the
pulpit clad in greatcoat and mittens, the student congregation,
similarly attired, attending the sermon. The trial of the spirit

seemed appropriate to a Puritanism that renounced softness and magnified duty.

These sermons might well have been a part of Dwight's series on theology. He worked out his theological system in detail and methodically presented it in a series of discourses, one each Sunday, that ran through an undergraduate's four-year course. Dwight built on Jonathan Edwards but modified the original form of the New England theology in the direction of greater emphasis on common sense and also on freedom of the will. Published later, Dwight's system of theology enjoyed a vogue.

The President emphasized theology frankly and continuously. For him it provided the framework of ideas and understanding that gave religion substance and quality. He despised the uneducated exhorter, either in the West or the East, as a ranter who had nothing but emotion to offer his hearers. Dwight would most certainly have approved the designation given at a later time to a region in western New York swept by a succession of violent revivals, namely the "burnt-over area." If theology of necessity must deal with the mysteries of God and of the meaning of human life, Dwight made his answers as simple as a hard subject would permit. He strove to achieve the teacher's goal of clarity.

Clarity might be important but, so far as the undergraduates were concerned, half the power of the President's sermons lay in the fact that Timothy Dwight pronounced them. An alumnus, a disciple of Dwight, recalled the man. "He was of noble form, with a noble head and body, and he had one of the sweetest smiles that you ever saw. He always met me with a smile."[5] Dwight looked upon the College as what, in fact, it was: a large family. Near the end of his administration, enrollment passed the three-hundred mark, not too many for the President to know personally every student.

To his critics in the party of Jefferson, the President was an autocrat. They pointed to the fact that one of their number, Professor Josiah Meigs, a man of liberal ideas and a favorite of

Stiles, found working under Dwight sufficiently trying to make the mathematician welcome the opportunity for an escape to Athens, Georgia. Yet, for all his aggressive Federalism, Dwight moved with the times. He abolished the rating of students in the class roll in terms of their supposed social standing. Stiles had continued and emphasized elaborate and formal courtesy. Dwight insisted that the college rules should require no more than good manners. Faculty and students alike were gentlemen; let them comport themselves accordingly.

Disturbances normal to a community such as that of a college continued, of course. Even Puritanism proved no substitute for sports in the matter of releasing excess energy. And organized sport was still unknown in American colleges. A familiar narrative continued even in the Dwight regime—rolling barrels down a tutor's staircase, shying a stone at his windows, cutting the rope of the college bell, decorating conversation with profanity, explosions in the commons, uproars caused by the consumption of too much wine, beer, or metheglin. Tutor Moses Stuart in 1802 in a letter to Benjamin Silliman, at the time in Philadelphia studying chemistry, enumerated the "convulsions" of the term just ended. He concluded his narration with a figure suggested, perhaps, by much listening to Dwight's sermons. "In short," said Stuart, "there appear to be more devils in the College at present than were cast out of Mary Magdelene."[6]

In dealing with all manner of offenses, petty or serious, Dwight allowed the elaborate system of fines that President Clap had worked out virtually to lapse. With common sense Dwight thought a fine punished the parent rather than the culprit. Dwight substituted in more flagrant cases the interview with the President. His ability on such an occasion to blend an exposition of the nature of evil with an appeal for better conduct made the session an ordeal to shake the most brazen sinner. Some left the presidential presence in tears. Rustication or even expulsion followed extreme dereliction. David Milford, in a letter written in 1806, gave an undergraduate's-eye-view of the government of the institution. "We who are in College,"

he wrote, "live in a kind of little Monarchy, the President with
his privy council (the professors and tutors) have full and absolute power to do with us what they please so far as it respects
the business and behaviour of College. Being however of a
Methodistical turn in their manner of governing us they will
admit almost anybody however bad into College as it were
upon trial, and then if we play any tricks which they don't
like, instead of inflicting any other kind of punishment, they
excommunicate us, or like the Quakers, spue us out of their
mouth."[7] Young James Fenimore Cooper from Otsego Lake
in New York, who entered college at thirteen with a preparation in Latin so good that he scarcely cracked a book in his
freshman year, was one of those whom President Dwight
spued out.

Dwight, who tried conscientiously to function as the father
of a great family, preached twice on Sunday and often in-
formally on other occasions. His student congregation knew
him to be honest, keen, forthright, and straightforward. They
knew also that he took time in a busy life to deal with the special
problems of students in trouble. As it turned out, the combination of man and sermon came dangerously near on one occasion
to making the Yale of Timothy Dwight itself a "burnt-over
area." To understand more clearly the atmosphere that Dwight
attempted to create in the College it is necessary to look more
fully at some of his rejections.

A passage probably written late in his presidency enables a
later generation to get a glimpse down the bleak and austere
corridor of the Puritan mind. If Hawthorne ever read the
paragraphs, as he may have done, it must have confirmed for
him the soundness of some of his own analyses. Dwight entitled the piece, "Characteristics of the Men and Women of
New England."

"On grave subjects," he wrote, "we are grave; and on such
subjects we are more accustomed to dwell with pleasure, than

men less disposed to admit the doctrines and duties of divine revelation." His thought turned to a question of growing importance for Puritan America, one which the seniors frequently debated in their exercises in rhetoric: the theater had made its appearance in New York and, with more robust life, in Philadelphia; an American play had been written and produced. "It must be acknowledged," Dwight continued, "that we [New Englanders] think, converse and write much less concerning theatres and actors than the inhabitants of London [or] Paris. . . . I shall be told that the drama includes within its precincts some of the first efforts of human genius. The names of Aeschylus, Sophocles, and Euripedes, of Corneille, and his splendid train of followers; of the immortal Shakespeare, and his; and perhaps too Schiller and Kotzebue; will be conjured upon the stage to refute these observations." In 1795 a Philadelphia press had begun the publication of the first complete American edition of Shakespeare. "I am not to be informed at this period," Dwight went on, "of the talents of these writers. The superiority of their powers I acknowledge in its full extent; but I assert . . . that they were employed in such manner as to produce little good and much evil. Among all their productions there is scarcely one which an Apostle would even read. How great a part of them are little else than splendid vehicles of vice . . ." Dwight knew he was rowing against the current. He did not care. "But I shall be charged with bigotry," he continued with that forthrightness that caused undergraduates to admire him. "The force of the argument contained in this accusation I do not feel sufficiently to wish to refute it. Finally, I shall be declared destitute of taste. From this decision I make no appeal. If it is the proper prerogative of taste to be sustained in the world at the expense of morals and religion; if it is the criterion of taste, to approve the stage; if it is the dictate of taste to prefer amusement to virtue, I shall feel no interest in repelling the censure."[8]

One suspects that Tutor Dwight did not read the Bard of Avon with his boys in the 1770's who were interested in modern literature. The Puritan mind focused on one, and only one, drama. The Author of the play was the Creator of all men and things. Its hero was sinful man. An evil and tempting world provided its stage setting. The climactic scene was the life and work of Christ, and the ultimate event was the Day of Judgment. What happened at Yale College after 1795 can be understood only in the light of the deep involvement, intellectually and emotionally, of Timothy Dwight in this cosmic drama.

When Dwight assumed the presidency in 1795, the humanism and rationalism of the Enlightenment strongly influenced the personal philosophy of life of great numbers of educated Americans. The faith of Franklin, as he described it in his letter to Ezra Stiles, represented a common view. Thomas Paine held some of the same positive religious beliefs as the great Pennsylvanian. In the 1790's the author of *Common Sense* lived in France. The French clapped him in jail after England attempted by force to confine the Revolution. Inspired by the uprising against the tyrannies of the *ancien régime,* Paine wrote the *Rights of Man.* Then, gathering his ideas from the contemporary literature of rationalism and deism, he turned out *The Age of Reason.* As a journalist Paine was an authentic genius. His book carried to the common people the ideas of thinkers who were abler than himself but who did not possess his ability to communicate. Perhaps many of his attacks on the Bible (unworthy of serious attention by the standards of modern criticism) were his own. For Protestants and especially Puritans they comprised his sharpest barbs. In America, Paine's book appeared in the homes of the people to the very edge of the frontier. Supplementing Paine's effort, Elihu Palmer attempted without too much success to organize popular deism into a kind of denomination.

Undergraduates at Yale in the early 1790's, feeling themselves part of a libertarian tradition that ran as far back as the Stamp

Act, welcomed any attack on ancient authority that seemed to restrict human freedom. They made the French *philosophes* their heroes. They bought and read *The Age of Reason,* the first part of which appeared in 1794 and the second, written in prison, in 1796. Student discussions before the open fires in the rooms in Connecticut Hall brought out the contrast between a freewheeling rationalist philosophy and the discipline imposed by an authoritarian Scripture. Inevitably the discussions moved round to the question: Was the authority of the Bible genuine or specious? Was it or was it not the literal Word of God? These were crucial questions on which the destinies of men in time and in eternity depended.

President Dwight began his war against rationalism on the day he first met the senior class to arrange the topics for the routine disputations in the practice of rhetoric. In the list of possible subjects submitted by the class a mischievous student had included the question: "Are the Scriptures of the Old and New Testament the Word of God?" The new President chose the topic dealing with the Bible. Informing the class that he would not assume the arguments presented by either side to be expressions of private opinion, he urged the young men to work hard, to do their best to find and to present every possible argument to support the answer they had chosen. Most of them chose the negative. When the debate concluded Dwight rendered his decision and the reasoning that led him to it. He had spent much of his adult life preparing to answer just that question. Dwight's method represents first-class teaching. But it was more than teaching. The President had begun a crusade. He considered "infidelity" a spiritual malady that threatened not only all order in society but the destruction of immortal souls. He was in deadly earnest.

The crusade revealed the man. Timothy Dwight was not a scholar, he was a prophet. He had read books about the philosophers of the ancient world. He had undoubtedly gone through much of the literature of the eighteenth-century Enlightenment. But he had familiarized himself with Tyndall,

Shaftesbury, Chubb, Hobbes, Hume, Voltaire, and Rousseau not that he might understand and weigh their efforts to find the truth about society or the cosmos but to prepare himself to confute them. He had no commitment to the scholar's code.

Sentences taken from a sermon entitled "Revelation" suggest the method of Dwight's polemics. The preacher had been discussing the proposition: "That man cannot find out a religion which will render him acceptable to God." "The ancient philosophers," said Dwight, "applied themselves to the task of devising a system of Duty . . . with intense labour, in a multitude of instances, and through a long series of ages. The men, who most diligently occupied themselves in this employment, possessed talents, not inferior to any equal number of those who have come after them." Naturally Dwight, the Puritan, was interested in the ideas of ethics of the ancients that he might compare them with his own. "Yet their efforts not only failed," Dwight went on, "but failed to such a degree, that their doctrines, taken in the mass, would not now be regarded with any emotion, but contempt and horror, by a Christian child twelve years old." The words were those of the President speaking in chapel at a time when the reading of the classics held a central position in the curriculum of the College. "Their best apprehensions," continued Dwight, "concerning *Virtue,* or moral excellence, were in many respects crude, gross, and false. What was done by these men [to answer the question posed in the preacher's proposition] was, in all probability, the utmost which man is able to do. If *Pythagoras, Thales, Socrates, Plato, Aristotle,* and *Cicero,* could not form just opinions concerning these subjects; who, in the same circumstances, could? If their opinions concerning them were, to a great extent, gross and contemptible where are the men to whom we could apply with confidence for such as were sound, profitable, and certain means of our acceptance with God?"[9] The conclusion followed inevitably. Only God, revealing himself, can point out the religion acceptable to him.

Timothy Dwight was later, in a rejoinder to the *Edinburgh*

Review, to praise his old colleague John Trumbull. But the advice of that discerning tutor made no contribution to the sermon on Revelation:

> Give ancient arts their real due,
> Explain their faults, and beauties too;
> Teach where to imitate and where to mend,
> And point their uses and their end.
> Then bright philosophy would shine,
> And ethics teach the laws divine.

Dwight entitled the two baccalaureate sermons he delivered to the Class of 1797 "The Nature and Danger of Infidel Philosophy." The reign of terror in the French Revolution, the tumbrils, the guillotine, the execution of Louis XVI and of Marie Antoinette provided the background for these discourses. The young men of 1797 were halfway through their course when Dwight assumed the presidency. The discourses must have stirred, even excited, the class that graduated in a time of uncertainty and of vehement debate. They saw the President of the College disdaining to remain aloof from the burning questions of the day. He attempted no pose of objectivity. On the contrary the new bachelors of arts saw him, his sword swinging, moving into the thick of battle quite literally for the Lord. ". . . in its nature," said Dwight, "must this philosophy [of Infidelity] be vain and deceitful. I shall attempt to show, that, in fact, it has from the beginning, been of this unhappy character. This will appear in the [first] Place, in the discordance and contradictoriness of its doctrines."

The President then noted briefly the varying ideas of God of nine philosophers of the ancient world. Eight "infidel" philosophers of the modern world received fuller treatment. But the preacher's purpose was the same, namely to show that the men of the modern world, like those of the ancient, had come to no agreement, but rather had produced a bewildering variety of ideas concerning all the great subjects; nature, deity, revelation, and ethics. Often they contradicted one another.

With incisive sentences Dwight presented what purported to be an epitome of the thought of man after man. He put together what must have seemed to his hearers, as he intended it to be, a kaleidoscope of confusion. That was "infidelity."

"Infidelity" for Timothy Dwight did not emerge as a novel speculation to be studied and understood, if not believed. He saw it rather as an infection. It brought about moral disorders. For the Calvinist president the moral argument offered the final and conclusive proof. He set forth the record, as he saw it, in the conclusion of the first of the two sermons.

The morals of Rochester and Wharton need no comment. Woolston was a gross blasphemer. Blount solicited his sister-in-law to marry him, and, being refused, shot himself. Tyndall was originally a protestant, then turned papist, then protestant again, merely to suit the times; and was at the same time infamous for vice in general, and the total want of principle. Hobbes wrote the Leviathan, to serve the cause of Charles I, but, finding him fail of success, he turned to the defence of Cromwell. . . . Voltaire in a letter now remaining, requested his friend d'Alembert to tell for him a direct and palpable lie by denying he was the author of the Philosophical Dictionary . . . Hume died, as a fool dieth. The day before his death he spent in pitiful and affected unconcern about the tremendous subject, playing at whist, reading Lucian's dialogues, and making silly attempts at wit, concerning his interview with Charon, the heathen ferry-man of Hades. . . . I shall only add that Rousseau is asserted to have been guilty of gross theft, perjury, fornication, adultery, and of abjuring and assuming, alternately, the Catholic and the Protestant religion; neither of which he believed. Thus, I have exhibited to you the nature, and the actual state, of this Philosophy.[10]

Thus also, it might be added, Timothy Dwight had exhibited the nature of his logic and the state of his temper. He published the sermons. But he had only begun to fight.

On July 4, 1798, Dwight gave, at the request of the citizens of New Haven, an address that he entitled "The Duty of Americans at the Present Crisis." The crisis was genuine. President John Adams had published the XYZ Correspondence that detailed the insulting demands for bribes made by emissaries of the French Directory to American envoys whom Adams had sent to seek better relations between the two countries. A wave of anti-French feeling swept the country. An undeclared war began, and privateers of both nations prowled the seas. Dwight mobilized an aroused nationalism as reinforcement in his battle with infidelity.

Dwight took his text from the Book of Revelation. He analyzed one of the great prophecies. "From this explanation," he said, "it is manifest that the prediction consists of two great and distinct parts; *the preparation for the overthrow of the Antichristian empire; and the embarkation of men in a possessed and unusual opposition to God, and to his kingdom, accomplished by means of false doctrines, and impious teachers.*" No argument could have been more persuasive in Puritan New England than that from prophecy. Dwight described the rise of anticlericalism in Catholic Europe. He saw the suppression of the Jesuits and, in some countries, of other orders as "mighty preparations for the ruin of the Antichristian empire." These events seemed to Dwight to be the fulfillment of the first half of the prophecy.

The activities of Voltaire began the fulfillment of the second half. "About the year 1728," said the preacher, "Voltaire, so celebrated for his wit and brilliancy and not less distinguished for his hatred of christianity and his abandonment of principle, formed a systematic design to destroy christianity and to introduce in its stead a general diffusion of irreligion and atheism." Dwight told his hearers about the "Encyclopedie" and about the "formation of a secret Academy, of which Voltaire was the standing president, and in which books were formed, altered, forged, imputed as posthumous to deceased writers of reputation, and sent abroad with the weight of their names . . . Nor were the labors of this Academy confined to religion. They attacked morality and government, unhinged gradually the minds of men, and destroyed their reverence for everything heretofore esteemed sacred." The President offered no proofs to substantiate his charges of alteration, forgery, and false attribution of texts to dead writers. The activities of the Academy clearly suggested the beginning of the fulfillment of the second half of the prophecy. They prepared the way for the terrible deeds performed at the crest of the revolutionary madness.

In the excesses of the French Revolution Dwight found the climax of his address.

The sins of these enemies of Christ, and Christians are of numbers and degrees, which mock account and description.... For what shall we be connected with men of whom this is the character and conduct? Is it that we may assume the same character, and pursue the same conduct? Is it, that our churches may become temples of reason, our Sabbath a decade, and our psalms of praise Marseilles hymns? Is it that we may change our holy worship into a dance of Jacobin frenzy, and that we may behold a strumpet personating a Goddess on the altars of Jehovah? Is it that we may see the Bible cast into a bonfire, the vessel of the sacramental supper borne by an ass in public procession, and our children, either wheedled or terrified, uniting in a mob, chanting mockeries against God . . .? Is it that we may see our wives and daughters the victims of legal prostitution; soberly dishonoured; speciously polluted; the outcasts of delicacy and virtue, and the loathing of God and man? . . . Shall we, my brethren, become partakers in these sins?[11]

Timothy Dwight printed this discourse also. During two years of semi-war his rhetoric took effect. The excesses of the French Revolution brought the rationalistic humanism of the Enlightenment into disrepute. The undeclared war against France produced in New England a revulsion against all things French. Dwight, who worked only in blacks and whites, contrasted religion with the doings of the Paris mob. After 1798, Puritan New Englanders recognized a champion.

In the spring of 1802 a religious revival began at Yale. It grew quietly yet steadily in intensity. Before the commencement in September half the senior class had publicly announced their faith and joined the College Church. A third went on to become ministers. The lower classes were profoundly moved. Tutor Benjamin Silliman knelt beside his students. In June he wrote his mother a letter that reflected the sentiment, sometimes merging into sentimentality, that characterized an emerging age. "Yale College is a little temple," said the young instructor, "prayer and praise seem to be the delight of the greater part of the students while those who are still unfeeling are awed into respectful silence."[12] There had been no special meetings. Dwight had not departed from his normal routine, namely to preach a theological sermon on Sunday morning and a practical sermon in the afternoon. The revival burned brightly for a time; then the flame died down. A succession of new classes entered the College. The mood of the summer of 1802 faded. But it would come again.

A sermon by Dwight which he called "The Youth of Nain" seems to have touched off the revival. Dwight urged the young men before him to "repent; believe; escape for your lives: or the night will be upon you, in which you will sleep, to wake no more."[13] But student initiative played a part in lighting the fires of that first Yale revival of the new century. In 1797 twenty-two undergraduates and three graduates organized the Moral Society. They created it a secret society. Eighteen years passed before they asked a member of the faculty to join. The new society stood in an old tradition of student enterprise and activities. The desire of undergraduates to make their own contribution to the life of the College had produced the literary societies, Linonia and Brothers in Unity, both originally secret. Later, in 1780, it had led to the establishment of Phi Beta Kappa, the second chapter of that fraternity of scholars.

The Moral Society appeared in the context of the time. The reaction against the French Revolution had begun. But a spirit of worldliness still dominated the life in the college yard. The usual amount of drinking continued in an age in which liquor was cheap and its consumption a commonplace among the males of all social groups. In the College a number of abandoned worldlings "played at Whist." Outside the College an American tendency to violent assertion of right or demands that had manifested itself before the Revolution in the riots of the Liberty Boys and the Tea Party in Boston harbor continued after that conflict in Shays' Rebellion in the 1780's in Massachusetts and the Whiskey Rebellion in the 1790's in Pennsylvania. One need not be surprised that in such an age freshmen, near the end of their first year, elected one of their larger and more combative members to the office of Bully. He functioned as class president, his symbol of authority being a long, stout club with a formidable knob on the end. By tradition he led the collegians, when occasion required, against the hostile roughs of the town. He remained in office throughout his course and, as Senior Bully, held a place of high prestige.

The social scene that brought forth the Bully produced also the Moral Society. If its organizers possessed the idealism of youth, they did not mistake themselves for saints. They shared as individuals in the life of their fellows. Members of the Moral Society could sometimes be found in the line-up of those subjected to discipline by the government of the College. But the Society at times disciplined one of its own members whose behavior suggested that the Old Adam was getting out of hand. The organization took itself seriously.

If their undergraduate predecessors a few years back had made heroes of Voltaire and D'Alembert, the young men of the Moral Society reflected a new mood just appearing and one that extended beyond the College. The brilliant and creative eighteenth-century Age of Reason was passing. After the turn of the century rationalism would have lost its old glamour and prestige. In Europe romanticism was emerging. Rousseau, who insisted that the impulses of the natural man are good and to be trusted, became a pioneer in creating a temper destined to affect mightily, in the first half of the nineteenth century, the literature and the fine arts of both Europe and America. The Enlightenment had emphasized the importance of the trained intellect functioning and creating in an ordered universe. The romantics pointed to the emotions as the wellspring of the human spirit. Within the heart of the individual man, they believed, lay unexplored depths out of which new truth and new life were destined to come. Evangelical Protestantism, rising in America after Whitefield and Edwards, carried at the opening of the nineteenth century the romantic's emphasis on the emotions into religious life. In many of the denominations that grew swiftly outside New England, Evangelical Protestantism played down the intellectual creedalism of an earlier age. It preached a simple Gospel. In the New England Theology the accent on feeling grew in importance in a dour system. Sensitive to the subtle alchemy that was dissolving an age of reason into one of romanticism, the undergraduates at Yale founded their secret Moral Society. It was destined to continue for more than a third of a century.

If the Society expressed an older tradition of student enterprise in Yale College, it also played the role of pioneer. Within a developing Protestantism it was a free and voluntary association of young men, an organization to facilitate serious discussion of religious questions and to further in a humble way the improvement of society. The Society appeared at a time when churches, such as the Baptist and the Methodist, were insisting that organized religion should follow the pattern of the free and voluntary association and should, where necessary, break away from all control or support by the state. The Moral Society stands in the historical record as one of the first in that series of societies and organizations—missionary, tract, Bible, peace, temperance, and antislavery—that, taken together, made up the extraordinary humanitarian movement in what Kenneth S. Latourette has called "The Great Century." If the preaching of Timothy Dwight provided the background for the appearance of the Moral Society, the undergraduates, with their principle of free and voluntary association for the furtherance of religion, were far ahead of the President. Dwight stubbornly held fast to the old idea that the state must provide support for the churches.

The revival of 1802 at Yale followed by some five years the
first manifestations of the new awakening west of the mountains. On the frontier unlettered and credulous persons interpreted the various types of hysterical phenomena that appeared
in the protracted meetings as proof that God had put his finger
upon human hearts. Into this region came the fame of Dwight,
challenger of infidelity. Some families in trans-Appalachia sent
their sons to Yale. These brought east with them news of
extraordinary and sometimes terrifying camp meetings, together with such names as James McGready, Presbyterian, and
Peter Cartwright, Methodist. At the turn of the nineteenth
century, revivalism tended to spread from community to community, as a new fashion sometimes sweeps unexpectedly
across the nation. In time revivalism came to Yale. The activities of the Moral Society, organized to promote and preserve
"morality among the members of this University," helped to
prepare the way. In the spring of 1802 a small group of students,
following the spirit of the times, began gathering to pray that
the stirring in evidence elsewhere might come to the College.
The revival of the same year was one of the earliest manifestations of what came to be called the Second Great Awakening
in New England.

The Moral Society provided a student background also for
the revival of 1808 that seems to have resulted more directly
from the preaching of the President. Still later the Society
justly claimed that the quickening of the spirit in 1813 was a
harvest that came from its own planting. Eighteen hundred and
thirteen was a year of many disappointments and some triumphs in the War of 1812. Under the date of July 4, 1813, the
scribe set down the following in the record book of the organization. "The year past," he wrote, "the Society has flourished in a manner superior to all other years. The number has
been great: the members have been spirited, peaceful and done
honor to the society. No member has been expelled or even
corrected. The last term ought even to be remembered by the
society, in which a great part of the Senior class awakened to

their eternal interest, as well as a number from other classes which greatly increased the society."[14] The happenings in the Yale microcosm reproduced those of the Second Great Awakening in New England communities.

Timothy Dwight cautiously used the revivalist technique within the framework of the New England Theology. Like his Congregational colleagues he discouraged excessive emotionalism. Dwight tried by personal contact with distressed students to prevent the concern for sin on the part of the individual from developing into hysteria. On one occasion the President sat at night by the bedside of an undergraduate stricken down by anguish and despair. Yet he preached revival sermons. Contemporaries credited one of these with initiating one revival and aiding in others. Dwight called it "The Harvest Past." It discloses both his style and his thought.

The preacher chose the theme of the busy and self-centered man who passes from youth through middle life and advancing age comfortable in the assumption that "repentance might yet be safely begun at some distant time." The concluding sentences of the sermon described the consequences of sin and of procrastination. Death comes unexpectedly. "The curtain now is drawn . . . his spirit . . . alone and friendless . . . ascends to God: to see all its sins *set in order before its eyes* . . . it is cast out as wholly wicked and unprofitable into the land of darkness and the shadow of death; there to wind its melancholy journey through regions of sorrow and despair, ages without end; and to take up forever the gloomy and distressing lamentation in the text, 'The harvest is past, the summer is ended; but I am not saved.' "[15] A junior in the Class of 1797 named Lyman Beecher listened one Sunday in the Chapel as Dwight preached that sermon. When the discourse ended, he wrote later, "a whole avalanche rolled down on my mind. I went home weeping every step."[16] In the following year the young man became one of the founders of the Moral Society. In a sense the New England Theology encouraged such experience as that of Beecher. Only through travail of the soul could weak and

erring man have any assurance that God had bestowed his grace
and that the former sinner was numbered among the saved.

Four years before the revival of 1813 a stranger became a
center of interest in the College. For several months in 1809
an Hawaiian boy came regularly to the yard to visit the room
of a senior named Edwin W. Dwight, who seems not to have
been related to the President. Captain Brintnall of New Haven,
who had ventured in the China trade, had given the boy
refuge when his ship had touched at the Hawaiian Islands.
Obookiah, who had seen his parents killed in a tribal war and
who was being trained by an uncle, a medicine man, in mysteries and rituals, fled the land where he had suffered so much
anguish. After the end of the voyage in New York, Brintnall
had brought the boy to New Haven where Dwight had discovered him. Finding the lad anxious to learn, Dwight became
his tutor.

The records permit a glance into a college room in the first
decade of the nineteenth century, where classmates of Dwight
gathered before the fireplace to see and talk with the brown-
skinned youth from the Pacific. He was a bright pupil with a
gift for mimicry, which on occasion he used to astonish the
guests. Obookiah brought to the college yard a glimpse of a
strange and a distant world. To Edwin Dwight and other religious members of the class he represented what was known
in the language of the time as heathenism. Dwight taught the
boy to speak English and to read and write.

Dwight's idea of what should be done for Obookiah's soul
provides a commentary on student attitudes. The senior
thought his pupil should abandon Captain Brintnall's home to
live with the President of the College. "This satisfied me,"
wrote Obookiah later. "I went with him to Dr. Dwight's
house. I lived with this pious and good family for some time.
Here for the first time I met with praying family morning
and evening. . . . I heard of God as often as I lived with this

family and I believed but little."[17] Timothy Dwight, as well as some of the boys in his College, came face to face with heathenism. In the following year, 1810, the President was one of the projectors of the American Board of Commissioners for Foreign Missions whose central office was established at Boston and which became the first American missionary society actually to carry its work beyond the boundaries of the nation.

While staying with the President's family, Obookiah came often to his teacher's room to continue his lessons. The Hawaiian boy met there one day the son of Samuel Mills, minister in Torringford—now Torrington. As a consequence the Polynesian became a member of the missionary-minded clergyman's household. Here he continued to study English and also learned to work on a farm. Here also, as in the dormitory at Yale, he became an object of lively interest. Ministers rode considerable distances to the Mills' home to look upon heathenism in the flesh. "I was told by them about heaven and hell," Obookiah recorded, "but I did not pay any attention to what they say; for I thought that I was just as happy as . . . those who do know about God much more than I do."[18]

The story that began when a Yale senior discovered an Hawaiian lad, clad in an ill-fitting sailor suit and wandering about New Haven, had a significant sequel: Obookiah experienced conversion, the emotional conversion of the time. He spoke in many Connecticut churches, where he stood before the congregations as the symbol of the heathen who had grasped the opportunity for salvation. There were other Polynesians in New England, flotsam left by the sea trade. Obookiah helped to raise money for a Foreign Mission School that came into being in 1817 at Cornwall, Connecticut. Here islanders and Asiatics in New England, together with Indians from the South and West, prepared themselves to carry the gospel to their respective peoples. Edwin Dwight became the first principal. When typhus brought death to Obookiah in 1818, Dwight wrote a *Memoir of Henry Obookiah* which the

American Tract Society published. The story it told illuminates the mind of the evangelical Protestantism that Timothy Dwight did so much to revive in Connecticut and at Yale.

One day in 1812 Timothy Dwight dictated, because of impaired eyesight, to an amanuensis in the President's office of Yale. Seventeen years had gone by since the Corporation had satisfied the ambition that never rested after his students had recommended their favorite tutor to succeed Naphtali Daggett. For seventeen years Dwight had been "Caesar." He had developed the College by giving it a new faculty. He had also made himself a major figure in the Federalist party of Connecticut. He wielded sufficient power for his political adversaries to refer to him angrily as "Pope" Dwight. As he formulated his paragraphs, he could look out on the college yard. The original building of the Collegiate School had long since vanished. A row of neat, brick structures stretched northward from Chapel Street. South College came first; then, at varying intervals, the Chapel, Connecticut Hall (now usually known as Middle), North, and, at the end, the Connecticut Lyceum, the first building wholly devoted to recitations. West of Connecticut Hall a new and inferior structure housed the commons, the place of origin of most of the student disturbances. Distinction had come to the College. By 1812 Timothy Dwight was not only one of the best known and most influential men in New England but his fame had spread beyond the Appalachians. Now, however, when he was dictating an essay in the form of a letter to an unnamed British friend, he was not thinking merely of Yale or of New England; he had all America in mind.

"In the Edinburgh Review of Ashe's Travels in America," Dwight wrote, "is the following passage, 'In short, Federal America has done nothing either to extend, diversify, or embellish the sphere of human knowledge. Though all she has written were obliterated from the records of learning, there would (if we except the works of Franklin) be no positive diminution, either of the useful, or the agreeable. The destruction of her whole literature, would not occasion so much regret, as we feel for the loss of a few leaves from an ancient classic.' "

Dwight, perhaps, paused to take in the obvious commentary on his own poems, *The Conquest of Canaan* and *Greenfield Hill*. "These declarations," he went on, "are certainly uttered in a sprightly manner. But they are untrue. The late President Edwards has more enlarged the science of Theology than any divine, of whom either England or Scotland can boast . . ." Dwight gave three spirited and cogent pages to his grandfather. Then he continued:

The talents of my countrymen have been exhibited, as I think, respectably in various other modes. Dr. Franklin is excepted in this very declaration of the Reviewer from the general disgrace. . . . Professor Winthrop [of Harvard] would have done credit to any country in the character of a natural philosopher; as would also Dr. Williams, who afterward filled the same chair in the University at Cambridge. Dr. Rittenhouse [of Philadelphia] merited this character in a still greater degree. . . . The best Orrery, it is believed in the world was invented, as well as made by Dr. Rittenhouse. . . . Many other specimens of ingenuity might be here mentioned, which have reflected not a little credit on the inventors of their native country. Such is the machine, invented by Mr. Whitney for cleansing the upland cotton of its seeds. [The boys of the College frequently walked past Whitney's gun works under East Rock where he pioneered in methods that were ultimately to make mass production possible.] Such also was the submarine vessel, invented by Mr. Bushnell of Saybrook [which actually submerged but failed by bad luck to blow up a British warship in New York harbor in the Revolution]. Such is the application of steam to the purposes of navigation.

Dwight turned his attention from theology and mechanics to the arts. He was determined to complete the picture of the America in which he lived and to demonstrate that his fellow citizens had taste and an interest in the "agreeable." His thought ran back to the "Hartford Wits." "The poetry of Americans," Dwight went on, "is treated by these Reviewers with not a little contempt. On this subject I shall say little. It may, however, be observed, that several Reviewers have spoken of it in more favorable terms. It may also be observed without any partiality, that McFingal [by John Trumbull] is not inferior in wit and humour to Hudibras; and in every other respect is superior. . . . The painters of this country have been holden in honourable estimation in Great-Britain. A high reputation has been attained by West and Copley, by Trumbull and Stewart . . ." Dwight added a final name to his catalogue. "The reviewer is disposed to speak contemptuously of Marshall's Life of Washington. Yet there is no piece of biography, written in Great-Britain, if we except those of Johnson, which would not suffer by a comparison with it."[19] Dwight, staunch Federalist, could not resist a plug for the Chief Justice who in 1803 in *Marbury v. Madison* had delivered a lecture on morals to President Thomas Jefferson.

Timothy Dwight was describing the intellectual world of America in which the undergraduates lived and the tradition of which the College was a part. His protest echoed the spirit of the nationalism that had spurred the young tutor to begin the writing of an epic which he hoped would bring honor to his country and then to resign his tutorship to become a chaplain in the Revolutionary Army.

Dwight lived and worked in the tradition of the Reformation. He supported the science of Silliman in the faith that it would further disclose the ways and wonders of the God whom the Bible revealed. Dwight insisted always upon the primacy of revealed truth. His treatment of the ancient philosophers in his sermon on "Revelation" makes clear the fact that the President of the College had no real knowledge of the method, discipline, or devotion of the scholar. Dwight's spiritual forebear was John Calvin. For Dwight, as for Thomas Clap, theology stood first among the arts and sciences. But Dwight, unlike

Clap, consciously shaped his theology to give it maximum utility for the evangelist.

But the President was a man of the New World, not of the Old. An ardent nationalism had taken him into the war, had made him support the Constitution, and through twenty-two years had impelled him as president to develop a college that would elevate and enrich the cultural life of the country. This achievement provided his real answer to the sneers of critics of the United States from across the Atlantic. Dwight also sensed that individualism which had been emerging in America since the first settlements and which had found its classic expression in the Declaration of Independence. "The piety of Hezekiah reformed and saved a nation," said the President as he faced the citizens of New Haven on that Fourth of July, 1798. Forty years later Ralph Waldo Emerson would preach in a new philosophical context the same doctrine of the potential power that resides in the individual man.

The "piety of Hezekiah" gave Dwight his model and his hope of accomplishment. When he died, he had not saved a nation. But he had raised the College to a position of leadership and he had made the plain, brick chapel that stood between South College and Connecticut Hall a sanctuary from which dedicated young men went out to serve the nation and the Lord. Through these spiritual sons and through the sermons preached in the College pulpit and read throughout the country in printed form Timothy Dwight contributed significantly to the re-establishment of Protestantism as a vital force in American life.

Chapter 5. The Last Days of the Old Chapel

To the men and women of 1817 the pulpit of the Chapel seemed empty indeed when Timothy Dwight no longer stood there. Jeremiah Day accepted the presidency of Yale with reluctance. The Corporation knew that the dying Dwight had expressed the wish that the Professor of Mathematics succeed him. They also knew that Day did not wish to serve. The Fellows elected the president of Middlebury College to be Dwight's successor but that officer declined. So Day, obeying the call to duty, took up the burden.

The moral thought of the Puritanism in which Day had been reared came to focus in the two words "duty" and "discipline." The Calvinist doctrine of the inherited depravity of the human soul emphasized the need for discipline. The College accepted the Puritan principles. Jeremiah Day seldom failed to occupy the President's seat at the Sunday services and was often present at morning prayers. The new president, like Timothy Dwight, considered himself the head of a great family. Day and his faculty looked upon the College as an institution that stood *in loco parentis* to the student until he received his diploma at commencement. A published statement of the policy of the faculty left no doubt as to the philosophy of the College. "In the internal policy of the institution," said the Report of 1828, "as the students are gathered in one family, it is deemed an essential provision that some of the officers should constitute a portion of this family, being always present with them, not only at their meals, and during the business of the day; but in the hours allotted to rest. The arrangement is such that in our college buildings, there is no room occupied by students, which is not near to the chamber of one of the officers." The authorities enforced a rigorous discipline, mental and moral. The College was a place where character, as well as intellect, was fostered. All students attended the same required classes and religious exercises. Undergraduates who could not or would not meet the required standards of moral conduct or intellectual achievement disappeared. Normally about half those who entered a class dropped out before graduation.

For the most part the students accepted the rigorous regimentation. But the liberal philosophy that Jefferson had written into the Declaration of Independence grew in importance in the early decades of the nineteenth century as the westward moving frontier gave more and more Americans experience with the liberty and rough equality of the new settlements. The developing mood affected life on the College yard where the authorities still governed, as Day's administration opened, in accordance with the ideas of an aristocratic Federalism and a demanding Puritanism. At times what Ezra Stiles called "tumults" rocked the little academic community. A "bread and butter" rebellion was followed by a "conic sections" rebellion. In the latter uprising, which occurred in 1825, Horace Bushnell, a sophomore, became a leader in an open revolt against the faculty which in student opinion had set an unfair examination in mathematics. One disturbance became an annual occurrence and acquired the status of a tradition. The fall term ended in January. Year after year on Christmas Eve enterprising undergraduates attempted measures to silence the college bell on the following morning. "The evening before Christmas," a member of the Class of 1849 later commented, "was made an occasion for special outbreak of disorder on the college grounds which had no equal in its peculiarities at any other season."[1] The custom did not end until, in the middle of the century, the authorities changed the academic calendar so as to put Christmas in the winter vacation. The change was part of a general relaxation of the old rigidities.

Jeremiah Day in dealing with boisterous undergraduates tempered firmness with sagacity and a sense of humor. On one evening the noise of a riotous student procession marching down College Street brought the President out of his house. Instead of attempting to quell it Day simply joined the last two students at the end of the line, saying nothing. When they became aware of their companion, they slipped silently into the night. The President then joined the next pair in front who, in their turn, disappeared. The process continued until Day came to the front couple and the procession had vanished.

The measure of the place of Timothy Dwight in the life of Yale is suggested by the fact that three men ultimately took over his work. Jeremiah Day became president. The Corporation appointed Eleazar Fitch as Livingston Professor of Divinity charged with the duty of preaching in chapel. Chauncey Goodrich, member with Fitch of the Class of 1810 and Professor of Rhetoric, became through his own volition religious adviser to the students—the chaplain, in fact, of the College. Goodrich had joined the College Church as a sophomore, Fitch in his junior year. The College had grown. The time had passed when the president dominated its life.

Fitch began his ministry in the Chapel in 1818 in a time of unusual difficulty. The students did not, however, cause the trouble. In 1818 a long and bitter conflict in Connecticut ended when the voters of the state abolished the privileges of the Congregational Church. They cast down the Standing Order. Timothy Dwight, until his strength failed, had fought powerfully to retain Congregationalism as an established church. Lyman Beecher had battled by his side and, when Dwight died, had assumed the unofficial leadership of the clergy in their campaign to retain their old position. Both Dwight and Beecher had used the revival as an instrument to win new church members and, incidentally, new supporters of establishment. In 1818 Litchfield's pastor read the election returns with dismay. "It was as dark a day as I ever saw," Beecher wrote later. "The odium thrown upon the ministry was inconceivable. The injury done to the cause of Christ as we then supposed was irreparable. For several days I suffered what no man can tell."2 Then the chastened Beecher and his Connecticut colleagues discovered the importance of a principle that William Penn had established in Pennsylvania as long before as 1681, namely that the cause of faith is best served when the support of religion becomes the responsibility of free churches which are voluntary associations of worshipers. Beecher learned the lesson well. In a time when a rising democracy expressed itself in the abolition of property qualifications for voting, Beecher became the champion of the principle that Christians, united as free members of their societies, should look only to their consciences and their wills to further the faith they cherished.

The Church of Christ in Yale College had, paradoxically, been founded in a special sense on the principle of voluntarism. In an institution that required attendance on daily prayers and at formal chapel services on the Sabbath Thomas Clap had initiated a voluntary church society, made up of undergraduates and graduates, of faculty members and their families, and of other spiritually qualified persons who cared to join. The law of the College had no relevance for this group. The undergraduate could join or ignore the Church; his conscience decided. The members of the Church assembled for the monthly communion service and for the midweek prayer meeting. From time to time the members gathered to conduct parish business.

Throughout the first quarter of the nineteenth century membership in the College Church remained small. An event that occurred in 1822 suggests a reason for the paucity of the membership and at the same time brings out the somber quality of the puritanism of the time. The brilliant Alexander Metcalf Fisher had recently been promoted from a tutorship to the Professorship of Mathematics vacated when Day became president. Young Fisher was engaged to Lyman Beecher's gifted daughter Catherine, sister of Harriet and destined to accomplish much for the advancement of women's education. Going abroad for advanced study, the promising mathematician lost his life in a storm which drove his ship onto the rocky coast of Ireland. When the news of the disaster reached New Haven, the shop-keepers closed their places of business, a gesture of mourning that reveals the impression the young man had made on the community. To Catherine the tidings from overseas brought a double tragedy. She had to accept her personal loss. But beyond that she knew that Alexander, though he had desired to do so, had never passed through that travail and final triumph of the spirit that was called conversion. Catherine, therefore, had to live with the conviction that the man she had loved could not in death join the glorious company of the saved. In her anguish she carried on a sad correspondence about the matter with her busy father, who tried to explain to her the theological meaning of the hard doctrine.

A "professing Christian" at Yale in the first quarter of the nineteenth century announced, either tacitly or openly, that he had passed through the torment and joy of conversion. To profess without such proof of grace might turn out to be blasphemy. The College Church remained small because no undergraduate or other person lightly joined.

Life in the College yard changed as an emerging industrialism and growing cities made that of the nation more complex. A mounting democratic spirit eroded the old Federalism. What came later to be called "Jacksonian democracy" won its first victory in Connecticut when a new state constitution put an end to the establishment of Congregationalism. New fashions in clothing suggested the emergence of a new era. The small clothes and the tiewigs of the eighteenth century had gone, replaced by less formal garb.

A member of the Class of 1821, writing in the manner of the popular novels of the second quarter of the century, has left a description of undergraduate apparel in the years after the War of 1812. "Passing down the college yard in front, with the observant eye of a newcomer," he commented, "I noticed a group who seemed to be much entertained by one around whom they were standing, and who was evidently a favourite. A small blue coatee, with gilt buttons; coarse brown linen trowsers, draggled and soiled at the bottom (for he had been rambling afield in the morning dew); a loosely tied cravat; and a broad-brimmed leghorn, drooping upon his shoulders and about his face, were his costume."[3]

Samuel Cowles, who had gone walking that morning, was destined to be elected by his class to be custodian of the Bully Club, an honor that made him a kind of class president. In an age when organized sports did not exist, walking provided almost the only outdoor recreation. The environs of New Haven offered varied and pleasant opportunities. Dirt roads led out through the countryside of well-fenced fields and substantial farmsteads. Trampers who visited the cave on West Rock where the refugee judges who had condemned Charles I had hidden in the seventeenth century recalled the antiquity of the town. On East Rock the college boys badgered the eccentric hermit who tended his half-dozen sheep in the meadow beside the hut he called his home. Samuel Cowles, who enjoyed risking his neck in attempts to scale its vertical cliff, was one of a long succession of adventurers.

Linonia, the oldest of the two debating societies, suffered from the tensions of the times. In 1819 a sudden and menacing controversy divided North and South, to be quieted in the following year by the Missouri Compromise. Most of the undergraduates from below the Mason–Dixon Line belonged to that society. In 1819, when the Southerners failed in a heated contest to elect one of their number president, many withdrew to organize a third literary society, Calliope. Change also affected the venerable Phi Beta Kappa when that organization voted to "explode" its secrets. A member who had favored the new policy later remarked that he did not "like to be charged with secrets which are of no importance and not worth the trouble either of keeping or revealing."[4] The Moral Society, now more than a quarter of a century old, continued to add to its library and to hold its debates. Leonard Bacon of the Class of 1820 was a member of the committee that ran the organization. But, as the second decade of the nineteenth century ended, interest in the society flagged. It was soon to disappear.

Bacon, whose father had been a missionary among the Indians of the Great Lakes region, planned to enter the ministry. He was one of that group of impecunious students who were assisted to prepare for the ministry by societies organized to further such a purpose. Some of the young men, however, who planned to serve the church came from more well-to-do families. The revivals which occurred from time to time added to the number of prospective clergymen; one such was Samuel Cowles.

Through the hot summer days of 1820 the college bell clanged its summons monotonously to academic and religious exercises. In their free time the undergraduates kicked footballs on the Green, strolled along city streets, and hiked into the country. On pleasant evenings groups on the College yard talked of College affairs and watched the quiet life of the town at the end of the day's activities. The doors of the shops closed. As the twilight deepened, lights came out in the houses beside the Green. The talk ran to the societies, to the idiosyncrasies of a tutor, to the unhappy fellow student who had felt the weight of College discipline. Later in the evening the undergraduates, sitting on the plain chairs and the beds of the dormitory rooms, continued the gossip.

Inevitably in that summer the talk of both students and faculty turned often to the *Microscope,* a Yale publication that had first appeared in the previous winter months. Its masthead announced that it was "edited by a Fraternity of Gentlemen." Undoubtedly, lively speculation tried to identify the authors of its unsigned articles. These included patriotic verses that recalled the victories of Perry and of Jackson. Some contributions dealt with religion. One deplored the lack of development in the United States of literary taste. The writer explained the absence of literary men of quality by pointing out that "almost all men in these States are men of business; each engaged in a variety of active pursuits, from which he expects his subsistence, his reputation, and his influence."[5] The author added that such writing as existed had been produced for particular purposes; ministers published sermons and doctors papers on the healing art. Only such men as those who had turned out an arithmetic, a geography, or a spelling book had been able to make a living by the pen.

Everyone knew that undergraduates did not do the principal pieces. The sponsors of the undertaking clearly had in mind as model the *North American Review*. At the end of the year the promoters disclosed that three recent graduates of the College, including James Gates Percival, had provided practically all the material.

Perhaps it was the interest of the *Microscope* in literature that inspired six seniors to organize themselves in 1820 into a literary and social club to which they gave the mathematical name of Hexahedron. Meeting each week in the room of one of the members, the group read English poetry. Its existence evidenced not only widening interests on the part of the undergraduates but a serious effort to supplement a curriculum whose study of literature did not go beyond the classics. Three of the members were destined to achieve distinction. Alexander Twining, engineer, located the line of the New Haven Railroad in Connecticut. Leonard Bacon served many years as pastor of the First Church on the Green and as member of the Corporation. Theodore Woolsey became President of the College.

The existence of the Hexahedron suggested a growing maturity in undergraduate life, but an essay in the *Microscope* discussed, gloomily, the condition of American colleges. The writer thought that the desire of each state to have at least one college tended to disperse the resources of the nation among

too many weak and struggling institutions. The Legislature of
Massachusetts had recently handsomely supported Harvard;
but the General Assembly of Connecticut had withheld needed
aid. The article pointed out the unhappy consequences of legis-
lative parsimony. "The [scientific] apparatus and cabinets of
most of our literary institutions," the writer continued, "are
small, while with the exception of the University of Cambridge
[Harvard], there is no one whose library amounts to more than
ten thousand volumes. The student has here a limited opportunity to consult the great masters of ancient learning. His
principal books of reference or reading are the Grecian and
Roman classics and the standard works of the last few centuries.
The knowledge acquired is comparatively superficial and . . .
[the student] seldom is able to 'drink deep' from the fountain
of learning or literature." The comment throws light on such
impromptu clubs as the Hexahedron. The colleges, the writer
concluded, must have more funds.

The young bachelor of arts who wrote the paper did not
despair. On the contrary, in spite of his pessimistic picture of the
educational scene of 1820, he looked to the future with a
typically American optimism:

Science and literature are beginning to engross the attention of
many of our young men of education, and several American publications have been well received on the eastern side of the Atlantic.
The public taste, although it may have been vitiated by the flood of
recent fiction and second rate poetry which has flowed in ceaseless
streams from our presses, is evidently improving. As the western
wilderness becomes peopled, the rage for emigration will lessen,
and eventually cease. The population of the country will become
more dense and the desire for improvement will be felt in old, as
well as the new states. The liberality there manifested will be more
strikingly visible east of the Allegheny, in consequence of their
greater wealth. It will become more fashionable for men of fortune
to part with some of their superfluous riches, in order to acquire
that reputation which those who evince this liberality so justly
merit.[6]

The authorities at Yale had already put to the test the theory that giving money to colleges was becoming fashionable among the more substantial citizenry. In 1817 Professor James L. Kingsley had taken time off from the teaching of Latin and Greek to write a brochure entitled, "Remarks on the Present Situation of Yale College, for the Consideration of its Friends and Patrons." As a result of the pamphlet, undergraduates in the summer of 1820 watched with interest bricklayers and carpenters as they began the erection of a new dormitory, North College. Kingsley revised the pamphlet in 1823 and, in the next year, a new chapel came into being between North College and North Middle. Jeremiah Day and his associates, good Yankees all, understood the meaning of pragmatism a century before William James put the word into the American language. But they gave thought to the spirit as well as to the treasury. Months before the builders had completed North College, the President and the faculty found themselves workers in one of the more important of Yale revivals.

Throughout the first half of the nineteenth century revivals provided the most spectacular and, sometimes, sensational aspect of American Protestantism. They flourished in a country where republican institutions put a premium on the ability of the political leader to persuade the electorate. The Protestant preacher might expound the very word of God but he spoke to a free people; he must persuade his hearers if his admonitions were to have force. At his best the revival preacher appealed to the reason of the men and women who came to hear what his message had to offer them. But emotion underlies reason. Just as the Republic brought forth at times the demagogue, so, on occasion, a religion dependent for support on voluntarism produced the ranter bent on swaying, by the use of any means, the minds of his unlettered hearers. Too often, camp meeting exhorters, particularly on the frontier, exposed to view unhappy aspects of American civilization.

Lyman Beecher recognized the rabble-rouser in the pulpit as a menace, not only to religion but also, when he turned vituperation against educated clergymen who criticized him, to the cause of learning. Beecher in 1828 published in the widely read *Religious Intelligencer* a letter to an evangelist in the West that mingled entreaty with rebuke. The eastern pastor urged upon his fellow worker the avoidance of "provoking epithets." "Did our Lord call the young ruler an Atheist or a Devil?" asked Beecher. "There is no need praying," he added, "as if God and man were deaf, or of wallowing on the floor and frothing at the mouth . . . nor any harm in kindness and gentleness. . . . There may be as great directness as is needed . . . without indecorum; and the Gospel may be preached faithfully and attended with the power of God, without groaning in prayer . . . and without that spiritual pride, which never fails to attend pressing the mass of community out of their place, and shaking together in one chaldron of effervescence, all the passions of all the classes in human society."[7]

Here spoke the Federalist as well as the restrained and cultivated man of religion. But Beecher did not renounce revivals. He knew the power of mass emotion when it moved at flood in a community. By wise direction it could be made a power for good. But some of his lay contemporaries disliked the revival phenomenon. In Yale College more than once in the first quarter of the nineteenth century student irritation flared up when some too eager worker attempted to loose the currents of emotion.

Nevertheless a revival came to Yale College in 1820–21. It was to be succeeded by others. A close look at the movement that started in 1820 gives to a later generation a sense of the impress made by evangelical Protestantism on nineteenth-century American civilization.

The revival began in the town in the summer. Lyman Beecher came down from Litchfield to help the clergy. The interest grew during the autumn. In the winter came the climax of a crescendo that had been building up for six months.

Crowds packed the churches. Lack of room caused some to be turned away. New Haven's was not an isolated phenomenon. A chronicler noted that revivals burned at the same time in forty contiguous communities in western Connecticut.

Naturally the fervor affected the College. New faces appeared at the Friday night prayer meeting which, for years, had been looked upon as the principal meeting of the Church. Another meeting of long standing came on Sunday morning an hour before the chapel service. Held normally in one of the smaller classrooms, this gathering grew so crowded that it had to be shifted to one of the largest rooms in the College. An observer commented on an "increasing stillness in chapel at morning and evening prayers," and spoke of an "unusual influence that seemed to be passing over the institution."[8]

This revival, in effect, produced a tract, though the publication did not appear until a few years later. The author of the narrative used the familiar theme of the brand snatched from the burning. He told the story of Samuel Cowles, the College Bully of the year, who had been converted in the awakening of 1820–21. Deciding on the ministry after his acceptance of religion, Cowles had gone on to Andover. Then, almost immediately after he had finished his course and been licensed to preach, tuberculosis had struck him down. To achieve his effect the tract writer painted the picture of the wild college boy— surrounded by irreligious and profane companions, joining in drunken carousels, rejected by the Moral Society when proposed for membership. The writer identified his hero by giving his initials. A classmate, himself a minister, came to the defense of Cowles. In a book on the college life of the times the writer pointed out that Cowles was, in fact, a decent, spirited, and very popular young man. The defender deplored the rejection of Cowles by the Moral Society, an organization which the classmate held in indifferent esteem. The sanctimonious Moral Society, the tract writer who felt called to magnify the sin that preceded the redemption, and the clergyman concerned with rehabilitating a reputation unjustly injured were all expressions of that evangelical Protestantism that worked so powerfully in American life in the early nineteenth century.

John Mitchell, the defender of Cowles, looking back across twenty-five years, described the scenes in September 1821 that marked the end of the four years' journey of his class. His account, written in an age when the moralism and sentimentalism of *Gody's Lady's Book* provided the standards that dominated popular taste, helps a later generation living in a different intellectual climate to gain some understanding of the emotional power of the old religion. "We who are of the church," wrote Mitchell in 1847, "are present for the last time at its stated evening prayer meeting; we review, mentally, and by allusion in what we utter, the religious history of the years of our residence there—in our case a most eventful one. . . . We give to our beloved brethren our parting exhortations, never more sensible of the prodigious interests that, under God, depend on their fidelity. We unite with them in fervent prayers, and our parting hymn is that so often sung,

> Blest be the tie that binds
> Our hearts in Christian love."

Commencement was a time when friends and families of the graduating class gathered in New Haven. Special ceremonies, the baccalaureate sermon, and the orations that preceded the awarding of the degrees, set off the time as a major event in the life of the young man entering upon a new phase of his career. The members of the graduating class had been associated for four years in a larger student community that emphasized class rivalry and class loyalty. All members had lived in the same dormitories and recited in the same courses. At the conclusion of the festivities they scattered. John Mitchell, clergyman, writing in a time when romanticism dominated American literature and art, described an aspect of his commencement still vivid in his memory. He portrayed a romantic Christianity:

There is another meeting, which time dissolves. It is the meeting of the religious members of the Class. . . . We had held such a meeting, on each Sunday evening, throughout our college life. We were few at first but our number had increased greatly during the recent revival. Let me present the last of these meetings as memory recalls it. It is held in "an upper chamber" of the old North, now North Middle College, at the closing hour of a delightful summer's day. The open windows look out upon the town. . . . There are about thirty-five members present. It is the last season of prayer they are to spend together within the college walls. . . . Nearly all of them have the ministry in view, and some are going to the heathen. They look thoughtfully abroad on the world, and see themselves scattered into various and distant parts of it; and anticipate that their graves will be as widely separate as their fields of labor. It is natural to think of the toils and sacrifices that are probably before them. It is natural to look forward to their meeting in heaven; and to anticipate, not only the joyful emotions with which they will greet each other there, but the deep interest they will feel in contemplating the results of their own and one another's labors—one coming from the distant land of the pagoda, his heathen converts with him; another from the forests of the West; another from the islands of the sea; and another, the shepherd and his flock from the midst of his own native land. All hope that, wherever their lot may be cast, they may be instrumental of the conversion of many souls, and believe that such a result will be among the purest sources of heavenly joy. They believe with the Psalmist, whose words they quote, that He that goeth forth and weepeth, bearing precious seed, shall doubtless come again with rejoicing, bringing his sheaves with him. Those delightful hymns,—The Pilgrim's Song, and The Parting of Christian Friends—conclude the interview.[9]

On November 20, 1824, Jeremiah Day and Eleazar Fitch dedicated the new chapel. Its walls were of red brick. A steeple rose above the eastern end. White columns stood before the entrance. In this New England meeting house the college preacher expounded the New England theology.

Already workmen were busy remodeling into classrooms that chapel which Thomas Clap had built in 1761. Within it prayers had been offered for the King, for the Commander-

in-Chief of the Revolutionary armies, and for the President of
the United States. Daggett, Clap, Stiles, Dwight, and Day had
preached from its desk. But it had become too small. The new
chapel served a college that, having overcome the worst of the
handicaps of poverty and of distance from the centers of
Western learning, was now, sure of its philosophy, moving
toward greater usefulness to the nation.

Chapter 6. The Liberal Arts, 1828

In September 1827 the Corporation held, as usual at Commencement, its annual meeting. As the members walked toward the President's room in the Lyceum, they observed changes that had come to the College. Judicious purchases of land and houses in the previous decade had enlarged the yard until it filled a city block. A new chapel and a new dormitory, North College, completed the "brick row." The college buildings, aligned in stiff formation like a company of Redcoats in the Revolution, faced east, toward the Atlantic Ocean—toward Europe, the place of origin of Western civilization. An unintended symbolism emerged from the orientation. Perhaps some of the Fellows, as they crossed the Green or the college square noticed the elms. James Hillhouse, treasurer of the College in the last decades of the eighteenth century, had persuaded his fellow townsmen to plant them. By 1827 they had acquired dignity. Dignity had also come to the College, now more than a century and a quarter old.

In this year, 1827, Noyes Darling of the Class of 1801 held the post of Assistant Judge in the Court of New Haven County. The town had grown steadily since his graduation. A steamboat made regular trips on Long Island Sound connecting the city with New York. Some of the more enterprising citizens mapped plans for a canal to Northampton, Massachusetts. New factories had appeared in addition to Eli Whitney's gun works. In the gossip of social gatherings was shop talk about styling and making carriages. Two years before, New Haveners had read in the newspapers of a canal barge that had left Buffalo carrying a cask of water from Lake Erie and had traveled to Albany, stopping at the more important towns where the in-

THE LIBERAL ARTS, 1828

habitants indulged in speech making and the firing of cannon. The canal boat had continued down the Hudson and the cask had been emptied into the Atlantic Ocean. For the manufacturers of New Haven the Erie Canal opened a route to a vast and expanding market beyond the Alleghenies. Already Yankee peddlers, vending Connecticut "notions," had penetrated the South and pushed into the West. A practical and hard-headed New England generation had begun the creation of what was to become a great industrial civilization.

Judge Darling shared sufficiently in the enterprise of his neighbors to get himself elected to the State Senate. As one of the senior senators for the year 1827–28, he found himself, *ex officio* by the arrangement made in Stiles' time, a member of the Yale Corporation. He knew the College better than the ordinary alumnus for, from 1804 to 1808, he had held a tutorship. He well remembered the weary grind of those days when he heard his boys recite in Latin, Greek, and mathematics. In 1827, as he looked about him in America, he felt that the old curriculum was out of step with an age that took progress for granted. What value had the classics for venturesome traders to China, for whalers whose snub-nosed sailing ships could be found on every ocean, for manufacturers throwing ever larger dams across New England rivers? Perhaps Senator Darling did not express his ideas in exactly those images, but they are faithful to his thought. He spoke, moreover, for many of his generation who saw the nation turning its back on Europe with its antiquated ideas and its reverence for the past. Americans faced a West that offered infinite possibilities. Senator Darling laid before his colleagues in the President's room a resolution that the College abolish the teaching of "dead languages" and emphasize in their place the modern tongues.

The startled Corporation referred the matter to a committee. President Jeremiah Day headed this body. For colleagues he had two distinguished clergymen, Senator Darling, and Gideon Tomlinson, governor of the state. The composition of the committee suggests the seriousness of the Corporation's concern over the question before them. The committee asked the teaching officers of the College to formulate their views and to present them before the next annual meeting.

The days when the President, the Professor of Divinity, and two or three tutors comprised the faculty of the College had passed. That body had increased not only in size but, under President Day, in authority. The teaching staff participated in decisions concerning the government of the student body. The professors recommended to the Corporation when new appointments became necessary. The custom became permanent. In 1832, moreover, the Corporation, under Day's leadership, had abolished the religious affirmation previously required of all appointees to the faculty. The action had ended the legal subjection of the teaching staff to theological doctrine. When President Day's committee asked the judgment of the faculty, it followed established practice. At the same time the request presented the officers of the College with a major challenge, for under Timothy Dwight the influence of Yale had extended far in growing America. Both President Day and his faculty colleagues recognized that, though the issue was technically parochial, the decision must have significance beyond the college walls.

Senator Darling's resolution confronted the men who met their classes in the brick row with a growing sentiment in the world outside the college square. The proposal required them to deal with a philosophy of practicality continuously reinforced by spectacular material advances. The test found them ready. Behind them in 1827 lay a quarter of a century of solid achievement.

Three men—James L. Kingsley, Benjamin Silliman, and Jeremiah Day— had carried on in the opening decades of the nineteenth century the work that Ezra Stiles had begun. Before the Revolution the colonial mind had dominated the College. President Clap had looked to the statutes of Oxford and

Cambridge for models for the laws he wrote for the government of Yale. After the war the College faced a new task. No longer a youthful, frontier institution in a powerful empire, Yale found itself a college older by three-quarters of a century than the new nation and situated on that eastern seaboard from which civilization moved westward. If the American people, now independent, had to discover themselves as a nation, Yale College, with responsibilities magnified, must contrive to grow into an independent and significant American institution while remaining part of the world of learning that knows no national boundaries. Kingsley, Day, and Silliman had to make a fresh start in the development of learning and had at first to be content with humble beginnings.

Jeremiah Day took up in 1803 the task of creating the apparatus for teaching a course in mathematics that would run through most of the student's four years. He turned out texts in algebra, trigonometry, logarithms, plane and solid geometry, and in the principles of navigation and surveying. Benjamin Silliman lectured on chemistry first to the senior class of which John C. Calhoun was a member in 1804. Then Silliman was sent by President Dwight for a year of study in Europe. There he purchased books for the library and fundamental apparatus for the laboratory. In 1818 he founded *The American Journal of Science and Arts* which promptly became a national institution for the exchange of information and opinion among a people immensely curious about science and keen to discover its practical uses.

In 1805 James L. Kingsley advanced from the post of tutor to a professorship that required him to teach Latin, Greek, and Hebrew and to lecture in ecclesiastical history. Later a new appointment in Greek lightened his burden. He served as librarian. In the first decade of the nineteenth century together with Day and Silliman he dealt with beginnings. He transformed the haphazard and sometimes perfunctory eighteenth-century instruction in the classics into disciplinary courses. For the college classes in Latin, his principal interest, he prepared

books of selections for translation. He edited and published
also a Cicero and a Tacitus. Of the three professors who built
the College in the early nineteenth century Kingsley alone
turned out original research. The poverty of the library during
most of his life prevented significant scholarly work in his
beloved classics, though some of his essays in criticism published in the journals called forth much comment in their day.
He pioneered in the writing of American history, doing,
among other things, a sound piece on the New Haven Colony
and a life of Ezra Stiles in Jared Sparks' *Library of American
Biography*.

Day, Silliman, and Kingsley transformed the College in the
first quarter of the century. They discarded some elementary
subjects such as arithmetic. They introduced new subjects such
as modern languages, science, law, and political economy.
They steadily raised the standards for admission. They improved the quality of the standard courses. Then in 1827 they
faced an unexpected challenge to their whole philosophy.
Senator Darling insisted that in a practical civilization young
men should be trained for practical tasks.

On Silliman and Kingsley primarily fell the burden of for-
mulating for the Corporation the thought of Yale College.
They missed the counsel of Alexander Metcalf Fisher. The College had called Denison Olmstead from the University of
North Carolina to replace the young mathematician. Though
a graduate of Yale, he was still a newcomer to the board of
professors when summons came to write the report. In the
winter of 1827–28 this small company of men in intervals
between teaching and lecturing set down their reasoning and
declared their faith. They shared the traditional religious outlook of the College. They now affirmed their belief in the
liberal arts.

"What then is the appropriate object of a college?" asked
the men who wrote the Report of 1828. ". . . its object," they

answered, "is to lay the foundation of a superior education." Speaking to a practical-minded generation, they urged a higher practicality. "The two great points to be gained in intellectual culture," the writers insisted, "are the discipline and the furniture of the mind; expanding its powers, and storing it with knowledge. . . . In laying the foundation of a thorough education, it is necessary that all the important mental faculties be brought into exercise. It is not sufficient that one or two be cultivated, while others are neglected. A costly edifice ought not to be left to rest on a single pillar." Silliman and Kingsley accepted the best psychology of the times, which pictured the mind as made up of separate faculties—reason, memory, imagination. The College must train them all.

Judge Darling had posed the challenge of popular materialism, an attitude that gained in persuasiveness and power as the frontier advanced and the national economy expanded. Ralph Waldo Emerson, six years out of Harvard College in 1827, would, in 1836, launch the campaign of the Transcendentalists against this same pervasive and almost overwhelming materialism. At that time he would, in effect, assail that Calvinism which seemed to him to further materialism. Calvinism, with its sanctification of work and thrift, declared that a man served God as well by faithful attendance upon his worldly calling as by his private and public devotions. Calvinism, in fact, required both kinds of service. Out of the Calvinist ethic, to be sure, came a theory of stewardship that called upon the successful man to give aid and succor to the less fortunate. But Calvinism offered only the duty of material aid and in addition such spiritual comfort as individual men could find in its austere doctrines.

Eight years before Emerson published *Nature* the writers of the Report of 1828 in public debate opposed to popular materialism a philosophy that derived from a tradition older than Christianity. From classical Greece by way of the Renaissance had come down an ideal and a vision of human possibilities. The Reformation had emphasized morality in the life of this world and faith as prelude for the life to come. The Renaissance emphasized knowledge, speculation, and beauty in the life of the here and now. The liberal arts at Yale carried both traditions. The authors of the Report accepted the New England Theology of their time. But they had dedicated their lives to the liberal arts. They turned the Report into a manifesto directed to their fellow citizens in America.

"Is a man to have no other object than to obtain a *living* by professional pursuits? Has he not duties to perform to his family, to his fellow citizens, to his country; duties which require various and extensive intellectual furniture?" With these questions the writers of the Report launched their argument. They wrote at a time when the College had already established professional departments for the study of medicine, law, and theology, but the central concern of the writers was nonvocational education. "As our course of instruction [in the liberal arts] is not intended to complete an education in theological, medical, or legal science," the Report continued, "neither does it include all the minute details of *mercantile, mechanical,* or *agricultural* concerns. These can never be effectively learned except in the very circumstances in which they are practiced." The writers argued for a general education.

The authors became specific. "The usefulness of mathematical learning is generally admitted; and few persons, perhaps none, would consider that course of education liberal, from which the mathematics are wholly excluded." The Report spelled out the importance of mathematical and scientific studies. Silliman, no doubt, wrote the paragraph.

The study of mathematics . . . is especially adapted to sharpen the intellect, to strengthen the faculty of reason, and to enduce a general habit of mind favorable to the discovery of truth and the detection of error. . . . The student who has laid up a fund of mathematical knowledge and has extended his inquiries to those sciences which depend upon mathematical principles, though he is employed in the practical application of no science, yet is brought into an important relation to those who are so employed. . . . He is able to judge the pursuits of others, to estimate the value of those pursuits, to understand the progress of science, and to feel an interest in the occupations of a large portion of mankind. . . . He is acquainted [through the study of geology] with the region where he is, acts more understandingly in what he undertakes, and is found in consequence of his knowledge, to be in all his transactions a more practical man. The student likewise by familiarizing himself with the general principles of the sciences . . . enlarges the circle of his thought, finds in his superior information new means of benefiting and influencing others, and his mind is thus far liberalized by liberal knowledge.

James L. Kingsley wrote the defense of classical study. He began with mention of the debt to the classics of the languages and literatures of modern Europe and America. At a time when the Greek revival in architecture influenced builders in North, South, and West to erect court houses, churches, and even private dwellings with columns and pediments in the style of the Greek temple, Kingsley remarked: "Architecture and sculpture, in their most approved forms, not only had their origin, but received their perfection in Greece . . . this [same] superiority belongs to ancient literature. . . . But [also] the study of the classics is useful . . . [because it] forms the most effectual discipline of the mental faculties. . . . The range of classical study extends from the elements of language to the most difficult questions arising from literary research and criticisms. Every faculty of the mind is employed; not only the memory, judgment, and reasoning powers, but the taste and fancy are occupied and improved."

Important as were the arguments in support of particular areas of study, the challenge of the Report lay in its basic point of view. Its authors proposed the liberal arts as the means by which to keep bustling, determined, and acquisitive Americans from sinking into that narrow, materialistic provincialism that comes into being when a man's interests and information fail to transcend his occupation. "Can merchants, manufacturers, and agriculturists," they asked, "derive no benefits from high intellectual culture? They are the very classes which, from their situation and business, have the best opportunities for reducing the principles of science to their practical applications. . . . Is it not desirable that they should be men of superior education, of large and liberal views, of those solid and elegant attainments, which will raise them to a higher distinction, than mere possession of property; which will not allow them to hoard their treasures, or waste them in senseless extravagance; which will enable them to adorn society by their learning, to move in the more intelligent circles with dignity, and to make such an application of their wealth, as will be most honorable to themselves, and most beneficial to their country?"

The writers climaxed their argument with a discussion of the liberal arts and the national interest. They wrote four years after President James Monroe had announced the doctrine that bears his name.

The active, enterprising character of our population renders it highly important, that this bustle and energy should be directed by sound intelligence, the result of deep thought and early discipline. The greater the impulse to action, the greater is the need of wise and skillful guidance. When nearly all the ship's crew are aloft, setting the topsails, and catching the breezes, it is necessary there should be a steady hand at the helm. Light and moderate learning is but poorly fitted to direct the energies of a nation, so widely extended, so powerful in resources, so rapidly advancing in population, strength, and opulence. Where a free government gives full liberty to the human intellect to expand and operate, education should be proportionately liberal and ample. When even our mountains, and rivers, and lakes, are upon a scale which seems to denote, that we are destined to be a great and mighty nation, shall our literature be feeble, and scanty, and superficial?

To the religious faith they had inherited from the Reformation the authors of the Report of 1828 added the humanistic faith of the Renaissance tradition.

The document submitted to President Day's committee by his colleagues on the faculty seems to have convinced even that skeptic Judge Darling. No minority report issued from the Corporation's committee. The Corporation at its meeting in 1828 not only approved the Report but ordered it, together with a supporting report by the Corporation's committee, printed as a pamphlet. Silliman reprinted both reports in *The American Journal of Science and Arts.*

The national setting of the Report of 1828 differed from that of Timothy Dwight's protest in 1810 to the article in the *Edinburgh Review.* Nine years had passed since *The Sketch Book,* published in 1819, had given Washington Irving an international reputation. He had followed that with *Bracebridge Hall* and *Tales of a Traveler.* In 1828 his scholarly *History of the Life and Voyages of Christopher Columbus* became a popular success. The year before this last book appeared James Fenimore Cooper, whom Timothy Dwight had thrown out of Yale, published *The Prairie,* his seventh novel. He had brought out that immortal tale, *The Last of the Mohicans,* in 1826. In 1828 Noah Webster completed a near lifetime's work of scholarship when he published *An American Dictionary of the English Language.* In this work, which quickly became standard, he included some five thousand words that had never before appeared in an English dictionary. American literature had made a beginning.

In such a time of hope and achievement Silliman's *Journal* distributed the Report of 1828 to the far corners of the nation. In the first half of the nineteenth century scores of liberal arts colleges appeared in North and South and in the broad valley of the Mississippi. Protestant denominations, to their honor, initiated most of these institutions. In that half century the independent liberal arts college, a unique American institution, became an important aspect of the civilization of the nation. The Report of 1828 had the significance for new and struggling institutions, whose managers sought guidance and encouragement, that comes from an ideal candidly argued and steadfastly proclaimed by a college with more than a century of experience behind it.

For Yale its significance lay in its demonstration that the men who led the College had achieved a measure of understanding of the meaning and importance of the liberal arts. It is true that the authors of the famous Report were not important creative scholars. For the most part these men were schoolmasters engaged in drilling students in the grammar and syntax of the ancient languages and in the equations and demonstrations of mathematics. But, working together, they had created a College where scholarship could take root and grow. In the Report of 1828 they proclaimed the faith that gave power and significance to their lives and to that of Yale. They had left behind the intolerance of Clap and the anti-intellectualism of Dwight. All these men of 1828 shared in the beliefs of evangelical Protestantism, but they did not look upon theology as first among the arts and sciences. In the spirit of Ezra Stiles they had achieved a balance between two faiths—that in religion and that in learning. With an equal sense of obligation they carried on the work of the classroom and of the College Church.

Chapter 7. Religion and the Liberal Arts, 1828-1846

In the first half of the nineteenth century the cultivation of the liberal arts in Yale College included at the summit of the four-year course what might be called an inquiry into the nature of the good life and into that religion which gave orientation to man and meaning to his existence. Three required courses—moral philosophy, natural theology, and the evidences of Christianity—dealt with subject matter deemed of supreme importance to young men about to pass from school to active careers. Jeremiah Day, as did his presidential colleagues in other colleges, taught moral philosophy to seniors. For a number of years Eleazar Fitch, college preacher, gave the courses in natural theology and the evidences. More important, however, than the teachers was a book, or rather three books. William Paley, whose father had been schoolmaster at Giggleswick, Yorkshire, England, had written them. Timothy Dwight near the turn of the century had first introduced them into the Yale curriculum. Paley, who never saw New Haven, has a unique place in the annals of Yale.

Graduating with distinction from Cambridge, Paley had taken orders. He had risen in the church to become Archdeacon of Carlisle. He was not a man of original thought. His genius lay rather in his ability to organize and to present clearly selected aspects of the thought of his age. He published *The Principles of Moral and Political Philosophy* in 1785, nine years after Adam Smith brought out *The Wealth of Nations*. Paley's book ran through fifteen editions before its author's death. Nine years later the Archdeacon published his *View of the Evidences of Christianity* to combat that rationalism whose

popular appeal had been so much augmented by the success of
the French Revolution. The work impressed the Bishop of
Durham, who suggested to Paley still another undertaking. In
spite of failing health Paley managed to bring out *Natural
Theology* in 1802. In these three works, finally brought together
in a single fat volume, the Anglican divine created a textbook
that became as much a fixture in the curriculum of Yale College as the writings of Cicero or Homer.

Reading Paley helps the twentieth-century man to recover
in imagination recitations and discussions in the bare, crudely
furnished classrooms of the Lyceum—or the Atheneum, as
the remodeled first chapel was somewhat grandiloquently
called. Sometimes the kindly and solemn Day pointed out
errors in Paley along with those of the students who recited
him. Probably the disability of Eleazar Fitch kept him from
being a very effective teacher. No matter. After both men had
passed to their reward Yale undergraduates still studied and
recited Paley. In the history of Yale College no textbook ever
approached the record of use for more than half a century established by the work of the Archdeacon of Carlisle. And no
textbook reveals more clearly the softening in early nineteenth-
century Yale of the doctrinal rigidities of the time of Thomas
Clap. Fitch preached in the Chapel a theology whose roots ran
back to Edwards but which a Yale group was making over in
a more liberal pattern. President Day taught Paley in the classroom. Paley asserted no dogmatics. The Archdeacon was a
product of English secular rationalism, not American evangelical Protestantism. In the spirit of the eighteenth-century
Enlightenment Paley brought reason to the support of faith.

To let Paley speak for himself enables one to get back most
surely into the intellectual climate of that vanished age when
evangelical Protestantism so strongly affected the thought of
America. Random sentences illustrate the ideas and suggest the
mood of the *Principles of Moral and Political Philosophy* that
introduced the student to the study of man in society. "Human
laws," said the Archdeacon, discussing the rules of life, "omit

many duties, as not objects of compulsion; such as piety to God, bounty to the poor, forgiveness of injuries, education of children, gratitude to benefactors." Paley warned against that dependence on the Bible as a compilation of law which had characterized the thinking of early Puritans. "Whoever expects to find in the Scriptures," he commented, "a specific direction for every moral doubt that arises, looks for more than he will meet with." The Scriptures merely lay down general rules which moral philosophy must analyze and develop.

In terse and didactic sentences Paley covered the whole range of social institutions and personal relations. He recognized that the institution of private property in land, the most important type of property in his day, had originated frequently in violence. But he enumerated the advantages of the system and argued the superiority of the system of private property over that in which land is held in common. "Inequality of property, in the degree in which it exists in most countries of Europe," he added, "abstractly considered is an evil; but it is an evil which flows from those rules concerning the acquisition and disposal of property, by which men are incited to industry, and by which the object of their industry is rendered secure and valuable."

The American generation that put the Bill of Rights into the Constitution could applaud Paley's concept of civil liberty. "Civil liberty," he said, *"is not being restrained by any law, but what conduces in a greater degree to the public welfare.* To do what we will is natural liberty: to do what we will consistently with the interest of the community to which we belong, is civil liberty: that is to say the only liberty to be desired in a state of civil society." Paley approved all humane measures and aspirations. He opposed slavery and urged its gradual abolition. He left no doubt as to the ultimate source of moral philosophy. "As the will of God is our rule; to inquire what is our duty, or what we are obliged to do, in any instance, is, in effect, to inquire what is the will of God in that instance, which consequently becomes the whole business of morality."[1]

When Timothy Dwight read Paley's *Evidences of Chris-tianity,* he seized upon it. Out of the Age of Reason had come a reasoned defense of Christianity. With the feeling that he had found a powerful ally Dwight set the college boys to reading Paley. Studying their assignments, the undergraduates found the Archdeacon's argument simple and direct. Paley noted that in New Testament times lived a considerable group of men who declared themselves to be original witnesses of the Christian miracles. The author pointed out further that, sub-sequent to the miracles, these same men passed their lives in labors, dangers, and sufferings that they undertook and en-dured voluntarily because they believed their witness to be true. At the same time and from the same motives they sub-mitted to "new rules of conduct," a new way of life. "If it be so," Paley contended, "the religion must be true. These men could not be deceivers. By only not bearing testimony, they might have avoided all these sufferings, and lived quietly. Would men in such circumstances pretend to have seen what they never saw; assert facts which they had no knowledge of; go about lying to teach virtue; and, though not only convinced of Christ's being an imposter, but having seen the success of his imposture in his crucifixion, yet persist in carrying it on; and so persist, as to bring upon themselves, for nothing, and with full knowledge of the consequences, enmity and hatred, danger and death?"[2] Dwight and his successors may well have urged their students to study Paley's prose not only for the substance of its argument but for its rhetoric. The orator flourished in the first half of the nineteenth century.

As soon as it appeared in 1802, Dwight introduced into the curriculum of the College Paley's last book, *Natural Theology.* In the mood and style of the Enlightenment it completed the argument begun in the *Evidences.* Its background was that picture of the order within creation that Sir Isaac Newton had completed when he discovered the laws of motion and worked out the mechanics of the heavens. The harmony of the move-ments of the planets about the sun and the predictability of eclipses gave to the eighteenth century confidence that men, through the use of reason, could push on and on into the mystery to read the once hidden thoughts of the Author of Nature. The Archdeacon shared the confidence of his age that men had made but a beginning. Turning to theology, as Newton had a century before, Paley used the argument of design to prove the existence of God. Order and law in nature imply, inevitably, a contriver, a designer, a Creator. In his chapters Paley discussed design as manifested in the inanimate world, in that of plants and animals, and, finally, in that of man. His reasoning carried him far. "Contrivance," he said, "if established, appears to me to prove everything we wish to prove. Amongst other things, it proves the *personality* of the Deity, as distinguished from what is sometimes called nature, sometimes called a principle. . . . Now that which can contrive, which can design, must be a person. These capacities constitute personality, for they imply consciousness and thought. They require that which can conceive an end or purpose; as well as the power of providing means, and of directing them to their end. . . . The marks of design are too strong to be gotten over. That designer must have been a person. That person is God."[3]

Year after year successive classes of undergraduates, with greater or lesser diligence, worked their way through Paley. They recited on what they read. They answered questions on final examinations. Some of his chapters were dull. Undoubtedly many a student went to sleep over the opened pages. But, given the prestige of religion that characterized the age, the cumulative effect of the Archdeacon's gentle arguments must have been great. More than sixty successive classes of the College learned at least the fundamentals of religion from Paley. The Civil War had passed before the use of the book was discontinued.

Benjamin Silliman, alone among the faculty who served with President Day, had a popular reputation that extended far beyond the College. He traveled widely delivering polished lectures on science to a generation to whom the material he presented came as a kind of revelation. He was the first Lowell lecturer in Boston in the 1830's. He spoke to audiences of fifteen hundred persons and had to repeat each lecture for the benefit of those who could not gain admittance. The *Journal of Science and Arts* made his name known in every state. In the time of President Day the scientist was a figure of such stature as to make the College a national institution. One piece of writing from his pen makes clear for his department the place of religion in the classroom.

As a young man Benjamin Silliman had not come to religion by way of natural theology. He had, in fact, experienced conversion in the year in which William Paley published his third and final book. The man who taught the sciences accepted the Bible as a revelation of truth and the source of ultimate authority. He accepted also the findings of the new science of geology. His popular lectures on the subject gave to his fascinated hearers new meanings to the landscape. Very early some Protestant literalists pointed out that the record of the rocks as interpreted by the geologist did not agree with the story of Creation in Genesis. For these objectors the matter had grave implications. Protestants who settled arguments by reference to the authority of a text took the position that to call into question any portion of Holy Scripture was to cast doubt upon the validity of the whole. In 1833 Silliman, in the interest of both religion and science, undertook to reconcile with Genesis that history of Creation that the pioneer geologists were beginning to unravel. He published a supplement to a British text, Bakewell's *Geology*.

Silliman dealt first with those defenders of Holy Writ who would balk at no affirmation necessary to maintain that the Lord had created the earth, its surface, and its creatures, as the men of the nineteenth century knew them. "We will not enquire," he wrote, whether almighty power inserted plants and animals in mineral masses, and thus exerted in working a long series of useless miracles, without design or end, and therefore incredible. The man who can believe, for example that Iguanodon, with his gigantic form, seventy feet in length, ten in height, and fifteen in girth, was created in the midst of consolidated sandstone, and placed down one thousand or twelve hundred feet from the surface of the earth, in a rock composed of ruins and fragments, and containing vegetables, shells, fish, and rolled pebbles; such a man can believe anything, with or without evidence. If there are any such persons, we leave them to their own reflections, since they cannot be influenced by reason and sound argument; with them we can sustain no discussion, for there is no common ground upon which we can meet.

Silliman had no knowledge of that biblical criticism, just beginning, which one day would bring the entire Old Testament into historical perspective. Silliman accepted the account set forth in Genesis as men had for centuries. He put that narrative beside the earth story beginning to be revealed by the geologists. He thought he saw fundamental similarities between the two. He insisted, however, that literal interpretation of the six days of creation must be abandoned. "The order of the physical events, discovered by geology," Silliman asserted, "is the same as that recorded by the sacred historian; that is, as far as the latter has gone, for it was, evidently, no part of his object to enter into any further details, than to state that the world was the work of God, and thus he was naturally led to mention the principle divisions of natural things, as they were successively created." Silliman saw no difficulty in accepting both the narrative pieced together by science and that of the Scriptures.

Certain aspects of the thought of the time impelled Silliman to write his supplement to Bakewell. "In this country," he affirmed accurately, ". . . the moral feeling of the people is identified with reverence for the scriptures." As a scientist he shared that reverence. He sought to defend both science and Holy Writ. He urged the geologist to respect the Bible and the

theologian to study and to take account of geology. If the
latter did not do so, he would send his students into the world
ignorant and unprepared to deal with the indisputable facts of
a rising science. But Silliman went further. Let both the scientist
and the theologian avoid the illusion that either had all the
truth. Let them both "remember that man is, after all his ac-
quirements of knowledge, a being so darkly wise and rudely
great, that he is in constant danger of deviating into error,
especially on subjects that have a moral, as well as physical
bearing."[4] Silliman, while remaining faithful to the old religion, rejected one of the most constricting dogmas of the
Protestantism of his day. For him both religion and science
belonged to the liberal arts and would ultimately be found to
be part of "the harmony *of all truth,* whether historical, moral
or physical." In addition to Paley, undergraduates after 1833
read Silliman's *Supplement.* In the brick college presided over
by President Day the Chapel and the laboratory were both
literally and figuratively close neighbors.

On the afternoon of October 21, 1846, as the elms on the
Green and the college yard blazed with autumn color, undergraduates and alumni who had returned for the occasion filled
the walks that converged on Center Church. Invited digni-
taries from other colleges and other cities joined the company
within the sanctuary. Jeremiah Day, well past seventy, gave
the charge to his successor, Theodore Dwight Woolsey. The
congregation—faculty, graduates, and undergraduates—understood than an epoch in the history of the College had ended. A
sense of the future, an expectation of achievements to come,
permeated the atmosphere. Events had provided sound reasons
for optimism. Silliman and his colleagues in science had that
year initiated what was soon to be called the Sheffield Scientific
School. In the College also a new spirit stirred in that fundamental department of the classics.

After graduation Woolsey had studied divinity at Princeton.

Called to Yale as tutor, he had completed his preparation in theology and had been licensed to preach. But humility as to his fitness for the work of the ministry had kept him from accepting ordination until his election as president. Convinced that that office carried religious as well as intellectual responsibilities, Woolsey asked on the eve of his inauguration to be ordained.

In his training and his mental outlook Woolsey united the new and the old. In the 1820's he had studied for some years in German universities. His professors in these institutions had roused his enthusiasm for classical philology and had unfolded before him the beauties of the poets, philosophers, and dramatists of Greece. He had mastered the exact philological methods of research that characterized German scholarship. Returning to New Haven, he trained, during fifteen years as professor of Greek, what became a notable group of scholars and teachers in the classics. In the classroom he laid aside Kingsley's volume of selections from Greek authors and introduced foreign editions of complete works of ancient writers. Inevitably Woolsey followed with deep interest the evolution of culture in the United States. As one of those who introduced disciplined scholarship into the College he contributed significantly to its development. After his years abroad he saw American civilization against the background of Europe. His dedication to the classics inclined him to judge that civilization by the standards of ancient Greece.

The company that gathered for the inauguration of the new president sensed strong and varied currents running in American life. Already in that year, 1846, James K. Polk had forced the negotiations that resulted in the division of Oregon between Britain and the United States. General Zachary Taylor had crossed the Rio Grande and Congress had declared war on Mexico. Territory of imperial proportions was about to pass to the Republic. The war, moreover, exacerbated the issue of slavery that increasingly threatened the unity of the nation.

In American letters a great age had begun. Hawthorne had

published *Twice Told Tales* and *Mosses from an Old Manse*. In these he had begun that probing into the Puritan mind that demonstrated a new maturity in the country. In 1846 a romace of the South Seas called *Typee* made Herman Melville the celebrity of the moment. American literature had begun to deal with a world already well known to Americans of the merchant ships and the whalers. Two volumes of verse had made Longfellow the people's poet. Europeans as well as Americans had acclaimed the extraordinary tales and verse of Poe.

But besides the works of these authentic artists the presses of the day turned out cartloads of romantic and sentimental pieces. Imitators of Cooper, writing fanciful biographies of Daniel Boone and, later, of Kit Carson, were creating the genre of the western in the format of the "dime novel." The pious tales distributed by the Tract Society set the tone of sentimentality and moralism that characterized a large volume of Eastern writing. Woolsey knew the books of Lydia Sigourney of the neighboring city of Hartford, the most popular poetess of the day. Mrs. Sigourney poured out, first and last, some sixty volumes of verse. Death was her favorite theme; she rarely let a funeral of one of the great pass without appropriate lines. Some remarked unkindly that one of the terrors of death was the inevitability of an effusion from the pen of the poetess. She yearned over the heathen Indian and wept for the Negro slave. In every sick child she saw a potential angel. In the pages of "The Sweet Singer of Hartford" the sentimental strain in the evangelical Protestantism of the first half of the nineteenth century reached its lachrymose climax.

No doubt Woolsey remembered that time in 1824 when Yale College had suffered as a result of this same sentimentality. In writing the account of the dedication of the new chapel in that year New Haven's *Religious Intelligencer* had surpassed itself.

We can hardly conceive of a more interesting Church and Congregation [wrote the reporter who covered the ceremony] than the one which is to worship in this house,—a Congregation comprising generally between four and five hundred young men nearly of an age collected from various parts of our extended country, are here united like a band of brothers. Here they meet as one common family, every day to offer up their morning and evening sacrifice, and here they meet with a few others, from Sabbath to Sabbath, to hear the Gospel preached. And when we reflect on the changing nature of this Congregation, it becomes doubly interesting. Every four years new members will occupy these seats and we can look forward to the hundreds and thousands who are thus brought under the droppings of the sanctuary—and may we not say to the hundreds and the thousands, to whom this place of worship, will prove "none other than the house of God and the gate of Heaven."[5]

Woolsey was a tutor when that piece appeared. The style and mood still continued when he became president.

Doubtless Woolsey had read in the 1830's the candid and shrewd comments of James Fenimore Cooper on the American scene. Cooper, traveling abroad, had defended his countrymen against uninformed and snobbish European criticism. At home he pointed out to his fellow countrymen that there were defects in the civilization of the Republic that should be recognized and, if possible, remedied. An intemperate newspaper attack was the thanks he received. Perhaps also in the following decade Woolsey read Poe's literary criticism, the only significant literary criticism of the time in the United States. Woolsey took a deep interest in such matters. He considered criticism vital. The new president believed that the American scene—exciting, hopeful, depressing, confused—presented a challenge to the College. He saw in the cultivation of the liberal arts a plan for giving Americans perspective in their outlook and standards for their judgments. His inaugural address, as he dealt with liberal arts in the College, disclosed a new depth of understanding when compared with the Report of 1828. It also emphasized his conviction of the importance of criticism, including criticism directed at the College itself.

". . . our teaching in the classics," said the former professor of Greek, "does little else but call into use those faculties which are concerned in discovering the sense of an author; and leaves the taste to imbibe that insensible and unconscious improvement, which grows out of familiarity with the beautiful; while our rhetoric, having a practical end—persuasion—in view, concerns itself rather with the most effective arrangement of words, thoughts, and arguments, than with the laws of perfection in art. And indeed we are able to do but little more; for strange as it is, there is a woeful deficiency of works in the science of the beautiful in our language." Woolsey specified the lacks. "The French school of taste," he went on, "and its English imitators are now exploded; the last century and its philosophy produced no works on taste, which at this time satisfy our minds; while the few specimens of just criticism with which the present age had supplied us, are chiefly oracular fragments of writers, who either judge intuitively and have no theory, or who have never published their theory to the world. And then even in the lower department of the history of literature, there are, I believe, no text-books accessible, which meet our wants."

Woolsey, no doubt, had noted Cooper's comments in the 1830's on the backwardness of the fine arts in American civilization. "As for the laws of the beautiful in music, architecture, sculpture, and painting," said Woolsey, "they are quite out of our view. . . . But we [of the College] can still make some resistance . . . to the evil [of too much emphasis on training the logical faculty]. We can teach the classics more with reference to elegance of style and artistic arrangement. We can bring the fine arts within the range of education." In 1832 President Day had opened the Trumbull Gallery, built in the rear of the new chapel. This pioneer art gallery of the United States housed the Revolutionary paintings of John Trumbull, all of which he had given to the College. In addition the gallery contained early portraits by other artists. In the Woolsey administration a school of the fine arts was to be established.

"We can," the new president continued, "make use of sound

works on the laws of taste as they arise, and thus oppose the influence of that unhealthy and unreflecting school which decides everything by feeling only, without being aware of a single law." In that sentence the classicist paid his respects to romanticism. He went on to consider the need of America. "That taste must be more and more cultivated in this country is apparent," he said. "But the danger now is that the vocation will fall into bad hands that either a taste will be promoted which has only to do with externals,—with sensual and not spiritual beauty; or that an erratic wildfire called taste, without laws or a rationale, will seat itself in the throne of criticism."[6] At the time Woolsey spoke, *Gody's Lady's Book* was the virtually unchallenged arbiter of taste in the United States. Woolsey saw in the liberal arts, properly developed and assiduously cultivated, the one hope for bringing sound standards to America. In the course of his presidency, however, Woolsey abandoned work in literature to become a pioneer in social science. He won distinction for his lectures and writings on political science and on international law.

Theodore Woolsey stood, like his predecessors, Day and Dwight, in the Puritan tradition. He had the Calvinist's sense of the pervasiveness and stubbornness of evil in the world. He believed in discipline and, in his personal life, he began with self-discipline. But Woolsey's Puritanism had mellowed. His theology had lost some of the severities of that of Edwards. Woolsey shared the humane spirit of the middle of the nineteenth century that led his generation to question Calvin's picture of the Almighty as a God who predetermined whom he would save and whom he would damn eternally. The Unitarians had insisted earlier in the century that such a god, were he to exist, would be immoral.

Woolsey not only espoused a gentler Puritanism but laid aside the sectarian spirit. He had studied Paley as an undergraduate. The Archdeacon's natural theology had a strong appeal to the new president who, next to the classics, was attracted to philosophy. Frankly conservative, Woolsey consciously accepted Aristotle's mean as his guide. The new president disliked radical sectarians, radical temperance reformers, radical abolitionists. He saw sectarianism as a danger to religion in the schools, threatening to drive it from the classroom. But on one position he stood firm. He refused to attempt an objective attitude toward one of the most important movements of the day in philosophy and religion.

Theodore Woolsey opposed that modern sorcery that would cause the God of his fathers to fade into an ether-like essence called the Over Soul. Transcendentalism had come to America primarily by way of Coleridge, whom Horace Bushnell of the Class of 1827 had read and by whom he had been profoundly influenced. In 1836 the publication of *Nature* had made that ex-Unitarian minister Ralph Waldo Emerson the leading prophet of the new faith. Trust thyself (said Emerson in effect to the young men of the day), for God is in you. Human nature, as all nature, partakes of divinity. The individual man, would he but realize it, possesses within his heart a power for righteousness that can enable him to move nations. In 1841 Emerson brought out the first series of his *Essays*. In the following year Theodore Parker published *A Discourse of Matters Pertaining to Religion*. The transcendentalist content of the book confirmed even the Unitarian clergymen of Boston in the wisdom of their earlier decision to bar their pulpits to this dynamic radical. In New England, Puritan ministers spoke of transcendentalism as the "new infidelity." Woolsey did not speak of transcendentalism. He used an ugly word, "pantheism"—meaning God is everything and everything is God. Woolsey saw pantheism as a menace to sound religion.

He saw also another danger to religion, materialism. Science had suggested its rationalism and the increasing triumphs of science had reinforced its appeal. Woolsey did not oppose science. On the contrary he strongly supported this aspect of human inquiry whose consequences for everyday life became steadily more important. Like Silliman, Woolsey saw no necessity compelling the man of the laboratory to embrace materialism. He thought, rather, that science could make its own great contribution to the achievement of the end the new president considered of prime importance. Woolsey's picture of the pyramid of the liberal arts set religion at the apex.

As he stood before them at the outset of his administration, President Woolsey urged his colleagues to lead the student, whenever possible, to the contemplation of those great insights that give meaning and direction to life. "There are, indeed," he said, "some departments where this can be done but in a small degree or not at all. Thus instruction in heathen literature, seldom finds good opportunities of raising the thoughts to God; and the same is true in a much greater degree of the pure mathematics, which have to do with abstract and necessary truth, such as does not involve the divine existence. But mixed mathematics, especially astronomy, all the natural sciences, psychology and morals, furnish a noble field for a devout mind to enforce the relations of the highest truths to truths of the lower order. When they are not thus enforced, when nature is treated by the philosophical man as a dead carcase, when he teaches that he has nothing to do with final causes, or marks of grandeur of conception in the universe, he not only fails of doing a great good, but he positively allies himself with a spirit which would banish God from creation." Woolsey had read his Paley to good purpose. But the Archdeacon's simple paragraphs on natural theology seemed a primer beside Woolsey's far-ranging vision. "I know," the President continued, "that some discard the search after final causes, on the ground that every new discovery in science tends to carry us back to some higher law unknown before, from which the final cause, as it is called, must necessarily arise. I know, too, what we call final is not really so, and that we must allow that there are infinite depths in the divine mind which we cannot explore. But is it any less a proof of the divine intelligence at work, that what we have called a contrivance is the evolution of the law? Or must we refrain from wondering at the divine counsels until we have explored them all,—that is until we become infinite ourselves? Or rather does it not present to us a higher idea of God, that his wisdom manifests itself through laws which rise in their generality until they span round creation, and that his purposes ascend, as we behold them, one behind another until to our eye they are lost in the clouds."

A sense of urgency filled the Woolsey argument. He saw the dangers of the day as immediate and great. "The tendency to materialism on the one side, and to pantheism on another, the literature of atheistic despair and sensualism, and the historic engines battering the walls of fact, must cause a multitude of minds in the next age to be assailed by religious doubts; and snares seem set for faith in revelation on every side. How desirable, if all this be not mere alarm, if the fears of many portending some crisis, in which the old shapes of things shall be broken up, be not entirely idle; how desirable, I say, that our educated young men should be taught a theology so liberal— if that might be—as not to pertain to the party but to universal Christianity, and so majestic in its outlines as to recommend itself to the consciousness, and make its own the presence of God."[7] So Woolsey would have the liberal arts direct men's minds in the end toward the grandest and most inspiring of human conceptions.

Time was to prove the accuracy of President Woolsey's premonitions of trouble ahead for religion. In 1859, thirteen years after the inaugural address, Charles Darwin published the *Origin of Species*. The new hypothesis of evolution broke up the "old shapes of things." It plunged Protestantism into a major crisis.

Chapter 8. The College and Its Church, 1824–1861

From 1824 until after the Civil War the chapel built by President Day served as a meeting house for worship and as a symbol of official deference to religion. The poverty of the College necessitated a multipurpose building. The top floor housed the college books until the erection of the library in neo-Gothic style in the 1840's. Students in theology also had rooms in the chapel building. Both outside and in, the structure had a simplicity that bordered on severity. It harmonized with the other plain and honest buildings of red brick that comprised College Row.

Inside, the chapel had three aisles, separating into blocks hard pews that each accommodated four persons. A high, traditional "meeting house" pulpit with double stairs stood at the front. Above the seats ranged a gallery. The very form of the sanctuary, devoid of altar or vain decoration, expressed the Puritan spirit and declared the Puritan faith. Pulpit, pews, and the bare walls enclosing them combined into a Protestant symbol. Here the people, assembled in the presence of the unseen God for prayer and praise, listened to the preacher as he expounded the Word and reminded them of those individual responsibilities to the Most High which no priest or church can assume.

But the chapel had features that grew out of its function as an essential part of a college. It contained eight boxes. The architect placed two in the rear and one on either side wall. Double boxes, one above the other, flanked the pulpit on both right and left. In a day when the college law required presence at religious service, these boxes provided conning towers for the faculty. They suggested the discipline that, since Puritan days, had been associated with religion.

The members of the College attended prayers twice each day. The bell on the top of the classroom building named the Lyceum called to service at five or six in the morning. This predawn clangor marked the beginning of a day in which the same bell announced all college exercises. In 1857 a contributor to the *Lit* described the dormitories and the chapel as they appeared on every week-day morning.

> How do the students go into prayers?
> From the rooms where they dwell, at the sound of the bell,
> Rushing and crushing and brushing downstairs,
> Rubbing their eyes in ghastly surprise
> At being obliged thus early to rise,
> Ripping the stitches in manifold breeches,
> And swearing and tearing, where'r the cloth hitches . . .
> They rush through the dark . . .
> For fear of a mark.[1]

Normally the President read the psalm and gave the prayer. There was no singing in the morning. At the conclusion of the invocation the three younger classes, and all the faculty save two, left by convenient doors. Then the President, followed by the two senior professors, passed down the center aisle between the ranks of the senior class, who bowed as the officers passed and then fell in behind them. Minor variations occurred from time to time but the essential pattern remained long after the chapel built by President Day had disappeared.

On Sundays members of the faculty sat, along with visitors, with their families in the gallery. Normally the Professor of Divinity preached. Occasionally a visiting clergyman filled the pulpit. Timothy Dwight the Second recalled preachers he remembered pleasantly from his undergraduate days in the 1840's: Lyman Beecher, President Eliphalet Nott of Union College, President Francis Wayland of Brown University, William Adams of New York, and Horace Bushnell of Hartford. Bushnell, who had served as tutor after his graduation, remained a favorite with the students to the Civil War. The President sat in the pulpit. At the end of the service the lower classes withdrew as at morning prayers. The minister left by the door behind the pulpit. Then the President, unattended, proceeded down the center aisle, where the seniors bowed as he passed and fell in behind him. Appropriately in what was a college exercise as well as a service of worship academic ritual blended with the forms of an austere Protestantism.

The young men who sat in the hard pews listening to the Sunday preacher came in the second quarter of the nineteenth century for the most part from families able to afford to give sons four years of nonvocational training in the liberal arts. But the college authorities, worried lest the student body be limited to the well-to-do, began to accumulate modest funds to make it possible for poorer boys to take advantage of the institution. The developing democratic ideals of the Republic opposed the practice in Europe of limiting opportunity for higher education to a privileged aristocratic class. Day founded his policy with respect to scholarships on the principle of equality of opportunity. The continuing need for a trained clergy, moreover, had called into being outside agencies which provided support for young men preparing for the ministry.

Under Day and Woolsey, Yale College attracted students in such numbers as to enable the faculty to require what were for the time high standards of admission and increasingly high standards for the degree. In the first half of the nineteenth century the appeal of the liberal arts came from the tradition, stemming particularly from Britain, that the educated man was one who knew Latin and Greek and the fundamentals of mathematics, and was trained in rhetoric. To this curriculum Yale had added, in generous and increasing proportions, science. The acquisition of an arts degree from one of the older and established colleges set off its possessor as a member of a small and highly selected group in the community. Along with the mental furnishings and training acquired in winning it the degree gave its holder status. As the decades passed, the College grew in popularity and in national reputation.

Yale College, however, in the time of Day and Woolsey did not stand in isolation. To meet the needs arising in a rapidly expanding nation and in a civilization steadily becoming more complex, the Yale authorities established outside the College embryo schools of divinity, law, and science. Timothy Dwight had initiated a school of medicine. But the College remained paramount. Jeremiah Day made that fact clear in his address at the inauguration of President Woolsey. "But whether we have or have not, in New Haven, a claim to the title of a university," said Day, "the labors and responsibilities of the President are almost wholly confined to the College proper. This is his appropriate sphere of action, though as a member of the Board of Trustees, he may have a nominal relation to the professional departments."[2] To this expanding Yale the College Church ministered.

It functioned in the second third of the century in an undergraduate scene greatly changed from the simple days of President Dwight. Basic features of the older Yale persisted in the separation of the student body into four classes. Each of these, a little over a hundred in membership, developed through four years of intimate association in dormitory and classroom a lively sense of the group. Set apart from the town, the undergraduates developed their own life and customs. Among the latter informal singing gave life in the college yard a distinctive quality. "The attention here paid to *music*," remarked a senior in 1851 speaking to an undergraduate audience, "is . . . deserving of note, exhibited as it is not merely in the singing of a choir skillfully trained . . . but manifested in the chorus which daily arises upon every side and from every company of students. Occasionally, with a chorus not unworthy of a German University, we join in singing

Gaudeamus igitur
Juvenes dum sumus,

while you well know that not an event occurs from the football game [on the Green between sophomores and freshmen]
to a successful 'biennial,' without some original song in its
commemoration,—not a society but has its ample private collection."[3]

Into the stratified society of the four classes came fraternities
and societies that, in course of time, developed an elaborate
pattern. The new period in undergraduate life opened with the
founding of Skull and Bones in 1832. A second senior society,
Scroll and Key, followed nine years later. After 1832 societies
peculiar to the junior, sophomore, and even freshman years
came rapidly into being. They expressed the desire for association in smaller groups. The senior societies became a means of
marking undergraduate distinction. Those of the three lower
years added to the gaiety, if not always to the dignity, of undergraduate life. All in their mottoes expressed the romanticism
of the time. The class societies existed beside the three older
debating societies which, together, included in their membership the entire student body.

The junior fraternities took a central place in undergraduate
politics. They electioned and maneuvered when the time came
to elect from the junior class the members of the "Wooden
Spoon Committee" and the editorial board of the *Lit*. This
publication, founded in 1836, not only expressed undergraduate initiative but reflected an interest in an American-produced
literature that had steadily been growing in the nation since
Irving's *Sketch Book*. To run through the volumes that appeared
in the 1840's and 1850's is to discover in the articles and notes
a more complex, sophisticated, and mature college life than
existed in the time of President Dwight. A considerable number of contributions in each volume revealed the continuing
impress of religion on the life of the yard. A piece on college
life in 1852 took a sentiment straight out of Silliman's lectures.

Speaking of the curriculum, the commentator said: "Geology becomes a hugh volume, whose pages are strata of rock recorded ineffaceably by the Creator with the story of Creation, an enduring evidence of the Bible's inspiration."[4]

In 1853 occurred an event that marked the beginning of organized athletics at Yale. For nearly ten years boat clubs, more or less ephemeral, had owned shells and had rowed them on the harbor. The boats were of several types, using four, six, or eight oars. Each club had its distinctive and colorful costume. In June 1853 the six existing clubs, Halcyon and Thulia of the Class of 1854, Atlanta and Nephenthe of the Class of 1855, Undine of the Class of 1856, and Ariel whose members came from the Scientific School joined together to form an organization known as the Yale Navy. They elected a commodore, who took the lead in bringing such order into the sport of rowing as to make progress possible.

The inauguration of organized rowing had consequences for the Chapel quite unsuspected at the time of the formation of the Yale Navy. In 1859 the Bible disappeared from the pulpit and turned up in Harvard, while, by a strange coincidence, the one from the Harvard chapel came mysteriously to New Haven. Letters went back and forth between President Woolsey and his opposite number, C. C. Felton, in Cambridge. In the end President Felton proved to be the better sleuth. On April 29, 1860, he wrote to the head of Yale: "In the course of my enquiries, I came upon a fact which was new to me, though it may be known to you: viz. that the enterprise of entering the Chapel and stealing the Bibles was concocted last summer between the Cambridge and Yale Boat-Clubs. If this was so we ought to scrutinize these societies a little more closely. I have long had the suspicion that they are not the excellent institutions that they are held out to be by the worshipers of the newly established Deity, Muscle."[5]

In such a busy, varied, and evolving college life that ancient

1. The first chapel, 1761–1824. The date of the print, 1786, suggests that President Stiles is represented. Approaching the chapel he passes on his left what are probably two tutors. Undergraduates salute him by doffing their hats as required by the College rules. Connecticut Hall stands beside the chapel.

2. The second chapel, 1824–76. North College appears at the right of the picture and North Middle at the left. The fence in the foreground extended along College Street as far as Chapel Street. The sophomore, junior, and senior classes each had a particular section of fence, at which members gathered.

3. Pulpit of the second chapel. In daily and Sunday chapel services members of the faculty sat in the high boxes on either side of the pulpit. The communion table stood under the pulpit.

4. The east end of the second chapel. A picture of the Class of 1872, painted for its class book. Note the first college organ above the entrance door.

5. Battell Chapel as originally built. The south aisle was added later as the student body grew in number. Note the elm used as a bulletin board.

6. Original pulpit of Battell Chapel. The choir sat below the high pulpit, the president and the preacher of the day on either side. The communion table stood at the head of the center aisle, down which the president made his exit as the members of the senior class bowed and fell in behind him.

7. Altar and pulpit of Battell Chapel in the mid-twentieth century. The choir area has been moved to the apse. The screen displays the coats of arms of the ten residential colleges. The north gallery, originally reserved for the faculty, is now occupied by the organ.

8. Dwight Chapel in the mid-twentieth century. In 1844 the College completed a library in the gothic-revival style. The picture shows what was originally the main reading room. Between each pair of pillars was a bay of open book shelves. Daily prayers are offered in the present chapel.

institution the College Church continued to play its traditional role. Throughout the period it remained important. Churches were important and religion was respected throughout the nation. The Yale community reflected the characteristics of the national scene beyond the limits of the yard. Many undergraduates brought with them to college convictions formed in religious homes. Some achieved their faith after they came to New Haven. Many were indifferent. Only a minority took a serious and continued interest in the meetings and affairs of the Church. Yet the undergraduates accepted the requirement of attendance at prayers twice each day and at preaching service on Sunday as a discipline normal and proper to a college. In the chapel that President Day built, the forms of what had become an evangelical Protestantism persisted little changed from the Puritan days of the eighteenth century.

In one respect the College Church felt the effects of that student desire for organization independent of the faculty that grew in strength in the nineteenth century. Undergraduate deacons appeared as early as 1812, when Stafford Ward had the office. Thereafter the records show sporadically the names of later deacons. Not until 1838, however, when the new society system was taking form, did the practice of electing deacons by the class become permanently established. From that time on, the sequence of class deacons remained unbroken.

The office of deacon sometimes had disciplinary responsibilities. That of pastor had even more. Three items in the minutes of 1833 illustrate the continuing character of the College Church as a parish institution together with the manner of dealing with problems of discipline. A husband and wife in the communion separated. The Church appointed President Day and Professor Chauncey Goodrich a committee to inquire into the circumstances. They reported that the separation resulted from the misconduct of the wife. Thereupon the Church suspended her from membership.

Under the date, June 28, 1833, the Minute Book contains the following item:

At a special meeting of the church this evening, the Committee in the case of Palmer [an undergraduate] stated that he had been cited to appear before the church and that they had evidence that the citation had been placed in his hands. He was called, when not appearing in person, nor by counsel, the Committee presented charges against him, and the evidence. Upon hearing the Committee the church voted, that they find Simeon Palmer guilty upon the following charges brought against him by the Committee. (1) Habitually neglecting the Ordinances of the Gospel; (2) Denying faith in Jesus Christ and expressing a wish to be released from the covenant of the church; (3) Contempt of the church in neglecting to obey a citation to appear before it. Voted also, that Simeon Palmer be hereby excommunicated from the fellowship of the church, and that the Pastor write to him informing him of this vote.

Another undergraduate, upon being accused, made in writing a "full and penitent confession of his sins." The meeting that dealt with the case accepted the declaration, restored the offender to the "privileges of the church," and spread the confession on the minutes.[6]

But times changed. After the middle of the century the officers of the College relaxed the stern discipline of the earlier decades. As part of the change they abolished evening prayers (1859) and set morning prayers after, rather than before, breakfast. In the same period references to cases of discipline disappeared for good from the minutes of the College Church.

A tough-minded Protestantism gave character to the chapel that stood between North College and the Lyceum. Here the preacher faced the great questions of the meaning of human life and the nature of human destiny. He pointed out man's duty to his fellows and to God. For the most part in the 1830's and 1840's Eleazar Fitch preached. But Nathaniel William Taylor sometimes took his place. In 1822 the Yale Corporation created a Theological Department that was, in fact, the beginning of the Divinity School. The Corporation then appointed Nathaniel Taylor to the chair of primary importance, the professorship of Didactic Theology. Taylor coöperated with Fitch in the presentation to undergraduates of theological material.

In a sense these men preached a simple evangelical gospel. As Timothy Dwight had done before them, they urged their hearers to repent and to seek redemption before time ran out. The ministers set out vividly the alternative of Heaven or Hell. The simplicity of the message they bore to their generation was more apparent than real. In reality Fitch and Taylor dealt with problems of infinite difficulty—the duty and destiny of man. They stood in the tradition of Calvin and Edwards. They took account of the universal and continuing problem of evil, not content to detour about it as their contemporary, Emerson, was doing in his transcendentalism. Fitch, with the aid of Taylor, dealt with the great questions in sermons on the Sabbath. The tradition of the College required the Professor of Divinity to expound the theology that gave bone and fiber to Calvinist Protestantism, not in isolated discourses but in a planned series of expositions. The Sunday service in chapel gave opportunity for more than worship. It made possible a course of instruction in some of the most difficult matter dealt with in the curriculum of the College.

When Eleazar Fitch succeeded to the chair of Divinity, he accepted a task that only a brave man would undertake. To instruct young men preparing for the ministry in a complex and dour theology was one thing but to present the same material to undergraduates ranging from seniors to newly arrived freshmen was quite a different matter. The student portion of the congregation was, moreover, a captive audience. The combination of theology and compulsory attendance had sometimes consequences all too obvious. On Sunday, January 9, 1825, Seabury Ford, a senior, wrote in his diary: "This forenoon had Prof. Fitch to preach—kept awake most of the time. This afternoon had Tailor—went to sleep soon after the sermon commenced, and I have been told since meeting that more than half of the class slept all the time." Ford seems to have been put off theology at least as early as his junior year. He definitely kept awake during one of the sermons he heard in the previous July. "Clear warm and pleasant," Ford noted in his journal.

The sermon in the forenoon I really do not know anything about though I did not sleep, yet my thoughts were much engaged on other subjects. This afternoon it was doctrinal points. Text "It must needs be that offences come, but woe to the man by whom the offence cometh." He went on and proved that Deity made sin, and could not have made the world without, also that it was necessary for man to sin according to the will of Deity, and that it was in the power of man to avoid sinning, and that he is damned because he does not frustrate the will of Deity and leave off sinning. Things which appear so inconsistent to me I esteem nonsense.[7]

Seabury Ford of the Class of 1825 was one of the first two students to come to the College from the young state of Ohio. One is not surprised to learn after his exercise in logic that he took up law following the getting of his degree. Entering politics, he became governor of Ohio in 1858. Ford represented the nonreligious undergraduate. His contempt for theology forecast a change in public attitude toward the ruling doctrines of the time.

In commenting on the sermon that dealt with sin Ford probably referred to Taylor. If so, he would doubtless have been astonished to learn of the controversy the Professor of Didactic Theology had already stirred up in Calvinist circles. Nathaniel Taylor refused to accept uncritically the doctrines of other men no matter how great the seers might be. As an undergraduate he had read and recited Paley. Studying divinity with Dwight after getting his degree, Taylor had come under the influence of a theology that drew back from the extremes of Edwardian Calvinism and substituted for the deductions of an uncompromising logic the more persuasive conclusions of common sense. But young Taylor, even when serving as Dwight's amanuensis, pushed out for himself to positions that must have seemed radical to his teacher, for

Dwight, though a moderate in theology, was always an aristocrat and always a Federalist.

Taylor, either in college or while preaching in Center
Church in New Haven at the end of his Divinity studies, must
have read Dugald Stewart's *Elements of the Philosophy of the
Human Mind.* The Scottish philosopher published the first
volume in 1792 and the second in 1814. He brought out the
third in 1827, five years after Taylor accepted his professorship.
Doubtless also Taylor had read the work of an earlier Scottish
philosopher, Thomas Reid, *Inquiry into the Human Mind on the
Principles of Common Sense,* published in 1764. Stewart built on
and popularized Reid. And what was this philosophy of common sense? Reid insisted that philosophy must depend on its
own scientific observation and that the scientist, looking inward, can observe consciousness. The self-evident intuitions
that introspection reveals are, Reid thought, the first principles
of morals. Moreover, Reid insisted with a side glance at Newton's system, nothing in the endless chain of cause and effect
can be an efficient cause in the proper sense save an intelligent
being. An inanimate object cannot be a cause of anything.
Reid was trying to exorcise the determinism of Newton's
celestial mechanics from moral science. About the time Taylor
came to the chair of Theology the College began to require
the senior class to read Stewart. The Stewart version of Scottish
common-sense Philosophy dominated the Yale classrooms for
a quarter of a century. Then Woolsey on becoming president,
discarded Stewart and required his seniors to go back to the
master himself and to study Thomas Reid. These developments
in Yale College provide a background for that New Haven
Theology created by Taylor and preached by Fitch in the College Church which in the 1830's and 1840's had a transforming
influence on the thought not only of New England Congregationalism but of Presbyterianism beyond its borders.

But examination of the Taylor system suggests that the revivalist–theologian felt also the impact of the secular thinking
of the age. By the time Taylor had come to his professorship,

Federalism, save for a handful of unhappy die-hards, was dead. What has been called "Jacksonian democracy" moved in the years from 1815 to 1840 to put an end to property qualifications for voting and to establish universal manhood suffrage. In 1829, with the inauguration of President Andrew Jackson, the age of the common man began in the United States. Democracy inevitably implies a measure of faith that, in the end, the common man can be trusted to choose with sense and with uprightness among the alternatives presented to him. A democratic faith emerged, a blend of the teachings of Protestantism and the philosophy of the Declaration of Independence with ideas born of the experience of the young Republic. This faith assumed that a fundamental law not made by man underlies society and is the ultimate governor of human relations. The faith assumed the freedom and the responsibility to the fundamental law of the individual who is at the same time the ultimate unit of society and the foundation of the democratic state. The faith proclaimed the mission of America to stand before the world as a witness that free men can govern themselves and as a beacon lighting for all men everywhere the hope of freedom.

By a subtle osmosis this democratic faith dissolved in the mind of Nathaniel Taylor that suspicion of the common man inherent in Timothy Dwight's Federalism. Taylor rejected the old Calvinist doctrine of the depravity of human nature and of man's inability to save himself. Taylor's doctrine of man affirmed the capacity for good as well as the propensity to evil in the heart of man. Each person feels in his inner consciousness a sense of freedom to choose between alternatives. Taylor, following the logic of Scottish common sense affirmed, that the sensed freedom is real and not an illusion created, as Edwards had suggested, by the strongest motive or "cause." Taylor defined the will as a power to choose between motives.

The New Haven theologian did not, however, go over to the attractive optimism of the Unitarian doctrine of man. Unitarianism centered in the Boston area and in 1819, three years before Taylor's appointment as professor, William Ellery Channing had announced its principal positions. The Unitarians, rejecting the Calvinist position, declared that human nature is inherently good. With a realism that had from the beginning been a strength of Calvinism, Taylor reminded his Unitarian contemporaries of the manifest and continuing evil in the world and of its source in the hearts of men. Eschewing utopian dreams, the teacher, who was more interested in the saving of souls than in theology, warned sinful man of that responsibility inherent in his freedom and held out hope to those who of their own volition choose the good life. In Taylor's thinking the doctrine of the free and responsible individual applied as much to the Christian as to the citizen.

Conservatives among Taylor's ecclesiastical colleagues read his arguments with dismay. They saw the Professor of Didactic Theology at Yale as a betrayer of the established orthodoxy, a renegade who had gone over to the camp of the Arminians with their easy doctrine of the freedom of the will. Some adversaries publicly demanded that the Corporation dismiss the heretic. But that body stood its ground. The New Haven Theology increased in influence. Its appearance and persistence proclaimed the decline of the old Calvinism. The strength of the New Haven Theology lay, however, in its affirmations rather than in its denials of old positions. It insisted on the need of the free man for religious faith and on his ability to choose the good life. When Taylor, an old man, lectured in the 1850's on the truths he had proclaimed in the 1820's, his students were astonished at his concern. A new generation could not believe that men had ever denied what now seemed axiomatic.

The chapel reflected the restrained liberalism of Nathaniel Taylor. The College Church backed his system with the prestige that Stiles and Dwight had given to its pulpit. Eleazar Fitch not only preached what was a new divinity but published papers in defense of its positions. Chauncey Goodrich purchased in 1828 the *Monthly Christian Spectator* to spread abroad the new ideas. The College Church, forward-looking and aggressive in furthering the cause of religion, had achieved one of its greatest moments.

As the event turned out, Fitch could not maintain the high level of the 1820's and the 1830's. In the earlier decades of his ministry he preached effectively. In his series of doctrinal discourses he presented ably his arguments and his conclusions. In his less rigorous "practical" sermons he sometimes rose to heights. One man who, as an undergraduate and then as graduate student, listened Sunday after Sunday to the College Pastor tried in later years to deal justly with his memory. ". . . for many years," wrote the second Timothy Dwight in 1903, "[Fitch] was held in the greatest esteem as a preacher by the entire academic community—his sermons being appreciated because of the intellectual force manifested in them and the spiritually stimulating influence by which they were characterized. He was certainly, in his mental gifts, one of the most remarkable men whom the college faculty ever had in the circle of its membership. He was a theologian, a metaphysician, a preacher, a poet, and a musician. He also possessed rare mechanical skill, and was a lover of nature in no ordinary degree. Considered in the full measure and the variety of his powers, he had no superior among the eminent scholars and teachers who were associated with him."[8] In a materialistic age that caused Henry Thoreau almost to despair, Eleazar Fitch interested himself in art and literature. At a time when florid and overblown oratory pleased the public taste, Fitch composed his sermons in restrained and carefully tooled prose. In an age when Unitarians were moving far away from the old orthodoxy and when the Transcendentalists were teaching a new theology of the Over Soul in nature and in man, Fitch held fast to an evangelical faith that offered hope while taking account of the realities of human nature and of society.

Fitch's description, on one occasion, of the transfiguration comprised a Protestant word picture worthy of the subject:

In this account of the Ascension of Jesus we are taught, that he desired still to promote the welfare of his disciples on earth, when
ascended to his throne in glory. How could it be, after all he had
done for the cause of God among them, and for their spiritual welfare, that he should for one moment forget their welfare, when he
went to his own joyous rewards? His heart was proved too com-
passionate and true, amid the toils and sufferings and death of his
ministry, ever to be absorbed in personal glory, so far as not to be
affectionate and true to them still. Therefore, when about to be
exalted out of their humble state, and to go to his Father's throne,
he engages to send down to them a powerful Comforter, the
Spirit, to supply the place of his bodily presence; he bids them wait
on him, with confidence that through the Spirit they shall be
strengthened for the duties and trials of their office: and, as he leaves
the earth, his last look is upon them: his hands are lifted up in blessing: his heart is directed to them in assurance of good will, in wish-
ing them to fare well in their earthly course.[9]

Had it not been for his strange nervous disorder (nowhere
named in the records) Fitch might have become one of the
great prophets of early nineteenth-century evangelical Protestantism. The disability made him a man of the study rather
than a pastor dealing intimately with his parishioners. The
trouble also rendered him virtually inarticulate without a
manuscript. It grew on him and seemed to sap his will. In his
later years his old power seldom manifested itself. An irreverent
undergraduate printed in 1849 in the *Yale Tomahawk* (a publication soon suppressed by the college authorities) some lines
he called "Sabbath Musings:"

> For full an hour good Rev. Dr. Fitch
> Obfusticates a point of doctrine, which
>   No apex hath.—
> The sinner sleeps, with but this anxious thought;
> If preaching be Heaven's Mercy, what
>   Must be its wrath?[10]

Three years later, at the age of sixty-one, Fitch retired.

What Eleazar Fitch lacked in ability to deal with people his classmate Chauncey A. Goodrich possessed in marked degree. Freshmen from the 1830's to the 1850's, when they first arrived in New Haven, probably knew more about him than any other member of the faculty. Many had admonitions from parents or graduates of the College to make his acquaintance at an early time. When he died in 1860 in his seventieth year, he was mourned throughout the entire company of Yale men.

After getting his B.A., Goodrich studied divinity with Timothy Dwight and also for a short time at Andover. Poor health forced his resignation from a pastorate he accepted at Middletown, Connecticut. Soon after this event he came to New Haven to fill the newly created chair of Rhetoric. He married a daughter of Noah Webster. Throughout his life he gave much time to getting out an abridgment and then a revision of the famous dictionary. On the faculty of Yale College, Goodrich pushed for the creation of a Theological Department. In 1828, six years after the initiation of the Divinity School, he purchased the *Monthly Christian Spectator* and during eight years used that journal to explain and defend the New Haven Theology. His continuing interest in the Theological Department led him in 1838 to propose the establishment of a chair of the Pastoral Charge and for its endowment he contributed a substantial sum. When the Corporation's first nominee for the post declined to accept, that body urged it upon Goodrich himself. His acceptance brought to an end his responsibilities as an officer of the College, and paradoxically, by so doing, freed him for the carrying out of a unique work. For more than a quarter of a century Goodrich exercised the most significant religious influence of any member of the College Church.

Goodrich labored actively in the periodic revivals, particularly after the impressive awakening in 1831. He was most effective in private conference. In these he listened to cases of conscience, and gave advice to burdened souls struggling for or against conviction. As he grew in years, he assumed a kind of paternal role among undergraduates desirous of guidance or assistance. His colleagues also, including President Woolsey, sought his advice on a multitude of matters. For three decades he led the meeting to which the undergraduates came on Sunday just after the evening meal, giving at such times an informal talk. After George P. Fisher succeeded Fitch as Professor of Divinity, Goodrich took an active part in the Friday evening prayer meetings for the older members of the parish. The life of this unofficial College pastor illustrates the power of that evangelical Protestantism in those simpler days before Darwin had changed the understanding of the origin of man and before historical scholarship had brought about a fuller knowledge of the ancient writings gathered together in the Bible.

In 1823 Jeremiah Day addressed at Boston the fourteenth annual meeting of the American Board of Commissioners for Foreign Missions. His discourse helps to explain a remarkable phenomenon in American history. Pioneers, pushing westward across the continental interior, had only recently crossed the Mississippi. Yet Americans, busy with the tasks of an expanding nation and facing a virtually empty continent beyond the new state of Missouri, gave thought to strange peoples who lived on distant islands and continents.

A group of undergraduates at Williams College initiated the foreign missionary movement early in the century. By 1823 eight graduates of Yale College had gone into service in Ceylon, the Near East, and the Hawaiian Islands. In the first half of the nineteenth century American Christians established in Asia, Africa, and the Pacific Islands the first of those hospitals, schools, and mission stations that carried to other races and cultures the ideals and faith of Western civilization.

A British movement had preceded that which originated in the United States, and the two developed together. But imitation does not explain the American effort. Rather it was the product of the dynamism of that evangelical Protestantism which had, long since, become indigenous in the Western Republic. Like most of his fellow countrymen, President Day, when he spoke to the American Board of Commissioners for Foreign Missions, was ignorant of other cultures. He saw the world simply as made up of Christians and heathen. The heathen needed help—urgently.

"The missionary cause is great," said the Yale President to the gathering in Boston, "when considered in reference to the numbers, to which its influence is to be extended. On how small a portion of the earth, has the sun of righteousness yet risen! Three-fourths of its inhabitants are still covered with the shadow of death. Year after year, multitudes from the nations, and kindreds, and people, are passing from the world of retribution, without even the hope of admission to the new Jerusalem; to the assembly of those who sing the praises of God and the Lamb."[11] President Day announced a hard doctrine. He called on Christians to take up the work of St. Paul and to push far out the boundaries of the area of light.

Eight years later in 1831, in the midst of a great revival, undergraduates and students in the Theological Department founded a secret society which they called The United Band of Foreign Missionaries in Yale University. Four years later the members changed the name to The Foreign Missionary Band of Yale College. The society continued for seven years.

Ten men founded the organization. Its numbers remained small. At the meetings the members discussed such subjects as "The Condition of China," "Heathen Nations Dying without Knowledge of Christ Are Lost," "The State of the Mohammedans," "History of the Sandwich Islands," and, on one occasion, whether they should abandon their secrecy and let the community know of their existence. The members turned down the last proposal. Committees were appointed to correspond with similar societies in Williams, Hamilton, Union, Dartmouth, Brown, Amherst, and Princeton. From the beginning the Band kept a "Sketch Book" in which each member set down his personal history. These small narratives with their intimate glimpses into the families of the writers assist a later generation to recreate in imagination the life of an age long gone. "Sketches" written by two of the members might almost have been conversations in a student's room.

Henry Sewall Gerrish French was born

at Boscawen, N.H. 27 April, 1807. Enjoyed the advantages of a common school, attending summer and winter until my 12th year. A few months before entering my 12th year left home and entered the Printing Office of George Hough Esq., Concord, N.H. where I continued 8 years. Was preserved from the many temptations to which I was there exposed by the kind warnings of my pious mother which I always received when I visited home. My Father and Mother were both professors of religion. . . . I gave my heart to my Saviour in 1824 and publicly professed my attachment to him in March 1827. I learned Latin grammar superficially while I was an apprentice but did not commence preparing for College in earnest till 1828, having spent more than a year at printing as a journeyman. . . . I spent 3 months at Phillips Academy, Andover, Mass. The remainder of my preparatory studies were completed in Boscawen, my native town.

Young French in his sketch told how he first became interested in the mission field. "My predilections for missionary life were apparently the result of circumstances though doubtless all written down in the book of Providence. I commenced my apprenticeship in January, 1819, 3 or 4 years after the establishment of the Ceylon Mission and also some of the Indian missions." The Concord shop printed a religious newspaper, with the consequence that the young apprentice had the "opportunity of becoming acquainted with the circumstances of these missions and the names of the Missionaries. . . . When I decided to live a Christian life, my resolution and desire was to be employed in some way for the salvation of the heathen. There was doubtless considerable romance connected with my resolution and desires . . . which subsequent prayer and examination of the subject has stripped off." French thought first of going out as a printer but friends urged him to complete his education first. "So soon as I could honorably disengage myself from my obligations as an apprentice, I commenced preparation for the work. A few years before this time my Father, who was engaged in a flourishing mercantile business, met with vicissitudes which rendered my family unable to supply me with the necessary means for pursuing my studies. I was therefore under the necessity of applying for aid to the American Education Society."

French entered college at the age of twenty-three. After graduation, he studied at Andover. Accepted as a missionary by the A.B.C.F.M., he sailed from Boston for Siam in 1839. He had learned the language and was starting his work as printer to the mission station in Bangkok when tuberculosis ended his life.

Jeremiah Root Barnes was born in "Meriden, Conn., March 9, 1809. From boyhood to 19 years was employed in various occupations of farmer, sailor, merchant and mechanic. Parents were pious and children of pious parents. Became professedly pious in New Haven, Conn., in the year 1828 soon after my father's death. The prayers and exhortations of my step-mother were the principal means. . . . Decided to study for the ministry. Fitted for college in New Haven and entered Yale College in 1831 [at the age of twenty-two]. Decided to be a missionary while in the Freshman class of YC."[12]

After getting his degree, Barnes studied in the Yale Divinity School, where Nathaniel Taylor instructed him in theology and Chauncey Goodrich in the art of preaching. He did not go to the foreign field. Rather he sought service in the new country beyond the Appalachians. In 1836 he took charge of a parish in what was still the frontier state of Indiana. It was no accident that Barnes in the Ohio Valley interested himself in schools and colleges. The cause of education on the frontier was at the time a primary interest of the Yale Divinity School. Barnes became financial agent of Marietta College in Ohio. He established a Young Ladies Seminary near Cincinnati in 1850 at a time when Catherine Beecher was pioneering in the cause of women's education. Finally Barnes became one of the founders of Carleton College in Northfield, Minnesota.

Jeremiah Barnes was one of an important company of men who left Yale College and the Divinity School to advance education in the West. They waged that age-old warfare against ignorance and lawlessness which enables a society to rise above barbarism. During the war that saved the Union and ended slavery, Barnes brought a career of service to a fitting conclusion as a worker in the Freedman's Bureau, aiding the ex-chattel to make a start in the adventure of freedom.

One day in 1859 Theodore Woolsey received a letter from a faraway mission station. After he read it, the President must have thought long before laying it aside to file. A young missionary of the Class of 1853 who had won academic honors during his college course had a burden on his conscience. In the epistle he spoke of his time at Yale as "happy years" but also of memories that would not down. "I was disposed," he wrote, "to take shelter under the practice and views of the great majority of professing Christians among my classmates. . . . Thus very many and among them professing Christians at times did not hesitate to request 'the monitor' to take off marks of absence or to take them off themselves. I remember . . . conversing upon the subject with one of our church deacons in Church Committee, who seemed to have no scruples of conscience on this point." The penitent could not forget that his father had been a missionary before him. "Is it not then strange," the writer continued, "that I could in any instance lend the influence of my example to the well-nigh universal practice of glancing more or less at text books during the hour of recitation? . . . I remember on one occasion—to have attempted wrongfully to answer *one* of the questions on *one* of our 'Biennial' papers, by copying from 2 or 3 very minute pieces of paper, which I wrongfully carried with me into the examination room. I now look upon my conduct as wrong

and ungentlemanly, and would consent to have my examination marked as a failure in that branch."

The missionary named and spoke with praise of two classmates who expressed to him moral scruples against the practice
of cheating. The final sentence of this confession to his former
president suggests a particular reason for the letter. "Let me
assure you," the young man concluded, "that were it again my
privilege to be a member of 'Honored Yale', I would earnestly endeavor to secure the approbation of my teachers and
especially of you who, with your hand upon my head, offered
that prayer in which I was set apart to the work of an evangelist . . ."[13] He made the amend honorable. He went on to a
career of distinguished service.

In the Commencement week of 1851, an event occurred
that attracted considerable interest. "On Monday evening,"
the *Lit* recorded, "the 25th anniversary of the Beethoven
[Sacred Music] Society was celebrated in the College Chapel,
on which Rev. Horace Bushnell, D.D. of Hartford, one of the
founders of the association, delivered an admirable address on
the subject of Sacred Music. The erection, then just completed,
of an Organ in the Chapel, gave additional interest to this anniversary. [The organ signalized a breach in the Puritan tradition
of New England.] A meeting of the past and present members
was afterward held and hereafter there will annually be a
similar gathering of the graduate and undergraduate members
during Commencement week."[14] The Beethoven Society originated in undergraduate initiative and represented a significant
undergraduate contribution to the religious services of the
College.

At a time when James Fenimore Cooper could point out to
his fellow countrymen, as he did in *The American Democrat*,
1838, not only that American culture lacked serious music
but that the public did not understand the importance of the
shortcoming, the Yale society took its place among a handful

of pioneering organizations. In its first quarter-century it provided, in the absence of an organ, instrumental music to support the singing. Even as Cooper wrote, an undergraduate, Richard Storrs Willis, worked to further the cause of music in America. Planning to devote his life to music, he served twice as president of Beethoven before he graduated in 1841. Before his commencement he had organized Yale's first orchestra. Later he studied with Lowell Mason in Boston and with Mendelssohn in Europe. He published the first collection of college songs arranged for tenor, baritone, and bass.

Meanwhile Beethoven pushed toward its objective, the installation of an organ in the Chapel. Benefit concerts added money to the organ fund. Members contributed. Near the end of the 1840's Irene Battell, wife of William Augustus Larned, professor of Rhetoric and English Literature, supported the cause of the Society with an infectious enthusiasm. When Bushnell came to New Haven to dedicate the organ, the event marked the culmination of a labor of a quarter of a century on the part of the Beethoven Society. The occasion, moreover, accented the fact that times were changing. Three years previous, Bushnell had delivered before the faculty and students in Divinity at Yale a lecture that presaged the passing of the old Calvinism and pointed to a liberal theology. In 1851 Bushnell celebrated the abandonment by Yale of an ancient Puritan prejudice against the use in public worship of the instrument of Sebastian Bach. Four more years were to go by before the elders of Center Church on the Green would consent to the installation of an organ.

President Woolsey had remarked in his inaugural in 1846: "We can bring the fine arts within the range of education." In 1855, putting to use a gift of Joseph Battell, the President appointed Gustav Stoeckel to be organist and choirmaster in the College Chapel. Formal instruction in music began at Yale. Stoeckel's publication in 1867 of a hymnbook for tenor, baritone, and bass voices seems to have been the first of its kind in the United States. The College Church had taken the position that beauty as well as preaching can enrich the life of the spirit.

With the appearance of an organized choir the function of the Beethoven Society had come to an end. After the Civil War Beethoven gave way to the new Glee Club.

For two years after Eleazar Fitch retired, the President added to his duties the responsibility of the chapel pulpit. Then, in 1854, George P. Fisher became professor of Divinity, expounding the traditional doctrines to the undergraduates and to the members of the Church and urging them to right living. In one important respect he differed from all his predecessors save Stiles in the chair of Divinity. Like Stiles, Fisher was more a scholar than an advocate of a particular system. He had a tolerance and balance that came from his unceasing attempt to achieve the broad view. He resigned the pastorate in 1861 to become professor of Ecclesiastical History in the Divinity School. It was the field in which Stiles took the greatest pleasure. Out of Fisher's researches came a notable book, the *History of Christian Doctrine,* published in Edinburgh in 1896.

Even before Fisher became pastor, the mounting tension between the North and South had extended to the Yale community. An undergraduate, Daniel Coit Gilman, vice-president of Linonia and later to be the first president of Johns Hopkins University, spoke of the class societies in an address he gave before Linonia on an occasion when the members of Brothers and Calliope were invited. The implications in his comments reveal some of the stresses in college life at midcentury. "I call your attention," he said in October 1851, "to the smaller literary associations that here exist, the 'class societies' as they are called and although it is not to be expected that I should enlarge on such a theme, yet I may be allowed to say, that so far as my acquaintance goes, they are both profitable and pleasant. Liable to abuses as these and all good things may be, yet even a casual observer can scarcely overlook the advantages they possess, in uniting together those whom the rivalries of the large societies would render hostile throughout the year, and those whom sectional and other differences might keep entirely apart."[15] Young Gilman spoke in the year that followed the Compromise of 1850, an intersectional arrangement that included the Fugitive Slave Law. Even as he spoke, Harriet Beecher Stowe's *Uncle Tom's Cabin* was running serially in *The National Era* and was to appear in book form in 1852. Southerners formed between 10 and 15 per cent of the Yale student body. The background of Gilman's remarks was provided by an event that had occurred a few weeks earlier. "We have to chronicle," recorded the *Lit,* "a movement of more than ordinary interest to our College Societies, and which more particularly affects the Calliopean. It is the withdrawal of the Southern members from the Linonian and Brothers Societies and their admission into Calliope. By this change, Calliope . . . has drawn more definitely the sectional differences of the students."[16] The times called for strengthening bonds of fellowship.

Fisher began his ministry in the College Church in a momentous year. In 1854 Stephen A. Douglas, senator from Illinois, brought about the passage by Congress of the Kansas–Nebraska Act. The measure tore up the Missouri Compromise that had lasted for more than a third of a century and opened to slavery broad western plains from which it had been barred. Tension among the undergraduates increased. The meetings of Calliope where Southern students stood apart from their fellows symbolized the ominous division developing within the nation. Fisher from the pulpit looked out on a congregation where anger smoldered. Before he had been a year in office his colleagues Benjamin Silliman and Nathaniel W. Taylor had, at a public meeting in New Haven, stood up to be counted among those who protested the Kansas–Nebraska Act. Leonard Bacon, pastor of Center Church, joined them. Jeremiah Day, Eleazar Fitch, and Chauncey Goodrich broke with the American Tract Society when some of its leaders tried to temporize on the issue that Douglas had forced on the nation. Two years later undergraduates and faculty pushed into a mass meeting held in United Church on the Green to say good-by and to give assistance to a company of young men who with their families were emigrating to hold Kansas for freedom. Three of the twenty-seven Sharp's rifles subscribed came from Benjamin Silliman and the undergraduates present. Fisher was the pastor of the members of Calliope as well as of Silliman, and of the undergraduates who had contributed rifles to the war that had already broken out in Kansas.

For five more years George Fisher preached on Sunday in the chapel. Tension grew. Chief Justice Taney gave Dred Scott his place in history. John Brown attacked Harper's Ferry and died on the gallows. In the last year of his pastorate Fisher delivered an address that revealed his quality. The governor of the state had designated January 4, 1861, as a special fast day. To an anxious congregation Fisher preached on the subject "Thoughts Proper to the Present Crisis." South Carolina had seceded and the Deep South was moving to follow the same course. President-elect Lincoln in Springfield, Illinois, waited to assume the direction of the government of a disintegrating nation. Conflicting counsels confused the citizens of the Northern states. Many insisted that it would be folly to try forcibly to hold an unwilling South within the Union. Uncompromising abolitionists demanded strong, even extreme action. To the fire-eaters Fisher spoke first.

"He who is conscious of strength and a just cause," the preacher said, "can afford to forego blustering and denunciation. Rant is the weapon of insincerity and weakness. We can consider the situation of our Southern friends, encompassed as they are with the fears of servile insurrection, and make it our own. . . . But conciliation must not go the length of surrendering principle. . . . In times of commotion, firmness in the magistrate and loyalty in the citizen are the prime virtues. . . . In such times, every good citizen should rally to the support of the government, if necessary with arms in his hands."[17]

In 1861 undergraduates loyal to the South withdrew from the College. The large company of its graduates also divided. The number of these on both sides who lost their lives proclaimed the character of this bloodiest of nineteenth-century wars. In the twentieth century the names of these men from the North and South who made the supreme sacrifice were to be engraved in the marble of the University's memorial tablets and to be set there once more side by side as they had stood in the college catalogues in the days of Jeremiah Day and Theodore Woolsey. At the Commencement of 1865 Horace Bushnell spoke the funeral oration not only of the alumni of Yale College but of all the dead who had fallen in the cause of the Union. His words recall the feeling of a people who had just emerged from tragedy.

As it is the ammunition spent that gains the battle, so the dead and dumb heroes are the purchase-money of our redemption. . . . We have now a new and stupendous chapter of national history. The story of this four year's war is the grandest chapter of heroic fact, tragic devotion, and public sacrifice that has ever been made in the world. The great epic of Troy is but a song in comparison. Our cause has been that of order, law, liberty, and right, and we have borne ourselves worthily of it. . . . By the blood of their sacrifices these dead have consecrated our free institutions. They are no longer mere human creations, but God's ordinances. . . . We are sworn to see that the perpetual, supreme sovereignty of the nation is established; we are sworn to see that every vestige of slavery is swept clean.[18]

Chapter 9. Evolution and the Old Orthodoxy

In July 1870 General Eugene A. Carr, commandant at Fort McPherson, near the North Platte in what was then the territory of Nebraska, said good-by to a small company of explorers as they started northward across the hot dry plains. Professor O. C. Marsh with nine Yale undergraduates and three recent graduates headed for the Loup Fork. Carr had given them a military escort to guard against roving bands of Indians. An army scout and two Pawnee guides picked out the way. For five days the party "marched over burning sand hills, without rocks or trees, or sign of water, while the thermometer stood at 110° in the shade of the wagons." Reaching the Loup Fork, the explorers searched the badlands along the river gathering fossils. The Indian guides balked at the business of collecting because of an old belief that the petrified bones found within their country were the remains of an extinct race of giants. "They refused to collect until the professor, picking up the fossil jaw bone of a horse, showed how it corresponded with their own horses' mouths. From that time they rarely returned without bringing fossils for the 'Bone Medicine-man.' "[1]

Darwin had published the *Origin of Species* in 1859 when Marsh was a senior. After graduating from the College the young man had returned to enroll in some of those advanced courses in science, provided for by the Corporation in 1860, which constituted the beginning of the Graduate School. Among other instructors Marsh had listened to lectures by James Dwight Dana, one of the best among the geologists of of the day, a scholar who blocked out the science of mineralogy and pioneered in the study of the evolution of the continents. But Dana, firm believer in traditional religion, rejected Dar-

win's theory of single-line evolution and wrote the great
scientist his criticism. Young Marsh went on to Europe, where
he studied science. He visited Darwin in the latter's home at
Down. The American student formed a lasting friendship with
that brilliant protagonist of Darwinism, Thomas Huxley. Appointed professor at Yale, Marsh in the summer of 1868 had
gone as far west as the then uncompleted Union Pacific would
take him. Fossils found in profusion at one place beside the
tracks where a well had been dug stimulated the professor to
organize the Yale College Expedition of 1870. Most of the
young men who joined him in the adventure paid their own
way.

For six months in the summer of 1870 Marsh and his company explored the western plains and mountains—Nebraska,
Utah, Kansas—examining every possible site where rumor
said that fossils might be found. Everywhere they gathered
treasure. In the several forts of the frontier they visited, Marsh
established with the commandants and their officers friendships
that were to prove invaluable for the expeditions that he was
to lead later into the plains. Newspapers in the West and East
reported the adventures of the party in the bison country. The
publicity appraised the public of the existence of a market for
fossil bones and established the professor as the most active
figure in it. In December the Yale College Expedition of 1870
returned to New Haven. It deposited in Peabody Museum
thirty-six boxes of materials, the beginning of what became the
greatest collection of the century of the fossils of ancient verte-
brates.

A few weeks after his return from the West, Marsh may have
read an unsigned review of Thomas Huxley's *Lay Sermons*
published in the January number of *The New Englander*. Yale
managed the journal. Three men, working in team, edited it.
George P. Fisher and Timothy Dwight were both professors
in the Divinity School. William L. Kingsley was to write a
history of Yale. The review, more than three pages in length,
found nothing to praise either in Huxley's book or in the man-

ner of its author. "He is positive," wrote the reviewer, "bold, sophistical even to self-entanglement, and contemptuous of all who dissent with him. He is so skillful in presenting one side of a case that he seems to deceive himself into the belief there is no other." Huxley's "case" was Darwinism. "The manifold ambiguities and hasty equivocations," the reviewer went on, "of his Physical Basis of Life, which have been so effectually exposed and answered, could never have been allowed by a man whose early education in logic had not been sadly neglected."[2] The temper of the review suggested the shock that Huxley's rationalism and agnosticism gave to conservative religious thinkers in midnineteenth-century Yale.

One wonders whether the great Darwinian met *The New Englander's* reviewer when he visited New Haven five years later. Huxley came to talk with Marsh. The conference extended into a week, a generous fraction of a seven weeks' lecture tour in the United States. With Marsh, Huxley pored over the trays that contained bones from thirty different fossil horses. From the evidence Marsh gave him Huxley rewrote the lecture he was to give on the horse in New York. He accepted gratefully for use on that occasion a chart that Marsh prepared for him which set forth the partial story of the evolution of the horse from a primitive four-toed species to the modern one-toed creature. Marsh had put together the first evolutionary sequence. But neither he nor Huxley thought it complete. The two men speculated one afternoon on the "dawn horse," not yet found. Huxley sketched the hypothetical animal showing five toes. He called it Eohippus. When the Bone Medicine-man later found the remains of the little creature, he kept the name. In the 1870's Marsh made Peabody Museum famous as the place where, in a cabinet that displayed the fossils of the horse's foot as it changed through geological time, the visitor could look upon the proof of evolution.

Six years passed after Huxley's visit to New Haven. Herbert Spencer, then at the height of his fame in America, came to the United States to lecture. But his health failed, compelling

him to cut short his visit. O. C. Marsh was one of those asked
to speak at the farewell dinner in honor of the celebrated visitor, given in New York on November 9, 1882. The Director
of Peabody Museum responded to the toast "Evolution, once
an Hypothesis, now an established Doctrine of the Scientific
World." "I can only reply," said Marsh, "that the battle has
been fought and won. A few stragglers on either side may still
keep up a scattered fire, but the contest is over, and the victors
have moved on to other fields." Marsh spoke of Spencer. In
his words of praise the paleontologist expressed a conviction
and a mood, derived in large part from Spencer, that was
bringing to educated Americans a reinforced optimism and a
new sense of direction. "Our guest tonight," said Marsh, "did
not stop to solve the difficulties of organic evolution, but with
that profound philosophic insight which made him read and
honored by all intelligent men, he made the grand generalization that the law of organic progress is the law of all progress.
. . . The evolution of life, and of the physical world, are now
supplemented by the evolution of Philosophy, of History, of
Society, and of all else pertaining to human life, until we may
say that evolution is the law of all progress, if not the key to
all mysteries."[3] Marsh had traveled a long road since that day
in 1870 on Loup Fork when he dispelled his Pawnee guide's
superstition concerning the fossil jawbone embedded in the
sediment.

At the Spencer dinner Marsh gave voice to the confident
secularism born in part of a science that each year added new
items to the knowledge of the history of life on the earth.
Aside from his praise of the Englishman, Marsh, however,
took little interest in the philosophical or religious implications
of the Darwinian hypothesis. These must be mentioned for
they impinged directly not only on the preaching heard in the
Chapel but on classroom instruction in the College.

The theory of evolution, particularly as presented in Darwin's *The Descent of Man* published in 1871, placed man wholly in the realm of nature, part of and the product of an evolutionary process. He had come up, Darwin thought, from antecedent mammals through a vastly long process of selection among tiny variations. The hypothesis seemed to undermine the ancient doctrine of special creation, the belief that God had created man above the animals and a little lower than the angels. The Darwinian hypothesis, in effect, relegated the story of the Garden of Eden and the fall of Adam to the category of myth. Inevitably the theory caused men to ask new questions about the idea of the unique spiritual nature of man.

The evolutionary theory posed also new questions for the scientists, for Darwin's theory had consequences for science as momentous as those for theology. The hypothesis sent the small but growing company of anthropologists into archeology to recover and to piece together what they could of the story of fossil man. The task proved long and arduous but in the twentieth century researchers produced an outline. The hypothesis also called into question the accepted dichotomy of mind and matter. Darwin's narrative of evolution began with organisms so primitive as to possess nothing that could be called mind. Yet, Darwin insisted, man ultimately evolved from them. For the great evolutionist, then, mind became not a separate entity but a psychophysical process, the functioning of the brain and its associated nervous system. The new approach sent investigators into human and animal psychology.

As for social thought, Spencer's evolutionary sociology was but an early example among countless attempts to reshape social theory in terms of Darwinism. Of these the most ambitious and most influential in the twentieth century was the "instrumentalism" of John Dewey. By 1900 "evolution" had become one of the two or three key words in American thought and discourse. To this consummation the neat and irrefutable sequence of the evolution of the horse that O. C. Marsh placed on display in Peabody Museum contributed significantly.

Through all this hurrying change James Dwight Dana,

Marsh's teacher, held fast to the faith in which he had been nurtured. For many years after the Civil War the geologist taught cosmogony to the undergraduates of Yale College. His lectures dealt with the origin of the earth, its continents and oceans, and with the development of life upon it. Inevitably he took account of the narrative of Genesis. He could do nothing else, for to him, as to his teacher, Benjamin Silliman, the Bible was a "Sacred Book." He reconciled the story as told in the Scriptures with that disclosed by the rocks. His last public pronouncement suggests the nature of the course.

On March 29, 1890, an audience gathered in one of the halls of Yale College to hear Dana lecture on "The Genesis of the Heavens and the Earth." He spoke with authority, for no geologist in any country surpassed him in eminence. His flowing white hair, piercing eyes, finely chiseled features made him an impressive figure. "The subject before us," he began, "is the bearing of the results of Nature's teachings on the character of ancient cosmogonic records. And since but one document has sufficient completeness and authority to merit consideration in this respect, and that is the opening chapter of the Bible, it is essentially a comparison between the teaching of God's Word and the teachings of Nature, or His works." "These readings of nature," the lecturer went on, referring to the geological timetable which he had set forth in his discourse, "are modern, the facts read are from records made during the ages to which they refer. A century since these ages were beyond the bounds of knowledge or thought. The earth in common belief had no past beyond man's birth day. . . . Now a volume of revelation is opening before us in which God has inscribed his wisdom and beneficence all along the ages . . ."

Dana took up the story as told in Genesis item by item and by skillful and effective interpretation harmonized it with geological history. He even included the development of life, though not in terms of the Darwinian theory. He came in his argument to Man and, in so doing, to a crucial question. "Science," he said, "has made no real progress toward proving that the divine act was not required for the creation of Man. No remains of ancient man have been found to indicate a progenitor of lower grade than the lowest of the existing tribes; none that show any less of the erect posture and other essential characteristics of the exalted species." Dana's statement was true in 1890. For Dana man was "made in the image of God." The lecturer concluded with a stirring peroration. "The degree of accordance between science and the Bible which has been made out should satisfy us of the divine origin of both Nature and the Bible . . . the stately review of the ages making the Introduction of the Bible stands there as the impress of the divine hand on the first leaf of the Sacred Book. The leaf carries the history, in sublime announcements, onward to Man. . . . Nature has her words of hope. For if myriads of ages were used in perfecting a single sphere in space and fitting it for its final purpose, and countless tribes of animals lived and died before the series reached a living soul, Man has reason to believe that this noblest form of life, whose likeness to the Eternal One is such that he is able to interpret and utilize His laws and find delight in the beauty and wisdom of his works, will not, after a few short hours, be blotted out forever . . ."[4]

Dana's lecture was the last significant attempt at Yale to reconcile Genesis with science. Even before he spoke, biblical criticism had put that ancient writing in a new perspective. At the same time Protestant theology was absorbing the theory of evolution. In fact three years before Dana's lecture, Henry Drummond, a Scotsman, preaching on the Yale campus, had demonstrated that evolution could be made a powerful aid to evangelism.

In that year of 1870, while Marsh prepared and carried out his first collecting expedition, a storm disturbed Yale circles. Younger alumni demanded a change in the composition of the Corporation, made up since Stiles' time of Connecticut Congregational clergymen together with the Governor, the

Lieutenant Governor, and six senior members of the upper house of the State Legislature. The "Young Yale" movement objected to the provincialism of the body. Anticlericalism appeared in the jeer about the "Rev. Mr. Pickering of Squashville" followed by the generalization that all ministers were an inferior lot. The critics suggested that alumni, elected to the Corporation by graduates, replace the Connecticut legislators. President Woolsey, about to retire, had already suggested a change. Alumni representation became effective in 1871 after the charter had been amended through separate actions by the General Assembly and by the Corporation.

The change was only one of many bits of evidence that an era in the history of Yale had ended. The initiation of the Graduate School in the previous decade was another. Discussion of the possible introduction of elective courses to reduce the rigidities of the old curriculum was a third. The men of the 1870's saw a new university rising about the College and assisted in bringing about fundamental alterations in that institution. The schoolmaster, with his faith in discipline and drill, had dominated the old College. Now the scholar's emphasis on freedom and responsibility in the search for new truth was beginning to introduce a new spirit to the institution.

In 1872 an Episcopal clergyman preached his farewell sermon at Morristown, New Jersey. William Graham Sumner had accepted the new chair of political science in Yale College. The creation of the new professorship to carry on a work that President Woolsey had initiated emphasized the broadening outlook of the institution. Sumner's abandonment of the ministry did not mean that he had given up his theological beliefs. His earlier experience as a tutor had persuaded him that he preferred the work of teacher to that of pastor. His parishioners at Morristown in that final service at which Sumner presided in their church heard from the pulpit an extraordinary summation of the position of religion in a troubled time:

Our modern society is deeply infected by philosophical skepticism and philosophical indifference. The number of men who are falling into a doubting position with regard to traditional religious doctrines is increasing every day. . . . A conflict is impending between the traditional dogmas and modern speculation and science in which it is possible that all religion may be lost. A chaos threatens the world of mind and spirit. Not two or three, nor a score, but a hundred claimants wrangle for the faith of men. It is to be apprehended that utter ruin may come upon all universal ideas and spiritual faiths. The great question is whether there is an historical revelation of spiritual and universal truths which has authority for man, or whether each man and each generation must reason out the whole problem afresh, or rest contented with such knowledge of the shell of things, as he can win through the senses. I say that this conflict is impending, and I believe and have always believed that it was the duty of the pulpit to prepare for it, to enter into it, and to win a victory in it. It is certain that every tradition and every inherited faith of mankind is to be stated on a re-examination of authority and evidence within the next fifty years.[5]

Theodore Woolsey at his inauguration in 1846 had sensed the crisis from afar. Before the Civil War he had noted the decay of faith in the old theology. In the final year of Woolsey's administration Professor Timothy Dwight in a little book called *Yale College—the New Era* discussed some issues raised by the crisis now at hand.

"We refer," said Dwight, "to the matter of religious instruction and the religious character of the institution." Dwight mentioned changes in the college system. He spoke of the strong desire of some to extend innovation into the area of religion. Dwight opposed the abandonment of tradition on grounds of both practicality and principle. "This institution," he reminded the would-be reformers, "was founded with prayer and consecration to God by the noble men of a past age. They established it as a place of religious teaching and influence, and not merely for the learning belonging to this world. They handed it over to the generations following them, that it might be as a light from God for all time. Every advance, which it has made since their day, has been made by the gifts and efforts of men who had their spirit. It has been as truly a power in the world for the extension of the Christian faith as for the promotion of any science. Its endowments would never have been given to it, but with the implied assurance that it was always to be what it was at first, a religious institution. If by any unfaithfulness of today, or of any future time, it should be suffered to pass out of such influence and take on a new character, it ought to lose its glory and its future. If those who do not believe in religion in college wish to establish institutions in accordance with their own views, they have abundant opportunity to do so."[6] Timothy Dwight followed his grandfather in taking up arms against secularism and infidelity.

In the year in which Dwight wrote, the Corporation, passing over the proposed names of Daniel Coit Gilman and Andrew D. White, President of Cornell, chose Noah Porter to succeed Woolsey in the presidency. Porter lectured in philosophy. Neither his reputation for erudition nor his preoccupation with scholarly work prevented him from having close relations with his students. A kindly man, he conspicuously abandoned the stiff formality of an earlier generation and achieved genuine friendships with some of the young men who came under him. In college as an undergraduate he had read and profited by Coleridge's *Aids to Reflection*. In the Divinity School, Nathaniel Taylor had trained him in a mild Calvinism. Porter had studied two years in Germany and had become familiar with German thought. As professor, Porter first used in class *Lectures on Moral Science* by Williams' Mark Hopkins. A believer in that faculty psychology that found such vigorous expression in the Yale College Report of 1828, Porter wrote a text for the course usually called Mental Philosophy. He published this book, *The Human Intellect,* in 1871, the year in which he became President. Executive responsibility could not keep him from his writing. He published a second book, *Elements of Moral Science,* in 1885, the year before he resigned as President to resume his professorship. Both texts achieved pre-eminence for a generation.

Carefully reasoned, though containing little original speculation, they presented a blend of old and new. Through these
two books Noah Porter influenced importantly the ethical and
religious thought of the students not only at Yale but throughout the nation.

In 1876, the year in which Huxley spent a week with Marsh,
President Porter dedicated Battell Chapel. Its location on the
corner of College and Elm streets between two new dormitories emphasized the acceptance by the authorities of the plan
to transform the college yard into a quadrangle.

One duty remained before the consecration of the new
chapel. On June 18, 1876, students, faculty, and friends assembled for the last time for Sunday morning worship in the
old chapel. The President led the service. Looking back to 1824,
he recalled the men who had preached from the chapel pulpit.
He emphasized the number of those who had gone out from
the College Church to careers of religious and educational
service in the nation and on the mission field. Porter understood the dangers to religion that lurked in the clash of doctrines that Sumner had described four years before at Morristown. As he said good-by to the old chapel the President spoke
with special earnestness of the faith that had been preached
there.

The theology which was taught and defended here was not taught
as a scholastic speculation, but as a living, energetic force, because
it was believed to be the power of God unto salvation. It was
preached with apostolic power. . . . The prominence which it gave
to the foundation truths of natural theology,—as freedom of the
will, and the moral government of God,—is explained by the conviction that Christianity presupposes these truths, that it must be
interpreted in harmony with them, and that it can never be rejected
by a man who intelligently and honestly holds them. The threatening aspects of modern unbelief bring daily and hourly confirmation
that these views in respect to the real strength and import of the

Christian evidences, and the nature of Christian theology, were eminently reasonable and just, and that they were not enforced too earnestly or too soon.[7]

In the afternoon of the same day the congregation that assembled for the dedication more than filled Battell Chapel. Many stood throughout the service. Many were turned away. Again the President spoke. Facing the "modern irreligious spirit" that had brought crisis to Protestantism he took his stand not only as an individual but as head of an emerging university. Higher education implies development of character as well as training of the intellect. A considered and balanced religious faith furthers both ends. The besetting sin of a community of scholars is intellectual pride and an intolerance toward religion akin to that which ecclesiastics have often exhibited toward the findings of science. Let the scholar remember that the "moral conditions of eminent success in scientific research are akin to those which admit to the kingdom of God."

Porter commented on the intellectual climate of the time. He did not mention by name Darwin, Spencer, or Comte, but he dealt with evolution, sociology, and positivism. John Stuart Mill was furthering positivism in British thought. European scholars, moreover, analyzing the books of the Bible and investigating the ancient world of which they were a part, proposed novel and disturbing hypotheses concerning the Scriptures. D. F. Straus, using the techniques of historical criticism, had proposed the hypothesis that the story of Jesus was a myth. Literary criticism of the documents had also led to conclusions that denied many old assumptions and beliefs. Porter, careful scholar, reacted against the revolutionary theories of the day. He stood fast on old positions. He believed that religion and learning could and should go forward together, bringing new knowledge to the illumination of old truth:

Hasty and superficial generalization is another characteristic of our times. It is seen on the one hand in the brilliant romancing of the eloquent scientific lecturer, in the flippant theories that characterize

our historical and literary criticism, and the confident dogmatism
of our one-sided theorists in psychology, ethics, and sociology. . . .
The new Voltaire is more decorous and respectful in his manner
than the old. The new Rousseau is less impulsive and more self-con-
trolled. The new Hume is more exact in his knowledge, more respectful and restrained in his tone: but the new Voltaire and the
new Rousseau and the new Hume shut their eyes as persistently to
the very same fact and relations which their prototypes rejected
with passion or ridicule or contempt. Atheistic and anti-Christian
theories of history, of government, of politics, of culture, of ethics,
and of human progress, are as narrow in data, as false in their conclusions, and as dangerous in their influence, in this generation as
in any other, and none the less because they are more decorous,
more learned, and more scientific.

Porter did not deny scholarship. He supported science but
he looked upon the new rationalism of positivism as a philosophical formulation. He accepted biological evolution but
denied the far-ranging implications expressed in social Darwinism. As a philosopher he criticized the empiricism of Mill.
At a time when O. C. Marsh swallowed Spencer hook, line,
and sinker, Porter in various writings subjected the empiricism
of Spencer to critical philosophical analysis. As it turned out,
Spencer did not stand the test of time. In his dedication address
Porter set forth his convictions concerning the relations between scholarship and religion. "A Christian university," said
the President, "is, other things being equal, the place of all
others in which truth is likely to be sought for with the boldest
and freest spirit, for the simple reason that those who believe
most earnestly in the Christian verities are the most fearless in
submitting them to the severest scrutiny. While it is true that
many religionists and so-called theologians are timid of new
light, suspicious of new investigations, it is also true that those
whose faith is strongest and surest, are the most eager for new
inquiries, and the most fearless of fresh investigations. On the
other hand whatever may be thought of the doctrines of our
modern scientific atheists and literary anti-Christians, their

spirit and temper bring little honor to the catholicity of Science."⁸ These words sounded in the new chapel on the day of its dedication.

Soon after he arrived at Yale the young Professor of Political and Social Science began reading with his students the only available book in English on the emerging discipline of sociology. Sumner, dedicating all his energy to the gaining of an understanding of society, felt it his duty to make available to undergraduates the harvest of scholarship contained in Spencer's book. The fact that religious conservatives considered Herbert Spencer the chief anti-Christian of the time, if it occurred to Sumner, was considered by him irrelevant. He read with surprise a letter from President Porter in December 1879, that concluded: "as I am presumed to authorize the use of every textbook, I must formally object to the use of this." The President made clear that he based his objections on religious grounds. "The freedom and unfairness with which it attacks every Theistic Philosophy of society and of history, and the cool and yet sarcastic effrontery with which he assumes that material elements and laws are the only forces and laws which any scientific man can recognise, seem to me to condemn the book as a textbook for a miscellaneous class in undergraduate instruction."⁹ In a private and amicable interview with the President the matter seemed settled. Porter did not change his opinion of Spencer's book. Sumner understood that he would not enforce his demand. The fact that an issue had arisen leaked to the New York press. The fame of Spencer and the prestige of religion made a tussle at Yale good copy. In the spring of 1880 the New York *Times* ran articles under the headlines, "Yale a Battle Ground" and "Two Parties at Yale." The news stories contained the usual journalistic exaggerations and inaccuracies. All parties in the College deplored the unhappy publicity. The newspaper flurry subsided.

A college year ended and another began. Sumner prepared

to use Spencer again in his term course on sociology. At some
time during the year a friend informed Sumner that the President in reporting to the Corporation at its June meeting on
the Spencer imbroglio had stated that Sumner had promised
to give up the use of the offensive book in his classes. This information had caused to be dropped a motion prepared by ex-
President Woolsey, now a member of the Corporation, that,
if passed, would have given the President specific authority to
rule on textbooks used in courses. The Professor of Political
and Social Science felt his position to be intolerable. Sumner
addressed to the President, the members of the Corporation,
and the professors a communication in which he defended his
decision to use the Spencer volume. He announced that he
was withdrawing from all committees and other faculty activities, save teaching. He made it clear that he was seeking a
position outside of Yale.

Friends, both outside the University and among his colleagues, rallied to his support. One of those among the latter
was young Henry A. Beers, who had abandoned the practice
of law in New York City to take up the pleasant work of
guiding students in his Alma Mater to the riches to be discovered in English literature. In a day when the classics held
undisputed supremacy Beers pioneered in a new and fruitful
field. Perhaps the experience strengthened his sympathies for
Sumner, also a pioneer in a virtually unexplored territory.

In the end Sumner did not resign. Neither Porter nor the
Corporation pressed to conclusion the matter of the denial of
academic freedom. Porter simply allowed time to correct his
original mistake. A few years later, when Sumner faced vicious
attacks, particularly by the New York *Tribune,* for his public
defense of the policy of free trade, President Porter did not
yield to demands for the dismissal of the offending professor.

The "Spencer Controversy" at Yale ranks as an event of
some importance in the history of American Protestantism.
For more than half a century Yale College had been a national
institution. Under an unbroken succession of clerical presidents

it had stood before the American public as an institution dedicated as much to the furtherance of the cause of Christianity
as that of learning. In his letter to the Yale officials Sumner had
stated his understanding of the issue as it related to religion.
"In my controversy with President Porter," he wrote, "I did
not defend agnosticism; I resisted obscurantism."[10] In the out-
come of the Spencer Controversy freedom of thought, of
teaching, and of inquiry had prevailed in a Protestant Christian
college.

Henry Beers, two years out of college, wrote a poem which
he called "The New Yale, 1871." The triumph of liberty ten
years later gave added meaning to his lines.

> All day we hear the chisels ring,
> The windlass creak, the masons sing;
> With every brightening moon there falls
> A longer shadow from the walls.
> We hope these rising halls may bring
> Some new event—some wished for thing.
> We look to see that not alone
> Of mellow brick-work or of stone,
> But reared of wisdom's magic wands
> Invisible, not made with hands,
> Yet stronger than the trowell builds,
> Her corner-stone's free-masonry
> As broad as this brave century,
> Our new regenerate Yale shall be—
> Our Yankee university.[11]

Chapter 10. From Orthodoxy to the New Theology

In the ferment of the 1870's when the University began to take form and when new ideas transformed the intellectual climate, an ancient institution of the College suddenly faced a challenge. Some members of the Yale community suggested that the requirement of attendance at chapel services on weekdays and on Sunday had served its usefulness. State universities had appeared and because of their public character had laid down no rules regarding religion. Andrew D. White, cofounder of Cornell in 1865, had left religion as the responsibility of the individual student. Should Yale, some asked, continue to be bound by a tradition that had originated in the early eighteenth century when Connecticut was a struggling Puritan commonwealth?

Undergraduates of the College made their opposition felt in varied ways. In 1870 the *Lit* began a crusade that lasted several years. Writers objected to inferior and inappropriate preaching. They would have no more of the old doctrinal sermons. One contributor pointed to the sorry state of the College Church when preaching was poor and when the College Pastor, being a member of the faculty, had only minimal contact with the students. In the bare and uncomfortable sanctuary that Jeremiah Day had dedicated the great majority of the student body of some four hundred expressed their attitude in an unconcealed indifference during the preaching. Many whiled away the hour by studying, novel reading, or sleeping. The faculty sat in the gallery. A note of exasperation crept into the comment of a contributor in December 1870. "And while we are speaking of the chapel," he said, "it may be well to mention another slight defect,—an error to which ministers from abroad are especially liable. It is unpleasant to see one at the end of his sermon, turn with a bland smile to the galleries and say 'and now, fellow-Christians, it is your duty to guide these miserable sinners (slightly contemptuous gesture toward the pit,) in the way of Life and Truth,' . . ." In the academic year 1871–72 the faculty abolished compulsory attendance at the afternoon Sunday service. But they would go no further.

As Battell neared completion in 1876, the *Yale Record,* a journal of news and comment, spoke of the "half a hundred years [that had] passed away since the old Chapel was dedicated." "As we look back," the *Record* continued, ". . . we cannot help having forcibly brought to us the consideration of what real advantage they have been, and whether they are worthy of being continued. A question by no means new, yet new in that on the eve of going into a building which presents so great a contrast to the barenness and plainness of the old Chapel, it seems only fitting to desire services which shall be free from the old Puritan ideas of compulsion and necessity. In our country now, colleges and schools are perhaps the only places where a union of church and government is maintained, and it is very difficult to see the real reason for such a course, especially where we see in the daily life and conversation of those around us, its evil effects." The writer in the *Record* went in for realism. He pushed an argument in the obvious hope that it might help to change the ways of Yale.

He reminded his readers that his fellow students were not schoolboys, but were at an age to doubt and to rebel at unreasonable authority. He wondered whether, as had been suggested, the purpose of chapel was to get the undergraduates up in the morning and to hold them in town on Sundays under the eyes of the college proctors. "If this explanation were true it would be as unworthy and unholy as when the heathen took the vessels of the temple for their drinking cups. . . . It is certain that nothing is more active in bringing religion and its services into disfavor than the belief, unfounded though it be,

that it is being made a means of worldly advantage . . ." The
writer concluded by calling attention to "the indifference and
distaste to religion" that prevailed among his fellows.[1]

Noah Porter undoubtedly read or was informed of the con-
tents of the *Record's* piece on compulsory chapel. He dealt with
the subject in his address at the dedication of Battell. The President had just completed his freshman year in Yale College
when Jeremiah Day's faculty issued the famous Report of 1828.
Forty-eight years later Porter had not budged from the basic
assumptions and principles of that document. As president he
had retained the fixed and required pattern of courses in the
classics and mathematics. Sumner's courses represented the
most striking departure from the old order. Porter still looked
upon the College as a great family whose head was the President. The issue of compulsory chapel evoked a disclosure of
the Puritan mind, tough, uncompromising, impervious to the
appeal for freedom of a new generation in a new age.

"Every college," said the President, addressing the great
audience that had crowded into the new chapel, "is a world by
itself, with its own peculiar atmosphere, its separate earth and
sky. It must have an altar of its own, or lose the advantage of
regular and formal worship." It must have its appointed hour
and place of public prayer or "stand as an offensive exception
to the ways of other organized human societies." Compulsory
attendance can be no hardship when it is practiced also by the
instructors. A wise education trains habits of method and regularity in "meeting the requisitions of life." Strict college rules
deliver the students from "hesitation and self-indulgence, from
dawdling and childish caprice, in controlling their time, and
meeting the stern demands of life." Having asserted the traditional position, the President concluded: "College prayers and
Sunday worship . . . are publicly dishonored by making attendance voluntary." Then Porter turned on those venturesome individuals who had suggested freedom. "Compulsion, I know,"
said the President, "is an odious word; but it seems to me that
it is never so odious as when it is wrested out of all propriety

in the spirit of the demagogue in education, or when addressed
to sectarian or libertine prejudices. We trust that no Christian
college will so far lose its self-respect in obedience to such a
cry, as to close or dishonor its house of prayer."²

The young men who sought a broader liberty might be defeated; they were not cowed. In spite of the fact that students
were, at the moment, occupied with annual final examinations,
the *Record* found time to reply to the head of the institution.
"We hope," said the writer in that journal, ". . . that we shall
not be thought presumptuous if we briefly describe the appearance of this question as seen from our own standpoint.
And in this particular we think we may fairly claim to represent
the prevailing view of the undergraduates. . . . We would ask
if it is not a little bit absurd to pretend to compel men to put on
the appearance of worship in the presence of the one who said
'They that worship Him must worship in spirit and in truth;'
and lastly we would speak of the moral government of the
Ruler of the Universe, who, we are told, has given us power
of choice in these matters, though 'compulsion' was doubtless
as easy to Him as to our respected Faculty. But we are not
fond of arguments, and if we were we would avoid them during annuals. . . ."³

The *Record's* anonymous Roger Williams continued to attend
compulsory morning chapel and Sunday service to the end of
his course. The law concerning chapel remained in force for
forty-eight more years.

The time came in the second Timothy Dwight's administration when the College more or less frankly used morning
prayers for worldly ends. As the University's bicentennial approached, a group of editors prepared a volume to which they
gave the title *Two Centuries of Christian Activity at Yale.* They
asked Charles H. Smith—"Indian," "Old One Lung" Smith
of history—to do a chapter. Among other things he dealt with
compulsory morning chapel. He wrote with care and candor.
"Public sentiment at Yale," he said, "supports the requirement,
but for reasons which are largely secular. Students and alumni

in large numbers express their approval of required prayers because of the inspiration which comes from seeing so many students together, and feeling one's self a member of a great institution." At the end of the century the undergraduate body of the College each morning filled Battell—the three upper classes occupied the main floor and the freshmen, the gallery. Monitors, as they had done for more than a century, listed the absentees. Smith noted that both students and alumni considered the morning chapel service as a "useful corrective to the disintegrating influence of the elective system upon the classes." Smith thought the reasons that were given for assembling the students had merit. He saw no satisfactory substitute for the traditional religious service. But he regarded as unfortunate the fact that a devotional exercise had been largely turned away from its proper use as worship. "Under existing conditions," he concluded, "which include the somewhat prevalent practice of studying the morning lesson during prayers, it may be questioned whether the exercise has much value as a 'daily recognition of the Supreme Being.' "[4]

Professor Bernadotte Perrin, who made the culture of ancient Greece come alive for his sophomores, was one of a group of chaplains who near the end of the century took turns leading morning prayers. One one occasion he addressed an eloquent appeal to a student audience in Dwight Hall to try to appreciate the values of the service. If they could not worship, let them appreciate its beauties, as they heard the music of the chants and hymns and listened to the noble prose and poetry of the prayers and the King James' version of the Scriptures. But the student body of the time added many Philistines to the large company indifferent to religion. Perrin's appeal, effective for a time, was ultimately forgotten. Compulsory chapel continued a quarter of a century after the classicist spoke, a relic of the eighteenth century persisting far into the twentieth.

The form of the service in what came to be called "daily chapel" remained virtually unchanged during the last half of the nineteenth century and, in fact, up to its abolition in 1926. Sunday chapel, however, saw not only modifications in the preaching service but important alterations in the theology presented in the pulpit.

The change in ideas was forecast as early as 1848, when Horace Bushnell, Yale-trained clergyman at Hartford, Connecticut, began to point out to midnineteenth-century Americans new religious vistas. In 1848, when Taylor's New Haven Theology was widely influential, the former tutor delivered at Yale, Harvard, and the Andover Theological Seminary a series of discourses in which he declared dogma to be an intellectual formulation that did not and could not express the meaning of religion. The lecturer implied that men must go beyond even the New Haven Theology. He urged further that preachers look to more important achievements than the revival brought about by the "friction of human effort and expectation." Bushnell, like Emerson, the transcendentalist, had fallen under the influence of Coleridge. The Hartford theologian saw religion as the Divine Spirit moving within the heart, "a new spirit of piety from God, such as we have never before realized." "One thing is clear," he added, "that the highest form of piety can never appear on earth until the disciples of Christ are able to be in the Spirit in some broader and more permanent sense than simply to suffer those local and casual fervors that may be kindled within the walls of a church or the boundaries of a village." Emerson could understand what Bushnell meant, for the thought of the two men had much in common. Bushnell, moreover, welcomed the geology that Silliman was teaching and to which Dana and Agassiz of Harvard were to make major contributions. The Hartford clergyman was convinced that the understandings achieved by reason would be found ultimately to be in harmony with the intuitions of the heart. Science, said the theologian, "opening to view new conceptions of the cosmogony of the universe, is destined gradually to assimilate with the Christian truth and to become part of it. For God is one, he is sure at last to be found in agreement with himself."5

Bushnell, forecasting a new theology, had long been under attack by the conservative clergy when George P. Fisher resigned as pastor in 1861 to accept a post in the Divinity School. The Civil War had already begun. For three years, while the shadow of the conflict lay across the college yard four men in rotation led the Sunday services in the chapel. Theodore Woolsey added this task to his other responsibilities. Three professors from the reorganized Divinity School—Hoppin, Fisher, and Dwight—shared the work with the President. Each of the four preachers took two successive Sundays, a responsibility that involved each time the writing of four sermons. The Sunday afternoon preaching service had not yet been discontinued but was to disappear within a decade. The wartime arrangement, though forced by a shortage of funds, turned out to be a pioneering experiment. The arrangement seems to have worked well. The Church and congregation expressed approval. Well they might, for Woolsey, Fisher, and the second Timothy Dwight were men of outstanding ability. The plan, moreover, gave evidence of a continuing close relation between the Divinity School and the College Church. Eleazar Fitch in the 1820's had pushed for the establishment of the school. Now, forty years later in a time of need, three of its faculty assumed the responsibility that he had once borne.

Of the four men who preached in rotation in the chapel in the early 1860's Theodore Woolsey spoke with the greatest authority. Did he not stand before the world as head of a college that for more than a century and a half had held fast to the Christian faith as that faith was expressed in some of the greatest doctrines to come out of the Reformation? Woolsey was worried by new currents in religious and secular thought. He saw the possibility of a greater calamity than that which threatened for a time because of the secession of the Southern states. After the surrender of Lee had ended the danger to the

nation, Woolsey reworked and developed a discourse he had
first preached in the chapel on the possible shipwreck of Christianity. It dealt with those intellectual currents which Sumner
was to mention at Morristown in 1870. Woolsey published the
sermon in *The New Englander* in 1869. He called it "The Religion of the Future."

The President dealt with what might pass for religion in a
post-Christian era and of that philosophy of positivism which
asserted that science was the final triumph of thought. He
spoke of the new deism arising from science. It alarmed him.
He saw science with every advance thrusting God to a greater
distance. The new learning was replacing the loving God of
his fathers with a remote deity who "has left the reins on the
neck of time and inhabits His eternity as a vital energy, without
concern or pity for man." Woolsey, insisting in the tradition
of Calvinism on the reality of evil and the enduring fact of sin,
suggested the consequences of the rising secularism. With a
shrewd forecast of social thinking to come he pictured a time
when "sin would be regarded as a transitional state of the necessary progress of human nature." "And it seems likely," he
went on, "that efforts against it would be confined principally
to the rectification of society, to the removal of ignorance, to
the relief of the lower classes, on the ground that human nature
is not bad, that evil emanates from society and can be effectively
obstructed and dried up by outward reformations." Woolsey
saw Rousseau's optimism concerning human nature reinforced
by the positivism of Auguste Comte. They acted together to
"plunge a demoralized world into atheism." The aging president called a generation that had slipped its tether back to
Christian fundamentals: Let men face the fact that Rousseau's
environmentalism will not purge evil from the hearts of men;
only redemption through divine forgiveness can achieve that
end. Woolsey set his face against both secularism and a new
theology. "If God ought to forgive because the best conceptions
of human virtue include forgiveness, He ought to have indignation against sin, because that too enters into our ideal of perfect

character. And how terrible that indignation."[6] That was the exit line of the last of the Yale presidents to represent the Old Theology.

In the time of Woolsey and Porter, Thomas A. Thacher, Professor of Latin, carried on of his own volition and in the tradition of Chauncey Goodrich, a kind of informal pastorate. Learned in the classics from study in Europe, he became in the classroom a stimulating and creative teacher. There his masterful presence subdued all undergraduates meditating mischief. Behind the formidable exterior, however, was a man who had a genius for friendship with persons of all ages, but particularly with young men. As each successive class left the College, it added a new and considerable number to that company of graduates who remembered "Tommy" Thacher as one who, through personal interest, friendship, and, often, affection had enriched their lives and had helped to shape their character. Thacher did not emphasize evangelical religion as Goodrich had done. The Latin teacher became friend and guide. He was more the humanist, interested in assisting young men to live rather than in preparing them to die.

During Thacher's service at Yale—he held the Professorship of Latin from 1842 to 1886—much of the old theology faded. One change was of fundamental importance. In the time of Thomas Clap old Wollebius had warned the college boys digging out their lessons in divinity: "But where Hell is we are not to search or enquire." If by some remote chance an undergraduate in the latter years of Thacher's teaching had stumbled on Wollebius' caveat, he would most likely have rejoined: "Why hunt for something that isn't there?" The disappearance of the age-old belief in the fiery pit and the burning lake necessitated of itself a change in Protestant thinking. But other influences equally important brought about a new conceptual structure. Thacher's emphasis on life in the here and now forecast an emphasis in Protestantism that grew in importance as the century neared its end.

A gift in the middle 1860's greatly enlarged the endowment of the professorship of Divinity and caused a change in its name. In 1863 the Corporation appointed William B. Clarke to the Chittenden professorship. For three years Clarke served as College pastor, then, after an interval, was succeeded by Oliver E. Daggett, who also served three years. From 1870 to 1877 Noah Porter was acting pastor. In the latter year William M. Barbour became Chittenden professor and held the post for ten years. In 1887, the year after the second Timothy Dwight was elected president, Barbour resigned to accept a post in a theological seminary in Canada.

The departure of Barbour brought to an end the old order of professors of divinity, successors to Napthali Daggett. During the previous two and a half decades the new university was taking form. The student body of Yale increased. With the growth of Sheff and the evolution of the professional schools the interests of the students became diversified. On each Sabbath the chapel preacher faced a varied congregation: the members of the College Church, the student body of Yale College, required to attend, a scattering of other students, and visitors with no University connection. The success of the rotation of the four preachers in the early 1860's seems to have encouraged invitations to more and more clergymen outside the University. During the period the University Church had a membership that compared favorably with that of earlier decades. Moreover, a new activity appeared.

In the autumn of 1860 two undergraduates began Sunday school classes in a large red house at the foot of Oak Street in a poorer section of New Haven. At the time, Sunday school was still a new and experimental addition to the traditional religious service. As the classes grew in size, the founders of the Bethany Sunday school recruited women teachers from the city. Success brought financial aid from prominent citizens in New Haven, and a new building housed what was now called the Bethany Aid Society. Students participated in the enterprise, along with workers from the city. The institution con-

tinued into the twentieth century. Before the Civil War men
had gone out from the College Church to undertake missionary
service on distant continents and in the West. Bethany Sunday
school initiated mission work in the evolving industrial society
that enveloped the College. The pastors, Clarke, Daggett, and
Barbour, watched with sympathy this outreaching of the
church they led.

When Barbour left in 1887, what had been an experiment
became University policy. A succession of visiting ministers,
with occasional clergymen from the University, preached in
Battell. Some of the congregation grumbled at the lack of
continuity of thought coming from the chapel pulpit. No
longer could those who attended Sunday service follow an
orderly and developed course of sermon-lectures in theology
such as Eleazar Fitch and the first Timothy Dwight had given.
Defenders of the new arrangement met the criticism by pointing out the value for the young men of listening to varied points
of view. Among other advantages the change enabled the College Church to deny the charge that it was tied to the Congregational denomination. Methodists, Baptists, and Episcopalians led the University service. In the presidency of Dwight,
Unitarians preached at Yale. The second Timothy had a sense
of humor. He doubtless enjoyed imagining what his grandfather would have said had he ever guessed that such a com-
merce with the Evil One would one day come about in the
college he had with such labor brought back to the straight and
narrow way.

The most distinguished preachers of the time came to
Battell. The list of visitors included the eloquent Hugh Black;
Joseph Twitchel, the Hartford friend of Mark Twain; George
Angier Gordon, pastor of the Old South Church in Boston and
writer on the New Theology; William Stephen Rainsford,
rector of St. George's in New York City, who also wrote
books on religion; Henry Van Dyke, poet and essayist, whose
allegorical and religious tales were widely read; and Lyman
Abbott, author of *Theology of an Evolutionist* and editor of the

Outlook, one of the most important journals of opinion at the turn of the century. To hear these men and others, the members of the College came together on Sundays. The President introduced the visitors.

President Emeritus Charles Seymour has left a picture of the chapel around the turn of the century:

the wooden barred cage enclosing the choir from which their heads popped when the "chant" opened morning prayers; the bare dais upon which sat the President and visiting preacher, raised well above the choir so that [after 1899] the continual winding and unwinding of Prexy Hadley's legs was in full view of the congregation; the forest of grey organ pipes, obviously never dusted, that rose behind in the apse; the "faculty box" in the north transcept with such reverend figures in the pews as George E. Day [Dean of the Divinity School], Samuel Harris [also of the Divinity School and possessed of] flowing white side whiskers; Franklin B. Dexter [librarian and historian of Yale] with beard well below the chest, George T. Ladd [of Philosophy], "Dog-face" Morris [of Classics], "Visi-Goth" Adams [of History], all well bearded but younger. And the imposing front row of the south gallery: George P. Fisher (blandly dominating and also with long white side whiskers), Bernadotte Perrin [of Classics] with red, bristling beard, "Buffalo" Wright [of Physics] with his Silliman and Trumbull connections, "Baldy" Wright, the impassive and benign Dean of the College. All these worthies the students saw regularly at close range in worship and the experience was part of their education.

After Woolsey's day sermons preached in Battell gave evidence not only that Protestantism had begun to assimilate the new science to the service of an old faith, but that the exuberent naturalistic philosophy of progress of Herbert Spencer had made an impress on Protestant thought. The preachers, however, insisted that belief, not doubt, opens the gate upon the good life. Back of their call to faith lay the continuing conviction that religion is the ultimate support of morals. Paradoxically, no one better illustrated the new emphases than conservative Noah Porter.

In 1880 President Porter, engaged in writing his *Elements of Moral Science,* preached in Battell a sermon he called "Agnosticism a Doctrine of Despair." It epitomized much of the argument of the book. Porter spoke of evolution, which had become one of the central concepts in the intellectual climate. He called attention to the larger history, "going backward into the remotest past, and unrolling its records, whether these are written on indestructable tables of stone, or suggested by the casual deposits of heaps of refuse." Porter and his contemporaries still lived in a Newtonian world. He saw the material universe as a great machine that functioned with the orderliness, the accuracy, and the dependability that Newton had found in the solar system. The preacher reminded his hearers of the logic of natural theology.

But history of every kind, even of nature is interpreted force and law; and force, to be interpreted by law, must be orderly in its actings; and order in nature, if it does not require a directing God, is, to say the least, best explained by such a God. Especially if the great law of evolution or development is accepted, and so a long story of progress is traced in the past, there emerges and shapes itself into being a continuous plan, a comprehensive thought wide enough to embrace all the events which have successively germinated into being, and long enough to provide for their gradual succession. This required a single mind as wide as that of one forecasting God, and as unwearied as his understanding.

The year before Porter preached on Agnosticism, John Fiske, lecturer at Harvard, had published a volume of essays on Darwinism. In 1884 he brought out the book *The Destiny of Man Viewed in the Light of His Origin,* which did so much to persuade American Protestant thinkers that evolution was a revelation by science of the Divine method of creation. Porter had, in effect, anticipated Fiske by four years.

The Yale President pushed on to the relation of religion to morals. He agreed with Spencer that science should stop at the border of what can be known. In opposition to Spencer he contended, however, that "atheistic agnosticism" could not give satisfying answers to the basic problems of life:

Strength and perfection of character are the supreme aim of all right-judging men. When they think of what man was made to be, and of what they themselves might become, they cannot but aspire. But strong as conscience is to elevate, control, and command, a personal God is needed by man to give his conscience energy and life. Personality without is required to reinforce personality within. . . . The theory that denies that God is a person, very naturally and logically denies that man is a person. It makes him only a highly developed set of phenomena flowering from a hidden root—the unknowable unknown. What we call his personality, his will, his character, are all as unreal as the clouds of a summer noon —one moment apparently as fixed as mountain summits, and another dissolving as you gaze.

Porter contended that Spencer's agnosticism must have despair as its fruit. Only Christian theism could provide the hope and the dynamism for that progress which Spencer insisted was an aspect of natural law. But Porter, careful philosopher, moved cautiously, permitting himself no extravagances of sentiment. "The developments of the past," he contended, "except as they reveal some plan of God, give no hope for the future. In the facts of the past, there is no security that the movement of man is onward. Manifold phenomena in human history suggest fearful forebodings of degeneracy, depravity, and retrogression." Porter did not live to see his forebodings realized in the moral retrogressions of the twentieth century. Unlike Sumner, however, whose uncompromising naturalism led him to dark and, as events turned out, surprisingly accurate forecasts, Porter shared the optimism of his day. He came to this optimism by way of the Christian tradition.

But so soon as we know that God rules over man for man's moral discipline, and that Christ is setting up a kingdom of righteousness and peace and joy in the Holy Ghost, then we lift up our hearts, and gather courage for man's future history. We find good reason to conclude that man will continue to make progress in the knowledge of whatever is true, and just, and honest, and of good report. We become well assured that the simple law of Christian love will in due time be expanded by Christian science into thousands and tens of thousands of those special precepts of Christian ethics, which future generations shall joyfully accept . . .[7]

Porter preached as early as 1880 many of the doctrines basic to what came to be called "liberal" Protestantism, namely the acknowledgment of science as a valid but partial discovery of the truth and the acceptance of the method of science as a dependable technique for the acquisition of knowledge. Nearly two decades before William James published *The Will to Believe* Porter rejected the rationalistic philosophy of positivism on the pragmatic ground that agnosticism leads to the despair of the man who looks out upon the universe disclosed by science and "muses upon the vastness of this great solitude, peopled though it be with the enormous agents that haunt and overmaster him with their presence, but are without a thought or care for his personal life." Despair provides no energy to activate the will to progress in the development and enrichment of human life. At the turn of the century James took exactly the same position in arguing the importance of faith. Porter also forecast the thinking of the social gospel, an aspect of Protestantism to achieve importance at the turn of the twentieth century. He affirmed the efficacy of the law of love. He suggested the idea of the kingdom of God, though he did not develop the doctrine into the form which later the social gospelers gave it. But the President expressed the optimism which powered that movement toward the regeneration of society.

Porter's sermon on agnosticism was a baccalaureate to the class of 1880. It came in the midst of the "Spencer Controversy," at a time when the President was making vigorous efforts to eliminate Spencer's *Sociology* as a text to be read in Yale classes. The address contained the President's criticism of Spencer's naturalism although he avoided the name of the British empiricist. Porter's assumptions concerning science in his argument help to explain why he never pushed his objection to what he deemed Spencer's offensive treatment of all religions to the point of formally denying freedom to the instructor. No doubt he profited by his observation of the consequences of his mistake in his original letter to Sumner. Six years later Porter addressed another graduating class. He spoke of "The Christian College."

We conclude as we began,—that a Christian college, to be worthy of the name, must be the home of enlarged knowledge and varied culture. It must abound in all the appliances of research and instruction; its libraries and collections must be rich to affluence; its corps of instructors must be well trained and enthusiastic in the work of teaching. . . . We do not contend that religious zeal can be a substitute for scientific ardor, but we do argue that it may and will furnish the highest aspiration when directed to scientific studies. We are not so simple as to hold that the culture of the religious feelings is a substitute for the training of the imagination; but we do contend that the imagination, when fired by Christian faith and fervor, rises to its loftiest achievements.[8]

Noah Porter, conservative almost to the point of reaction in educational and administrative policies, developed and preached a religious philosophy that not only looked forward but helped to shape the more liberal religious thinking of later decades.

Timothy Dwight succeeded to the presidency in 1886. His outstanding capacity for organization was no whit impaired by his quiet, genial manner. The University moved swiftly forward under his leadership. Occasional preaching in the University Chapel he considered a responsibility of prime importance. His approach to the task and the ideas he expressed throw light on important aspects of liberal American Protestantism at the end of the century.

Dwight, who had graduated in the days of Eleazar Fitch, noted the differences that the events of three decades had brought to the preaching in the chapel. Dwight had been brought up on the long sermon compounded of closely argued theology. He recalled that in the first half of the century the

preacher almost invariably came back in the end to the theme
of personal salvation, the preparation for the life beyond the
grave. Shortly after his retirement the last of Yale's clerical
presidents commented on changes made manifest by the
preaching of the final quarter of the century in both the intellectual and religious life of the institution. "The entire movement of men in both spheres of living," said Dwight in 1903,
". . . is more external now, whereas it was more internal fifty
years ago. Certainly this is true of the religious life. . . . The
thought of the personal soul of the individual man—how it is
developing—is less prominent than it was in the earlier days.
What are its outgoings in efforts for other men? is the question
that is now asked with all interest, and with constant repeti-
tion. The evidence of love to God is sought for and discovered
through its manifestation of itself in love of mankind. To many,
if not most, minds this change seems, in and of itself, to be an
indication of progress toward the highest Christian ideal." In
this discussion Dwight described the ethos of the social gospel
movement, getting under way as his presidency closed. The
new Protestant leaders thought in terms of the salvation of
society. They were no longer convinced that the conversion
of individual men represented the sole obligation of the church.

The retired president saw another change, this one in the
realm of personal religion. He spoke of the difficulties he saw
impeding religious life when he was an undergraduate. "I
refer," he said, "to the hindrances which were occasioned by
the theological and Christian thought of the former time. The
legal side of Divine truth, rather than the loving side, was then
presented, and the gateway of the new life was made so narrow
that even the most serious souls were fearful as to their entrance. Religion became, in undue measure, introvertive in
character, and self-examination was attendant upon every stage
of growth." The President probably never knew of the travail
of Catherine Beecher after she learned of the death of her
fiancé, Alexander Fisher. But Dwight, the student, had seen
the suffering of individuals, endured sometimes to the verge

of hysteria, that sometimes occurred in revivals. "The Christian life of today," the ex-president continued, "is happier for thoughtful men than it was. The winsomeness of the Church for those who are turning towards that life is greater."[9]

When President Dwight preached in the chapel, he did not emphasize the social gospel. Doubtless he thought the succession of visitors who occupied the pulpit developed sufficient variations on that theme. He called a little book of sermons he published *Thoughts of and for the Inner Life*. He gave the sermons in the Chapel. They express the mind of the University Church at the end of the century. "The idea of the Christian life," said Dwight in his preface, "which, in large measure at least, underlies the suggestions of the sermons, is that of a personal fellowship, a Divine-human friendship, if we may use the term, between the believer and Christ. This is the Johannean idea, as set before us in the Fourth Gospel and the First Epistle, and is, to the mind of the writer of these discourses, one of the most beautiful and inspiring of all the thoughts presented to us in the New Testament." One recalls his grandfather's sermon, "The Harvest is Past," given a little more than a century earlier. Preoccupation with death had been replaced by attending to life.

The growing University fostered the altered outlook. The developing arts and sciences strengthened the humanistic emphasis. In the natural sciences Dana and Marsh made spectacular contributions to useful knowledge. Their younger colleague, Josiah Willard Gibbs, moved in his researches so far into the unknown that his out-distanced colleagues never suspected that his work would help to shape the twentieth century. The labors in the science of language of William Dwight Whitney, Sanskrit scholar whose fame spread across the Atlantic, deepened the understanding of the origins and the nature of the languages of Western Europe. In the science of society "Billy" Sumner, indefatigable in amassing data, forthright and gruff in announcing his conclusions, sought to map the course of evolution. Economics, religion, and politics were all grist to his mill. Applying the naturalistic technique of the scientific method, he attempted to assess the function and significance of each in the common affairs of men. In the arts Thomas R. Lounsbury, digging into the writings and times of Chaucer, discovered a poet who knew and enjoyed the vagaries of human nature and recovered for the nineteenth century an age that had a zest for living. The University found its center in the liberal arts. And the men who cultivated the arts and sciences conceived the purpose of their disciplines to be to add quality and to give power to the lives of men.

President Timothy Dwight labored effectively to develop the University. In fostering learning and teaching he gave aid to a maturing humanistic effort. But Dwight, unlike Sumner, did not lose his faith. "Life has its own laws and its own forces," he remarked one Sunday morning in Battell.

Doubts and questionings are not life. They are, rather, its opposite. Life is movement. Life is faith in the reality of things. Life is love which animates and inspires and glorifies the soul. . . . The peace of the soul is the result of faith. The man who doubts and questions cannot be at rest. The settlement of his questionings must be secured before quietness and truest happiness can be his. But when faith enters the heart as an active power, and puts forth its energy through love, and unites the soul with God,—then the Divine gift comes in answer to faith. The man lives, and works, and moves in all his movements after the Divine manner. There is peace in believing— an ever-abiding, ever-deepening peace.[10]

Chapter 11. Dwight Hall, 1881–1914

In its October number in 1880 the *Lit* ran a brief note: *"Linonia,* The question was decided in the negative and the society has been declared dead . . ."* Undergraduates had created it in the time of Thomas Clap. They had built up its library to supplement the meager collections of the College. At its meetings they had debated subjects they chose without asking leave of the faculty. Before the Civil War, with Brothers in Unity and Calliope, Linonia flourished in a time when the oratory of Webster, Clay, and Calhoun influenced the course of history. After 1865 the political chieftain, so important before the war, gave way in prestige to the captain of industry and the master of finance. In 1880, when Linonia died, the political orator had lost his former importance.

At Yale the College yard evolved into the University campus. Rowing, begun in the 1850's as a result of influences from Oxford and Cambridge, developed steadily after Appomattox. The annual race with Harvard provided a colorful climax to the college year. Baseball, of American origin, appeared almost casually after the war. Henry Beers recalled that his Class of 1869 in its Freshman year put the first baseball nine of the College on the diamond. "I fancy there was something a little impromptu about these early matches, anyway," he commented, "and that, when a challenge was received from Harvard or elsewhere, a nine was hastily extemporized to go out to Hamilton Park to play the visitors."[1] Baseball, however, quickly became a serious matter. A home run in a crucial inning brought fame beyond anything the simple life of the old College had known. In the fall of 1880, when the *Lit* recorded the passing of Linonia, Walter Camp, who had graduated in the previous June, began to assume a leadership that was to transform Rugby football into the American game. Two years before, the *Yale Daily News,* the most ambitious of all undergraduate journalistic enterprises, appeared. Beers, looking back from 1895, recorded with astonishment and some regret the change that had come over the campus. Organization had replaced the old, impromptu spontaneity. "The number of clubs and organizations in a modern *Banner,*" he commented, "is something wonderful: glee clubs, chess clubs, Andover clubs, Ohio clubs, Berkeley societies, etc., etc.; most of them all undreamed of in the simple structure of undergraduate life in the sixties. . . . It sometimes seems to me . . . as if . . . everyone was enrolled in some organization or other, was in training for something, and carried on his amusements strenuously and in a corporate way."[2]

In the lighthearted years from 1880 to 1910 (to use approximate dates) the undergraduates of the University lived in a closed community that they or their predecessors had organized and which they ran. They looked inward, absorbed in the doings on the campus and largely oblivious of the outside world. Only when senior year neared its end did the young man peer seriously outward through the college gates, and even then his purpose was to discover the implications for him of the world outside. The classes separated campus society into four smaller communities. These remained more or less aloof from one another, partly because each class occupied its own set of dormitories and partly because social honors were bestowed on the lower class by the one immediately above it. Class loyalties, stimulated by intramural athletic contests, evolved to the point of exaggeration. At the same time upper classmen indoctrinated each in-coming freshman class in that larger romantic loyalty that demanded of every individual that he "do" something for the honor and glory of Yale. Loyalty, the code of sport, and the necessity for cooperation in other extracurricular activities provided sanctions that reinforced undergraduate ethical standards. Individualistic competition powered undergraduate life. Senior societies, the older two now nearly a century old, selected the winners in the race for prestige.

The young men of the College and of the Scientific School, with some help from graduates and faculty, shaped the life of two student communities. The social systems of the two schools differed. A moat separated the College Campus from "Sheff Town," bridged only by the cooperation of individuals in extracurricular activities. But undergraduate society manifested an essential unity in that each school produced its own replica of the life of the nation. The hustle, the joining, the individual competition, and the corporate activity were as American as Plymouth Rock. Inevitably religion adjusted itself to the new mores of the new era.

Henry Beers in enumerating the student organizations in late nineteenth-century Yale did not include Dwight Hall—a strange omission, for in 1895, when he wrote, Dwight Hall, though younger than the Berkeley Association, was off to a vigorous start. In 1878, two years after the dedication of Battell, Dwight L. Moody, famed evangelist of the time, carried on a campaign in New Haven. In Moody's message an old theological orthodoxy blended with a new sense of urgency for the poor and the disadvantaged—by-products of a burgeoning and unregulated industrialism. Moody defined the Christian life in terms of action as well as of faith. The influence of his work extended to the campus where, in 1879, a group of undergraduates organized the Christian Social Union. In the middle of the century the YMCA had come to the United States from England. In the latter years of the 1870's student YMCA's, part of the larger movement, appeared in many colleges and universities. In 1881 the Christian Social Union rewrote its constitution and changed its name to the Yale Young Men's Christian Association. Interested alumni gave advice and assistance. Four years previously Barbour had become college pastor. Undoubtedly he gave friendly help and counsel, for some of his contemporaries later recalled that much of his pastoral work consisted of guiding student activities. In 1886 a benefactor gave funds for a building of red stone erected on the west side of the campus to provide a center for the Association. It contained living quarters for a resident secretary. An auditorium gave opportunity for large meetings. Four small rooms, each assigned to a particular class, provided places where committees could deliberate and where class prayer meetings could be held. Called Dwight Hall in honor of the first Timothy Dwight, the name became, in effect, that of the Association.

When college opened in the fall of 1886, Chauncey Goodrich, who had received his B.A. in June, moved into the rooms provided in the new building. Grandson of the first Chauncey and nephew of Theodore Woolsey, young Goodrich was not only the first secretary of the Yale Association but the first full-time secretary in the United States. Goodrich, from a family of moderate wealth and of high social position, took off a year for work on the campus before going on to the seminary to prepare for the ministry. He was the first of what became a long line of young men who were really student pastors.

Student initiative created Dwight Hall at a time when undergraduates were transforming college life into a complex of organizations. The Alumni Council, which gave advice and assistance but never direction, was the counterpart of similar more or less formal alumni groups associated with various extracurricular activities or with fraternities and societies. Undergraduates ran their own show. After the manner of the YMCA they organized committees and through these they carried on a varied work. They coordinated their activities with those of the undergraduate deacons of the University Church. A class elected three deacons in sophomore year. They served at communion and acted as ushers. Members of Dwight Hall elected officers, chosen at the end of their junior year, who as seniors directed the affairs of the Association. An executive committee, called the Cabinet, came into being.

Student initiative brought about a YMCA in the Sheffield Scientific School. It, too, had a graduate secretary. When at the end of the century a benefactor made possible a building that was not only a home for the Sheff Association but a kind of student union for the school, the Sheffield organization came to be known as Byers Hall. A graduate secretary, as in Dwight Hall, guided the work. A general secretary appeared who co-ordinated and supplemented the work of his two colleagues.

In conformity with the trend of student life at the end of the century the undergraduates gave religious work on the campus a high degree of organization. Goodrich, knowing while a junior that he would become the first graduate secretary of Dwight Hall, refused an election to a senior society on the ground that the office required him to be above all campus politics. The gesture did not establish a tradition. Leadership in Dwight Hall ranked as leadership on the campus, and the president normally became a member of a senior society. This aspect of Dwight Hall which made it, along with other activities, a part of organized and competitive student life provided the basis during the great years from the 1890's to World War I for some lifting of eyebrows on the part of non-members of the Association when they looked at the behavior of some of their classmates. For the most part, however, religious loyalty was genuine. As the old century came to an end and the new one began, Christianity took on significance for many men.

The period in which Dwight Hall played its most conspicuous role in student life began in 1887 and ended with World War I. In the autumn of 1887 William Lyon Phelps of the Class of 1887 succeeded Goodrich as Dwight Hall secretary. When the college year had gotten well under way, Phelps learned that the Scottish layman Henry Drummond was in Hartford. The new secretary promptly took the train for that city to persuade the visiting Britisher to come to Yale to speak to the students. Drummond, a geologist by training, had published in 1883 *Natural Law in the Spiritual World*. The American edition of the book, brought out in 1884, had enjoyed an extraordinary success. This reasoned and inspiring work, perhaps even more than the writings of John Fiske, had persuaded American Protestant theologians to accept evolution as the Divine method of creation. Drummond sent Phelps back to New Haven with the word that he would come on the condition that he be permitted to address the entire college student body in the Sunday morning service. President Dwight stuffily refused on the ground that the visitor was not a clergyman. Drummond, disappointed and inclined to by-pass New Haven, finally succumbed to the blandishments of the young secretary. It should be added that this same secretary would one day become a vastly popular Yale professor of English and a national figure as lecturer and commentator on contemporary literature.

A word needs to be said about Drummond's book, for it suggests the ideas that had power in the last two decades of the nineteenth century. At the time educated Americans saw in the warfare between science and theology, to use the phrase of President Andrew D. White of Cornell, one of the most important developments in American thought. Geology had started the conflict more than half a century earlier. The entry of Darwin's theory of evolution into the fray seemed to many to have made the struggle a war to the death. Americans heard in the last two decades of the century Mark Twain's bitter rejection of the Calvinism in which his parents had reared him. But Twain's ubiquitous admirers also sensed the pessimism into which the acceptance of scientific determinism had plunged the humorist.

In his book Drummond introduced every segment of his argument with a scientific concept, such as biogenesis, degeneration, growth, environment, conformity to type. A trained scientist, he handled with sureness and authority the scientific theories important at the time. Then in each chapter he carried the concepts of science into the spiritual realm. "The position we have been led to take up," he said, "is not that the Spiritual Laws are analogous to the Natural Laws but that *they* are the same Laws. It is not a question of analogy but of Identity." In chapter after chapter he moved from the consideration of nature to striking conclusions regarding the spiritual life. He mentioned, for example, the law which causes the protoplasm of the acorn to eventuate in the oak—the law of "conformity to type." And the application? "Bird-Life makes the Bird. Christ-Life makes the Christian."

In his last chapter Drummond dealt with "Classification." He concluded a long argument with a picture of evolution. "Modern Science," he said implying that theology must go beyond it,

knows only two Kingdoms—the Inorganic and the Organic. . . . Studies in Classification, beginning with considerations of quality usually end with references to quantity. . . . [In the process of evolution] mineral, but not all becomes animal; some animal but not all becomes human; some human, but not all becomes Divine. Thus the area narrows. At the base is the mineral, most broad and simple; the spiritual at the apex, smallest but most highly differentiated. So form above form, Kingdom above Kingdom. *Quantity decreases as quality increases.* The gravitation of the whole system of Nature toward quality is surely a phenomenon of commanding interest. . . . To Science, defining it as a working principle, this mighty process of amelioration is simply *Evolution.* To Christianity, discerning the end through the means, it is *Redemption.* . . . And these Kingdoms rising tier above tier in ever increasing sublimity and beauty, their foundations visibly fixed in the past, their progress and the direction of their progress, being facts in Nature still, are the signs which, since the Magi saw His star in the East, have never been wanting from the firmament of truth, and which in every age with growing clearness to the wise, and with ever-gathering mystery to the uninitiated, proclaim "the Kingdom of God is at hand."[3]

Phelps wanted to get a man with such an approach to religion on the campus.

On a Sunday afternoon in the fall of 1887 Henry Drummond addressed a crowded assemblage at Yale. He stayed in New Haven to give talks every night for two weeks. "Billy" Phelps has described the man who stirred the indifference of the Yale community. "I have never seen," said Phelps, "so deep an impression made on students by any speaker on any subject as that made by Henry Drummond. . . . He was a gentleman and a scholar; his method was new, fresh, original. He spoke in quiet conversational tones, never raised his voice, made no gestures, but was intensely earnest. He changed the emphasis from death to life. 'We come not to save your souls, but to save your lives. We want you to be Christians, not because you might die tonight, but because you are going to live tomorrow,'" Billy described Drummond's eloquence as Mommsen had described Caesar's, namely as the eloquence of deeply felt thought. "He told us too much introspection was bad; to keep our eyes not on ourselves, but on the Master. By contemplation of him, we might gradually be transformed into his likeness."⁴ Drummond came more than once to the campus. He initiated an extraordinary period in campus history.

In 1887 when Drummond first came to Yale, Americans were reading William Dean Howells' realistic study of the late nineteenth-century self-made man, *The Rise of Silas Lapham,* published the year before. As the Drummond meetings were going on at Yale, Edward Bellamy was finishing the romance *Looking Backward,* which was to have within a year an astonishing vogue and was to familiarize Americans of that generation with the idea of socialism, though the book avoided the term. In 1890 a New York journalist, Jacob Riis, published *How the Other Half Lives,* a mosaic of stories of slum life in "Mulberry Bend" and the "Five Points" of Manhattan. The success of the book added its title to the list of colloquial phrases in American English. Three years later an unknown young New York reporter for the *Herald* and the *Tribune* named Stephen Crane published *Maggie, a Girl of the Streets,* a study in the Zola manner to illustrate a philosophy of uncompromising natural- ism. A generation whose taste and conventions had been con- ditioned by the Genteel Tradition ignored the book until two years later Crane's *Red Badge of Courage* brought him fame. Then *Maggie,* gaining a reading, became important in intro- ducing a new outlook and a new genre in American writing.

Crane, Riis, Bellamy, and Howells pointed up in their writings social issues that time would sharpen. Observers, con- cerned with the future of America, they began to give thought to the plight of the poor and to the concentration of untaxed wealth into the hands of the few. At a time when evolution provided the key word of the intellectual climate, Crane's philosophy of naturalism, a by-product of science, suggested an outlook that increasing numbers of educated Americans found reasonable. For Mark Twain naturalism by the time of the 1890's had become unavoidable even though it drove him into a dark pessimism.

The naturalism and the social issues of the end of the century challenged Protestantism. In New England, in the Middle West, in New York men emerged who took a stand—for the rights of labor, handicapped in bargaining with a powerful employer; for a Christian socialism to substitute cooperation for what the reformers described as a dog-eat-dog competition; for a law of love to spread through society the Kingdom of God. In the early years of the new social gospel Walter Raus- chenbusch, a young graduate of Rochester Theological Semi- nary, ministered to the poor, the demoralized, and the hopeless in "Hell's Kitchen" in western Manhattan. In the first decade of the twentieth century his criticisms of the economic and social order in terms of Christian principles and ideals made his the most significant expression of the aroused conscience of American Protestantism. The social gospel provided the con- text for the evolution of religion at Yale at the turn of the century.

Campus religion developed also in another context. William

James at Harvard hammered out the philosophy of pragmatism and gave form to its central thesis that the truth of an idea can be found only in its results. Pragmatism gave to James a defense for his religious beliefs, a defense that Protestant leaders soon learned to use. Naturalism leads to despair and kills the motive for doing; religion gives ground for hope and energizes the man. Noah Porter had anticipated the argument in 1880. But even as some Protestant leaders looked for help to pragmatism, John Dewey, pioneer with James in the formulation of the philosophy, moved from the religion in which he had been brought up into a frank secularism. A thoroughgoing naturalist, he undertook to demonstrate that morals in reality depend not on supernatural religion but, rather, on experience.

At Yale, Sumner's laborious research was leading him in the 1890's to the concept of mores, those basic and enduring customs that condition the lives of individuals in society. In 1906 Sumner published *Folkways* in which he pointed out that moral codes are merely an aspect of mores, that mores can make any type of behavior right or wrong. At the same time, in his course to seniors Sumner lectured on religion. He saw religion —for subliterate peoples, a ghost-fear—as one of the four basic civilizing forces. The others were hunger, sex love, and vanity. The four drives create mores and lead to social organization. At the same time he began the study of the evolution of religion from its beginnings in a primitive animism. He applied the techniques of scholarship to what he saw as a social phenomenon—a phenomenon that expressed itself in creeds and in rituals, in taboos, and in complex institutions. In an exuberant and optimistic age in which the religious-minded gained hope from faith and the secular-minded from science Sumner warned his colleagues of a rough road ahead. He pointed out that the individual cannot prevail against mores, that men cannot by the use of reason make over society as Bellamy thought they could. After the turn of the century he saw forces gathering strength in an apparently peaceful world that forecast a dark time of revolution and war ahead.

Seven years after Sumner's death in 1910 the Yale Divinity School invited Rauschenbusch to give the Nathaniel Taylor lectures. The former pastor in Hell's Kitchen, now a professor at Rochester, proposed a theology for the social gospel. In addition to the natural forces working in human institutions Rauschenbusch saw a Divine force, an immanent deity, moving through society bringing to pass, with the aid of men, the Kingdom of God. To Sumner's relativism he opposed the old doctrine of eternal verities. Rauschenbusch gave new content appropriate for the age to the doctrine announced in Paul's text: "And the greatest of these is love." The lecturer spoke in 1917 after the United States had entered the war against Germany. Rauschenbusch did not see that conflict as a holy crusade. He declared that the great and continuing struggle was the one between the Kingdom of God and the ever-present, ever-menacing Kingdom of Evil. Rauschenbusch was no sentimentalist. He saw the law of love as a hard doctrine that demanded fortitude and sacrifice. When Rauschenbusch spoke in New Haven, a chapter in the history of religion on the campus was ending. Its narrative disclosed the impress of the social and intellectual forces of the time.

Henry Drummond in 1887 and in his later visits gave new life to evangelical Protestantism on the Yale campus. The University Church felt the new life, but the center of activity passed from the Chapel to Dwight Hall. When Barbour resigned in 1887, the Corporation appointed no full-time pastor to replace him. Pastoral work among the students became the obligation of young men who stayed on for a year as secretaries for the Associations in the College and in the Scientific School and also the general secretaries who normally for a three-year term coordinated and supervised Christian work on the campus.

In time the University appointed Benjamin Bacon of the Divinity School to the part-time post of pastor of the Church.

The selection disclosed several characteristics of the thinking of the Yale authorities of the end of the century. The new appointee, relative of Leonard Bacon, came out of the soil of New Haven. The pastor had been a back on some of the early teams of Walter Camp and his prowess had won him the nickname "Boanerges," Son of Thunder. He had been tapped for a senior society. His undergraduate career seemed to make him an ideal leader of the University Church. As a man he was amiable and courtly. He had studied biblical criticism in Germany. Returning to the Divinity School, he turned out scholarly papers and books that gave him a place in the forefront of the students of the New Testament documents and of the writings of the early Christian centuries. His careful research led him to reject the Pauline authorship of many epistles generally ascribed to him. Bacon brought distinguished scholarship to the pastorate. The appointment evinced the acceptance of biblical scholarship by the authorities who controlled the Church. They selected a gentleman as pastor.

Bacon chose to be pastor in little more than name. He presided with dignity each month at communion. He did not appear in the pulpit either as preacher or as the one who introduced the minister of the day. President Dwight and later President Hadley assumed that responsibility. Bacon left pastoral work with the students to the secretaries of Dwight Hall. His scholarship and teaching filled his life. "There is no greater service," said Bacon in a concluding lecture at Oxford in 1920, "men like ourselves can do for our age than to sweep away the fogs and obscurities which gather round the figures of Jesus and Paul. Jesus and Paul are the champions of the only gospel that has real promise for our struggling world."[5]

While Benjamin Bacon was still a student of divinity learning the techniques of research, a young man of the class of 1884 was carrying evangelical religion to Europe. If Bacon went to Germany to study under scholars, James B. Reynolds crossed to Europe to work with students. As an undergraduate Reynolds had been superintendent of the Bethany Sunday School and, in his senior year, president of the Christian Association. At the end of the 1880's he established headquarters at Paris and from this base traveled to universities in the United Kingdom and on the Continent. Where Christian student groups existed, he joined his activities to theirs. He worked to found new groups where none had hitherto appeared. He furthered the work of summer student conferences. He had a vision of an organization of Christian students that would transcend both denominational differences and national boundaries. Reynolds' was a bold dream to come out of an America preoccupied with domestic concerns whose people had little interest in world affairs. Reynolds did not achieve his goal but he prepared the way for another.

John R. Mott completed the work that Reynolds began. From the late 1890's through World War I he came to the Yale campus practically every year that he was in the United States. He preached in chapel. He talked before special meetings. He had conferences with individual undergraduates. His influence was a powerful force in determining the character of Dwight Hall religion in his day. As an undergraduate at Cornell in the 1880's he had chosen Christian service in place of the career in industry to which he had looked forward and for which family wealth and connections provided opportunities. Mott attended the Northfield student conference in 1886 at which one hundred young men and women founded the Student Volunteer Movement. In the middle 1890's Mott, following the pattern of Reynolds, traveled in Europe and in Great Britain. He was ponderous and heavy as a speaker but he had a genius for organization. Of commanding presence, his personality never failed to impress. He worked among students in Protestant countries. He traveled in eastern Europe, where he established close connections with leaders of the Eastern Orthodox Church. He made friends in liberal Catholic centers. Largely as a result of his labors the World Student

Christian Federation came into being in 1895. When Mott came to Battell and to Dwight Hall, his words extended the horizons of young men in college at a time when the United States was emerging from a century of isolation and, with some awkwardness and confusion, was beginning to assume the responsibilities of a major power.

Mott had an ally whose influence at Yale was as important as his. Robert E. Speer as an undergraduate at Princeton had come under the influence of Drummond. Some time after graduation Speer became Secretary of the Board of Foreign Missions of the Presbyterian Church, a post whose primary responsibilities were working with students. Like Mott he remained a layman. Widely read and of a scholarly turn of mind, Speer had effectiveness in dealing with students. When he appeared in Battell, as he did with regularity through the years, his sermons were evangelical to the point of being sentimental. Students called him "Weeping Bob." He published small books—on the person of Christ and on the obligation of Christians to evangelize the world. Mott and Speer, close friends, supplemented each other. The brand of Protestantism which they and Reynolds before them sought to further became to a great extent that of Dwight Hall.

The second Timothy Dwight had summed up the religion of the campus when he described the Johannean idea of "a personal fellowship, a Divine-human friendship between the believer and Christ." Such a faith could give strength. Because it lacked the discipline of a rigorous theology it could also degenerate into sentimentalism. At the turn of the century it did both on the Yale campus. A majority of undergraduates in an age moving toward greater emphasis on secularism remained outside Dwight Hall, respecting but uninterested in its activities. But the power of the Dwight Hall religion manifested itself each spring when year after year students assembled at the Northfield Conference noted that by far the largest delegation came from New Haven.

In the years between Reynolds and World War I, deeply felt

Christian concern tended most often to express itself in work in the mission field. Sherwood Eddy, 1891 S., became an evangelist to students and the intelligentsia in India and in eastern Asia. Henry W. Luce, 1892, went to China to become a major figure in the creation of Cheeloo and Yenching universities. Horace Tracy Pitkin, 1892, worked in Peking until the Boxers killed him in 1900. Edwin C. Lobenstine, 1895, helped to form the National Christian Council of China and through it to make an impress on the development of Christianity in that ancient country. Sydney K. Mitchell, 1898, became one of that pioneer band of teachers who went to the Philippines to establish American ideals and methods of education in the Archipelago. Four men, Edward H. Hume, 1897, John L. Thurston and Brownell Gage, 1898, and Warren Seabury, 1900, combined activities that ultimately brought about the creation of Yale-in-China. Anson Phelps Stokes, Secretary of the University, gave support to their undertaking, and the institution had its formal beginning in his house. At the height of its influence, Yale-in-China, established in the ancient and cultural center of Changsha, consisted of a middle school, a college of arts and sciences, a hospital, a nursing school, and a medical school. Dickson H. Leavens, 1909, who went out to Yale-in-China to teach English and to aid with athletics and other extracurricular activities, became the first of a long succession of "Yali bachelors." Leavens stayed on to become a teacher of mathematics and treasurer. Lorrin Shepard, 1914, prepared himself to carry on what became after World War I an important medical work in the Near East.

This corporal's guard (for in numbers they were no more) who went as doctors and teachers to service overseas came from a university in which science flourished and in which cultivation of the social sciences and the humanities had been extended into new areas and achieved depth and sophistication. The audacity of the various designs of those who set out for work abroad reflected the mood of an optimistic age—an age when Europeans still thought of themselves as leaders, if not the masters, of the eastern continents, and Americans, still naïve in world affairs, saw only progress ahead. But the enterprises demonstrated also that evangelical Protestantism had not lost its power and that faith could be a creative force furthering human brotherhood.

Some men in the period between Drummond and World War I undertook work at home. Alonzo Stagg, football and baseball hero of the Class of 1888 and successor to Phelps as graduate Secretary, founded the Yale Mission as a social and religious center in a blighted section of New Haven. From Stagg's time onward, students under the direction of Dwight Hall helped staff one or another boys' club in the city. In 1907 John Magee, 1906, while Secretary of Dwight Hall, conceived and founded the Yale Hope Mission. William Borden, an undergraduate, provided the original funds that made the undertaking possible. The institution was a rescue mission similar to the McCauley Mission in New York. Serving homeless men, it grew into a useful social agency. The Yale Mission of Stagg, the boys' club work, and the Yale Hope Mission suggested the influence of the social gospel movement on the campus. Such activities, however, implied no criticism of the economic and social order. They expressed in a new age that doctrine of stewardship as old in America as seventeenth-century Puritanism. Let the strong and the successful in the competition of a free economy lend a hand to their weaker and flagging brethren. After the turn of the century this doctrine came to be compressed into the word "service." President Arthur Twining Hadley emphasized an ideal that extended beyond the limits of the Dwight Hall membership. "The true worth of a man," said Hadley in 1905 to the graduating class, "is to be measured not by things he has done for himself, but by the things he has done for the world around him and after him. Every man who has consecrated his life to an ideal larger than he can hope to compass has the kind of faith which moves the world; whether he calls it faith in God, or faith in duty, or shrinks from calling it by any name at all and goes on living for his fellow men without ever being able to formulate the reason why. Each man finds his highest spiritual development, not by working out his salvation alone and for himself, but by losing the thought of self in the thought of others. This is the Christian life; this is the faith by which men are saved."[6]

If Dwight Hall in the years from the 1880's to World War I displayed interests and activities characteristic of liberal evangelical Protestantism at the turn of the century, it also disclosed the extremes which that religion could produce. In 1925 George Stewart, Jr., a former general secretary of Dwight Hall, published a biography of his close friend Henry B. Wright. John R. Mott wrote a foreword. The book narrates the events of a short life and one lived with a special intensity. H.B.W. was the son of Henry P. "Baldy" Wright, dean of Yale College and a man with a multitude of friends. The younger Henry, Class of 1898, was president of the Association in his senior year. His membership in a senior society was evidence of a successful undergraduate career. For three years he held the post of general secretary. Taking a doctor's degree in the classics, his father's field, he taught Latin and Greek. He became Assistant Professor of Ancient History. He was appointed to a newly established chair in Christian Methods in the Divinity School. Through all his years of teaching, however, Dwight Hall remained his primary interest. For more than a decade Henry Wright was the central figure who provided the driving force behind its work. The entry of the United States into the war caused Wright to undertake for the YMCA work first in Plattsburg and then for the duration of the conflict at Camp Devens. He returned in 1919 to the Divinity School. Death came suddenly in 1923.

Henry Wright lived the doctrine that the second President Dwight called "the Divine-human friendship . . . between the believer and Christ." John R. Mott, who had known well the General Secretary and the later teacher, spoke after the death of his friend of "the career of a man who resolutely, consistently, and sacrificially made the touchstone of his life and the controlling factor in every choice or decision, What is the mind of Christ? What is the will of God? To him these two questions were synonymous."[7] Mott did not exaggerate. He described a mystic.

The Dwight Hall Bible classes offered Wright his opportunity, not only when he held the office of General Secretary, but later. He taught freshmen. Dean Wright's gift for friendship appeared in the son as a talent for personal evangelism. He taught the Scriptures as an evangelist. No biblical scholarship impeded his full acceptance of the Gospel record. Speaking as an historian on one occasion he declared the physical resurrection of Christ to be an event as well attested as any that occurred in the ancient world. He used proof texts to drive home his points. Henry Wright had a faith akin to that of the first Timothy Dwight, though more mystical and at the same time devoid of a reasoned theology. Though he could be effective before a large audience, Wright worked best with the small group. The Bible class led frequently to the personal conference. When talking with a young man face to face, Henry Wright's manifest sincerity and implicit faith made an impact that sometimes re-directed human lives.

In the academic year 1912–13 Sidney Lovett, President of the Association, attended each week in Dwight Hall the "Wednesday at Five Meeting" over which Henry Wright presided. Benjamin Bacon was usually there. So was Charles Reynolds Brown, the new Dean of the Divinity School. Dwight Hall secretaries and a few students swelled the number to ten or twelve. Prayers were offered and testimonies given. During the weeks one after another narrated a personal odyssey of the search for faith and of the vicissitudes that followed its discovery. The young men still in college found themselves on the same level of human frailty and hope with older men exalted by position and reputation. It was a strange and affecting experience. The participants in these group confessionals

put emphasis on conversion and commitment. The Christian
was the dedicated man.

Henry Wright published a little work book which he called
The Will of God in a Man's Life Work. The volume set forth the
ideal of absolute perfection. Wright taught four absolutes—
purity, honesty, unselfishness, and love. He urged the re-
pentant wrongdoer to make restitution, as nearly complete as
possible, for injuries he had inflicted. In this case, it must be
added, the preacher gave himself in the causes he espoused
with the same abandon that he asked of others. At Camp
Devens in the summer and fall of 1918 when an epidemic of
virulent influenza, often resulting in a lethal pneumonia, filled
the regular and improvised hospitals with stricken soldiers,
Henry Wright, unmindful of danger, was constantly at bed-
sides performing services for the sick and praying with the
dying.

A letter the camp secretary received that autumn suggests
not only the nature of Wright's mysticism but his influence on
the man who took over his ideas and techniques and by use of
them created a cult. In the summer and fall of 1918 Frank N.
D. Buchman traveled in the Far East as a member of a team
led by Sherwood Eddy. The evangelists worked primarily
with university students. "I have used the triangle and the 'On
Top' phrases [of H.B.W.]," wrote the disciple to his long-time
friend and acknowledged master, "and also the outline of your
'Diagnosis' lecture in China using my own laboratory experiences. . . . I have always given credit to you. . . . The triangle has caught all over the Far East. Bible women, students,
evangelists, pastors, and missionaries all quote it and most of
them know that it is your thought." Henry Wright's "triangle," often put by the teacher on the blackboard, illustrated
his theory of prayer. "I used to pray," he told George Stewart,
"O God, help John Jones or Sam Smith. There was a flash up
to the Almighty and another from him toward the man prayed
for. In later years I have prayed that, wherever possible, God
would show me how to help my friends and work out through

me the answer to my petitions. God is helpless unless He can find human wills willing to do His will."⁸ Wright often told to friends stories of how the answer to a prayer had come in the form of guidance to perform some specific act or to undertake a particular enterprise. In course of time Buchman, promoter extraordinary of religion, took over from Henry Wright the four absolutes, the technique of the group confessional, the idea of guidance, and the emphasis on personal evangelism, but not Wright's self-forgetfulness. Eventually a movement emerged called first the Oxford Group and later Moral Rearmament.

Occasionally as they crossed the campus Henry Wright and William Graham Sumner met and passed one another. No contrast could be greater than that between the worlds in which these two men lived. Wright personified the ultimate position of an evangelical Protestantism whose faith was rooted in emotional experience and whose emphasis was on the individual. Sumner, the rationalist whom the students called "Old Mores," talked to the men of his classes of the rigors of the scientific method and warned them, if they had any hope of staving off the disaster threatening the world, to get an understanding of the hard and uncompromising forces of nature. Wright preached the absolutism of eternal verities; Sumner the relativism of custom born of experience. Wright belonged in the company of Dwight L. Moody, Henry Drummond, John R. Mott, and Robert E. Speer, though he was more mystical than any of them. When Sumner died in 1910, this individualistic, romantic, evangelical Protestantism stood at its zenith on the Yale campus. In that year Kenneth Scott Latourette supervised the work of student-led Bible classes in which a thousand undergraduates were enrolled.

But change was on the way. If Sumner was interested in society, so also was Walter Rauschenbusch. Men on the campus began reading his book *Christianity and the Social Crisis,* published in 1907. Henry Wright put Sidney Lovett in touch with a young man from Union Theological Seminary named Norman Thomas. In the summer of 1910, at the end of his freshman year, Lovett worked with Thomas at Christ Church, a branch that the Brick Presbyterian Church had established in Hell's Kitchen, where Rauschenbusch had worked a decade and a half before. At the same time evolution in the humanities and the sciences expressed itself in the Yale classrooms in richer, more varied, and more significant course offerings. A new questioning attitude toward religion appeared. It had only begun in 1914 when war broke out in Europe and a new era opened.

In the early 1930's James Rowland Angell, Hadley's successor as President of Yale, set about the writing of an address on religion that he hoped might be useful in an age of disillusionment and skepticism. Having no experience with the Yale community as undergraduate or graduate student, he asked some colleagues on the faculty together with selected alumni to outline for him the religious history of the institution since the 1890's. As a result he gathered a sheaf of appraisals of evangelical Protestantism as manifested in student life at the turn of the century from some distinguished churchmen and educators. Henry Sloane Coffin, '97, President of Union Theological Seminary, Dean Clarence W. Mendell, '04, Bishop Henry Knox Sherrill, '11, and the Rev. Morgan P. Noyes, '14, later to be a member of the Corporation, replied to the President's request. Reading the letters, later generations can get a firsthand sense of campus life and religion in the decades immediately preceding the opening of an epoch of wars and revolutions.

"In the decade 1900–1910," wrote President Coffin, "I should say that the solidarity of the classes at Yale was very strong and also that the unity of the College was well maintained by the presence of everyone daily at Chapel. This had a great effect upon the religious work of Dwight Hall. There were class meetings immediately after morning service which were fairly attended . . . there was a strong programme of Bible study . . . there was much interest in evangelistic work of various kinds . . . and there were large groups of students, between a hundred and a hundred and fifty, that went every summer to the conference at Northfield. The main interests of the boys were in the religious adjustments of their religious beliefs in the light of new knowledge, particularly new views concerning the Bible, the historicity of miracles, the divinity of Christ, prayer, etc."

"The situation when I came to college [in 1900]," Dean Mendell recalled,

seemed to me to be that a certain religious observation was traditional and that it was the religion that appealed to me as normal. The voluntary meetings at Dwight Hall of a Sunday evening would bring out three or four hundred men who enjoyed, I think, the singing of gospel hymns and went through the rest of the motions almost unconsciously because they had always done so. The men who were definitely connected with Dwight Hall were a smaller group. From these were chosen the deacons and officers of the Christian Association. When a man received a tag of this sort it was quite respectable to be religious and, in fact, it was expected of him to carry the religious responsibility of the class and relieve the rest of most of the obligation. . . . Outside the recognized Dwight Hall group there was not a very active body of opinion for or against religion. I think it safe to say that religion was pretty much thought of as the church regime and that, while it was already slipping, it was still considered the right thing for the world at large, even if it was not heartily supported. I think it also safe to say that there was practically no intellectual inquiry into religious matters. Prayer meetings and even Bible classes were places of exhortation and not intellectual training. As I look back on that particular phase nothing could very well be worse, from the intellectual point of view.

Bishop Sherrill thought of religion at Yale before World War I in terms of an "established" church.

Before the war there was compulsory chapel ... when I was in college, there was considerable but certainly not organized grumbling in regard to Sunday chapel, but weekday was regarded as a *Yale institution*. If I recall, successive senior classes voted in favor of compulsory weekday chapel. Without regard to the devotional aspect, it was felt on the part of a large majority to be a *Yale tradition*, which should be retained ... there were fewer rebels, greater acceptance of tradition and authority before the war. The same might be said of Dwight Hall. The emphasis in the college of those days was on *doing*. Every social pressure was exerted to make a man try for a team, or a paper. The basis of judgment was largely how much he *did*. Dwight Hall was one of these activities. The President of Dwight Hall was an outstanding man in the established order along with the football captain, and the chairman of the News, generally sure of an election to a senior society. The election of Class Deacons was an important event and participated in by a large proportion of the class. For Dwight Hall played a considerable part in the established order. This brought Dwight Hall a great influx of numbers, certainly a proportion who came in the same sense as they might have tried for the News.

Morgan P. Noyes, of the Class of 1914, was the most recent graduate from whom the President sought historical enlightenment. Noyes noted that when he entered in 1911 Dwight Hall rather than the College Chapel was looked upon as the center of religious life. "At Dwight Hall," he went on, "it was the day of well-attended meetings and popular religious interest. Class prayer meetings were held each Sunday morning after chapel, the attendance at the freshman meeting numbering from perhaps sixty to one hundred men each week. I think it was indicative of the lack of intellectual vigor at Dwight Hall that the attendance grew smaller as one went up the scale of the four classes. Professor Henry B. Wright taught a Wednesday evening class for freshmen which was attended by one hundred or more men each week. His message was very single and direct, covering such personal questions as gambling, drinking, honesty, and the like, based on the teachings of Jesus." Noyes mentioned the vogue for Bible classes.

It was also the day of philanthropic social service [he continued], and large numbers of men led boys' clubs and taught English to foreigners. Religion was eminently respectable, so much so that for those who became religious leaders it was the high road to social success. There was in each class, I suppose, a small number of men who deliberately espoused religious work as their extra curriculum activity for the sake of social rewards. There were more men, I imagine, who were unconsciously influenced by such considerations. It was the period of "the manly Christian." There was very little to stimulate intellectual activity or to disturb the complacency of "The Dwight Hall Heelers." The world was all right if men would not drink or swear, would give some of their spare time to helping those less fortunate than themselves, and would go to church.

Noyes stayed on to spend a year after graduation, the year 1914–15, as a Dwight Hall Secretary. His candid observations of the Yale scene add evidence to the conclusions of some historical studies made in the 1950's that the intellectual and social revolutions that characterized the 1920's began actually before World War I. Said Noyes:

There was a marked change during the five years of my residence on the campus. It is sometimes said that the great change was after the war, which may be true, but the changes were revolutionary even before the middle of that decade. Attendance at meetings in Dwight Hall shrank to very small numbers and the class prayer meetings and Wednesday evening Bible classes vanished. The voluntary Bible study groups were confined to the freshman class because the upper class men ceased to enroll. An occasional communication would appear in the News questioning the validity of the Christian religion. Religion became much more a topic for spontaneous discussion around the fireplace in the dormitory and much less a thing to be taken for granted. Professional religious leaders became very much suspect and it was in the occasional class room, where religion was discussed in an unorthodox fashion by some professor whose vocation was something else, that men turned for their religious interpretations. When the war came it found religious life at a rather low ebb. The influence of Dwight L. Moody and Henry Drummond, which for years had been mediated through men whom they had influenced, was pretty well spent. The pietistic atmosphere no longer fitted into the intellectual climate of New Haven and men were no longer willing to devote so much time to being told to be good.[9]

Chapter 12. Religion and the Wilsonian Crusade

On July 4, 1914, another student conference at Northfield was nearing the end of its ten days of meetings, conferences, and play. Sidney Lovett, at the close of his year as Dwight Hall Secretary, had come north with the delegation from Yale. He joined the high-spirited crowd that tramped into the auditorium as the sun went down behind the Vermont mountains. The Reverend Charles E. Jefferson of the Broadway Tabernacle in New York spoke. Ugly rumors were circulating, he said. The newspapers reported that the German Emperor was making threatening gestures against England and France, following the murder of the Archduke of Austria at Sarajevo. Lovett in later years recalled the scene: "It is . . . before the huge bonfire is lighted with wood provided by the Conference management. . . . In his speech, Dr. Jefferson takes brief cognizance of the German menace, but goes on to discount the possibility of war; and why? Because of the solidarity of the working classes in England and France and Germany. With a vision of the workers in these three countries, linking arms together in a fraternal determination to maintain peace, we go out into the night reassured, and frolic about the bonfire, unperturbed by current rumors of conflict."[1]

The Rev. C. E. Jefferson's appraisal of European events typified a naiveté in international affairs characteristic of most educated Americans in 1914. When a month later Europe's long peace ended as German soldiers marched into neutral Belgium, America could scarcely credit the news that civilized nations had begun to fight. Americans defined civilization in terms of the restraint and the rationality implicit in a high level of moral and intellectual achievement.

Midtwentieth-century Americans find it increasingly difficult to recapture in imagination the developing mood that finally, in 1917, interpreted American participation in the war as a crusade. In that year with a unanimity unparalleled in their history Americans responded to the call to push back the German aggressor and to overthrow that authoritarian militarism whose triumphs on the battlefield posed a major threat to democratic freedoms. President Wilson mobilized the wills of his countrymen and led the nation in what proved to be a successful war effort. He hoped to achieve a League of Nations when the conflict had been won. The phrases "make the world safe for democracy," and "the war to end war," epitomized the mood of the time. The clergy, with negligible exceptions, became prophets of the crusade.

More than the threat to democracy motivated their actions. Unsophisticated along with their generation in the realities of war, they read with astonishment and horror the news from across the Atlantic. To be sure the standards of an age just ending enabled them to sympathize with a despoiled Belgium, but no previous training or conditioning prepared them either to understand or to accept the logic of military necessity that caused the decision of the German High Command to strike at France across the flat plains of Flanders. Americans seethed with righteous rage when a German submarine sank without warning the *Lusitania,* carrying a valuable cargo from the neutral United States to embattled Britain. Civilized nations did not make war on noncombatants, let alone women and children. President Wilson demanded of the Imperial Reich that such barbarism cease. In excoriating the Germans, Americans failed to take account of the fact that the characteristics of the submarine make it inevitably a weapon of stealth and ambush. The German practice in World War I of sinking enemy ships without warning followed the logic of the weapon, just as Americans were to follow the logic of the atom bomb at Hiroshima. But the latter sad event was not to come about until thirty years had passed. With clear consciences the American generation of 1914–17 lashed out at German fright-

fulness. The anger did the generation honor, even if it demonstrated a lack of understanding of the nature of war.

President Hadley, who saw more deeply than most of his
countrymen into the realities of the crisis, not only pioneered
in making military training possible on their own campus for
college men but saw to it that they got training in that essential
military arm, artillery, which the antiquated army of the United
States had neglected. The President also encouraged a company
of undergraduates to learn at their own expense to fly the
primitive airplanes of the time and, by so doing, to take the
first steps in the development of naval aviation. The passing
months saw students and instructors quit the classroom for
service overseas in the driving of ambulances purchased with
American money for service in medical units hurried by the
hard-pressed Allies to the front.

In such a time of excitement, adventure, and idealism Dean
Charles R. Brown of the Divinity School preached one Sunday
in Battell. "And nowhere," said the famous pulpit orator,
"has this response of young manhood to the call of duty been
more complete or more satisfying than in our colleges. We
have seen it here on the Campus at Yale as other men and
women have seen it in all the colleges and universities of the
land. The spirit of it has been finely expressed in these lines.

> 'I saw the spires of Oxford
>   As I was passing by,
> The gray spires of Oxford
>   Against a pearl-gray sky.
> My heart was with the Oxford men
>   Who went abroad to die.
>
> . . . .
>
> 'God rest you happy, gentlemen,
>   Who laid your good lives down,
> Who took the khaki and the gun
>   Instead of cap and gown.
> God bring you to a fairer place
>   Than even Oxford town.' "

The Dean looked out with those piercing, dark eyes over the silent congregation. "And when those young men," he went on, "who have been striving to do the will of the Father, have fought their good fight and have finished their course, and have kept their faith, they will find laid up for them a crown of rejoicing. They will find that they have filled the hearts of their fathers on earth and of their Father in Heaven with a joy unspeakable."[2]

The sermon reflected the mood of the campus. Kenneth MacLeish, 1918, expressed the same mood in a letter from over-seas. He was one of the Yale pioneers who founded Naval Aviation. He was shot down over Belgium in combat with a superior number of planes on October 14, 1918. A letter to him from home after he had joined the service raised frankly the question of possible death. His reply is a classic statement of the idealism of World War I. "If I find it necessary to make the supreme sacrifice," said MacLeish, "always remember this —I am so firmly convinced that the ideals I am going to fight for are right and splendid ideals that I am happy to be able to give so much for them. I could not have any self-respect, I could not consider myself a man if I saw these ideals defeated when it lies in my power to defend them. So I have no fears! I have no regrets; I have only to thank God for such a wonderful opportunity to serve Him and the world."[3]

If Billy Phelps was in the congregation that listened to Dean Brown's call to arms, he remained unmoved by the Dean's eloquence. He had early made public his conviction that no Christian can reconcile his faith with the despoiling and the killing of war. At the end of March 1917 Phelps sat on the plat-form before a hostile audience that packed Woolsey Hall. David Starr Jordan, President Emeritus of Stanford University, had come to speak for peace. Phelps had insisted, and the Presi-dent had agreed, that the most famous pacifist of the day should be permitted to have his say. Though they rejected his arguments, the undergraduates allowed a man to speak who had been turned away from every other eastern university. When Jordan had finished, a band led the audience in a patriotic procession from the building. Billy Phelps always remembered the cost to him of that evening—the fear of being tarred and feathered and run out of town on a rail as a letter in the *News* of that morning had threatened—the fear that, if the threat were carried out, he would never be able to recover from the ridicule and the humiliation.

Phelps later changed his mind and supported the war, but not before he had paid the expenses to Washington of a junior in the College, E. Fay Campbell, who joined with other objectors in a protest against the declaration of war. Campbell represented a tiny minority. Henry Sloane Coffin, writing to President Angell in 1933, summed up accurately the situation at Yale as the war got under way. "There was some heartsearching during the first years of the War, and the question of pacifism came to the fore, but on the whole the Yale group was pretty much a unit behind our participation in the War and I do not think many boys had serious conscience difficulties. Those of us who were pacifists like William Lyon Phelps and myself never had much following."[4]

During the winter and spring of 1917 Billy Phelps had sometimes attended meetings in Fay Campbell's room in Berkeley Oval, dormitories occupied by the junior class. The group met there because the Christian Association denied it the use of the Dwight Hall building. By invitation Sidney Lovett sometimes came up from Union to talk with the little group of conscientious objectors.

Lovett later described the origin of his ideas. "Curiously enough," he remarked in 1956, "it was the firmly established confidence in religious and moral absolutes that attracted a few of us to the position of absolute religious pacifism. . . . Norman Thomas was an absolute pacifist in those days, and I imbibed my own views largely from him and a small group of men and women of similar mind. We were reinforced by the visits to this country of Leyton Richards and Richard Roberts, the latter to remain permanently, and the consequent extension of the British-born Fellowship of Reconciliation to these shores. The pacifist position was greatly strengthened by the Quakers, men like Rufus Jones and Harold Hatch, who represented the fine flowering of a long and unremitting devotion to peace."[5]

Lovett spoke of the gulf that yawned in Protestantism between the handful of pacifists and the clergy, in overwhelming majority, who preached, like Brown, the Great Crusade. On one trip to New Haven Lovett fell in with his one-time friend, Henry Wright. As they walked together, Lovett asked his companion how he could be sure that the war was the will of God. Wright replied with his usual earnestness that all had been solidified for him by a dream. The war was on. Wright saw the trenches, filled with soldiers of the United States. He saw Jesus, in the uniform of an American doughboy, go over the top. After that dream Wright insisted that the only line for a Christian to take was to do his bit. Wright's absolutism led him to reject the conscientious objector, even though it meant the breaking of friendship. Charles R. Brown took a similar position. World War I split American Protestantism into a majority and a small, rejected minority. "Nothing in our religious education and nurture," Lovett remarked later, "had prepared most of my generation for this particular rending of the veil of the Temple, a structure of spiritual hopes and aspirations which had seemed to us inviolable."

Benjamin Bacon, College Pastor and New Testament scholar, faced the issue raised for the Christian by the war. In 1918 the then young Yale University Press published his hard-won conclusions in a pamphlet that Bacon called *Non-resistance, Christian or Pagan?*

Non-resistance under some circumstances and conditions if not under all, is a duty which Jesus undeniably taught. Moreover, his conduct was fully in accord with his principles; otherwise his following could not have maintained their unparalleled loyalty to him. The manifest inconsistency between these non-resistance sayings (taken by themselves) and the method advocated and used by our Government in defense of democracy and righteousness remains ever present. The grave extent of its [pacifism's] inroads upon the national morale may be judged by the circulation attained by a typical pacifist book [*New Wars for Old* by John Haynes Holmes] whose principal basis of argument is nothing else than these non-resistance sayings, and which if it does not attempt to square them in all cases with the conduct of Jesus, but rather accords to Buddha, Confucius, and Lao-tse the merit of greater consistency, nevertheless owes all its real effect to the fact that its author speaks as a well-known and authorized exponent of Christian teaching . . .

Bacon pointed out that the book created the over-all impression "of an absolute and unqualified doctrine of non-resistance as supported by both the teaching and the conduct of Jesus."

In Washington the Red, White, and Blue Pamphlets turned out by the Creel Committee detailed the crimes of the Imperial German Reich and pictured the "blonde beast" whose home was central Europe. President Wilson's moving addresses called on all citizens for acts of dedication and sacrifice. The pamphlets and the addresses provided the background for Benjamin Bacon's argument as, in the midst of world crisis, he tried to discover the Christian's duty.

"It is true," Bacon went on, "as Tolstoi finely says, that Jesus' noble depiction in the Sermon on the Mount of the forbearance of God as the standard of the highest righteousness means that we should never do anything *contrary to the law of love*." But the great Russian, Bacon pointed out, had omitted from "that 'law of love' its first and great commandment"— namely to seek first the Kingdom of God. "It is because Jesus sought *first* the Kingdom," Bacon continued, "which means righteousness, peace and good will among men, sovereignty of right over might, overthrow of the powers of darkness . . . that he could teach as the best means of its attainment forbearance and loving kindness to the limit. For a limit there is—the *divine* limit of the welfare of all. . . . Jesus teaches *unlimited* non-resistance where only personal and selfish interests are at stake; but resistance unto blood for the sake of the Kingdom of God and His righteousness. In this he *is* inconsistent with non-resistant pacifism that can see no difference between this doctrine and that of Buddha or Lao-tse."[6]

Bacon argued cogently and a majority of Americans agreed with him. But a few, listening to the still, small voice within, were not persuaded and chose the hard course of fidelity to their convictions.

After the Armistice, time and the dying down of wartime emotions made it possible at Yale for charity to close the rift in the Christian ranks. When the conflict had ended, both Brown and Wright repented of their stiff-necked positions. Before Wright died in 1923, Fay Campbell, who as a senior had managed Dwight Hall on a depleted campus and to whom the older man would not speak while the fighting continued, became a close and helpful friend. In the 1920's also Campbell worked closely with Dean Brown in the direction of the affairs of the University Church.

Not all the religious leaders of the Yale community took in wartime the extreme stand toward pacifism that Brown and Wright did. Charles Campbell, '09, became General Secretary of Dwight Hall in the year in which the war began. His appointment came as a result of adoption a year or two earlier by the Advisory Board of Dwight Hall of the policy of making the post of general secretary a permanent one. In preparation for his service at Yale, Campbell had studied theology at the University of Edinburgh. He had barely entered upon his duties when the United States entered the conflict. In the academic year 1917–18 he left the campus for war service of a religious nature. Though he disapproved of pacifism, he asked Fay Campbell, who was working as leader of a small group of undergraduates, to carry on. After the Armistice family considerations compelled Charles Campbell to give up the career of General Secretary to which he had looked forward. He was a member of the Advisory Board which in the autumn of 1921 appointed Fay Campbell, then a student in the Divinity School, to the post. Fay Campbell held the office for more than a decade and a half.

In January 1919 Yale, no longer the armed camp of the Students' Army Training Corps, resumed normal work. The Professors of Latin, History, and English quit with relief the teaching of the physics and mathematics of the science of artillery and dusted off the familiar books of their trade. At first singly and then in larger and larger numbers, discharged veterans returned to the campus. Members of the faculty, abandoning war jobs no longer necessary or separated like the students from the Armed Forces, came back to resume the old routines in the classroom, laboratory, and library. There was improvisation in an effort to salvage an academic year one-third of which had been lost when the undergraduates were organized in a students army training corps. There was some confusion as new students kept turning up in the classroom almost to the end of the year, and occasionally as returned instructors suddenly stood at the desk. The treadmill of extracurricular activities creaked into motion.

In the spring Dwight Hall became the center of a significant undertaking. A national committee of distinguished citizens headed by John R. Mott organized and carried on a drive originally planned as a wartime venture. Throughout the United States, using methods developed in the Liberty Loan drives, the committee raised a great sum for work with the soldiers overseas and at home for the YMCA, the Salvation Army, and Catholic and Jewish organizations. The committee advertised the plight of students, particularly in Belgium and the new Czechoslovakia, caused by the dislocations and the destruction of war. A Student Friendship Fund accumulated as part of the drive provided immediate relief and substantial long-time aid. Yale's participation in the fund-raising got under way when Sherwood Eddy addressed a mass meeting that filled Woolsey Hall. Dwight Hall, with the vigorous support of the *News,* organized for the first time in the history of the University a door-to-door canvass in the dormitories. A faculty committee solicited their colleagues. In a week the Yale community raised one hundred thousand dollars. The achievement marked a high point in the history of Dwight Hall, comparable in idealism to that which in earlier years created the Yale Hope Mission and Yale-in-China.

Dwight Hall continued to support the Student Friendship Fund. In each of the following two years this voluntary religious organization raised a little less than ten thousand dollars for the men and women of European universities. In the autumn of 1921, as Fay Campbell began what turned out to be a nineteen-year term as General Secretary, Harry Allen, a sophomore member of the *News* Board and a member of the Dwight Hall Cabinet, proposed a Yale Budget Drive modeled after the Community Chests appearing at the time. The Drive raised money not only for Dwight Hall but for Yale-in-China, the Yale Hope Mission, and other agencies and charitable undertakings. In these first years after the war Dwight Hall initiated and to a great extent managed a student undertaking that in time grew into an autonomous activity, independent of all the agencies it served. The Yale Budget Drive of 1921 was the first undertaking of its kind in American universities.

Chapter 13. The Chapel in an Age of Disillusionment

In 1920 Yale's Sinclair Lewis published *Main Street,* an examination with inventories of civilization, such as it was, in Gopher Prairie. In 1925 he brought out *Arrowsmith,* a study of a medical scientist. In the same year H. L. Mencken, editor of the *American Mercury,* reported the Scopes trial at Dayton, Tennessee. He ridiculed the "yokels" who tramped out of their crossroads churches to vote into office the men who wrote and passed the anti-evolution law. In 1930 Mencken, become the scourge of the complacent and the prophet of all those young men who believed themselves to be sophisticated, published *Treatise on the Gods.* Lewis' *Arrowsmith* was the best literary expression of the cult of science in a civilization becoming rapidly secularized. Mencken's *Treatise on the Gods* marked the high tide of the attack on religion in an age of disillusionment and cynicism.

In the 1920's the Great Experiment laid the foundations for the empire of Al Capone; the Ku Klux Klan, attracting a membership of millions, rode at night against Catholics, Jews, and Negroes; William Jennings Bryan assumed the leadership, ended only by his death, of an anxious and embattled multitude who held fast to a literal faith in the Bible; and the Commonwealth of Massachusetts executed two Italians, Sacco and Vanzetti, for the murder in Braintree of a payroll clerk. In this decade when schism weakened Protestantism and secularism endangered all religious faith, when gangsterism threatened the stability of society and anti-intellectualism challenged learning, Yale College broadened and deepened the curriculum of the liberal arts. Inevitably the liberal arts made religion,

Christian and non-Christian, a subject of study in some class-rooms.

Courses in the great living religions and in biblical literature had been carried over from the prewar era. So had the work of Albert Galloway Keller, Sumner's pupil, successor, and literary executor. In pungent lectures Keller outlined to large and appreciative classes the science of society. A significant portion of the course dealt in the manner of positivism with the evolution of religion. In addition to his teaching, Keller labored during the decade of the 1920's to complete the work on the *Science of Society* that Sumner had begun. When it appeared, though Keller had done the greater part of the labor, he put his name second to that of his master on the title page. The story of the development of religion from animism to monotheism comprised its most interesting and challenging section. There in detail, supported by an impressive accumulation of evidence, appeared the completed argument of the lectures he gave to his undergraduates for a quarter of a century. But with publication came tragedy. Sumner in his day had been a pioneer who had provided new insights in the study of society. But by the time the volumes called *The Science of Society* had appeared, anthropologists had given up the attempt to explain societal phenomena in terms of single-line evolution. The investigations of the newer anthropologists, trained in the first-hand study of subliterate cultures, had outmoded the work of Sumner and Keller before it came from the press. Yet, though the newer men discarded the simple evolutionary formula, they retained the scientific approach used by Sumner and Keller with religion as an aspect of society. They strove to discover the significance, in terms of useful function, of the beliefs, the rituals, the taboos, and the institutions of the religions in the cultures they studied.

If the social sciences treated religion as an aspect of society, like governmental or economic institutions, other departments dealt with Christianity as part of the tradition of Western civilization to which America was heir. The philosophers traced the course of speculative thought from the ancient Greeks through the scholastics of the Middle Ages to the metaphysicians of the modern world. The brilliant Charles Bennett studied mysticism.

In basic courses in English literature undergraduates read Carlyle's chapter "The Hero as Divinity," Milton's *Paradise Lost,* and Tennyson's *Idylls of the King.* Under the guidance of William Lyon Phelps, large classes read further in Tennyson and most of Browning. Phelps agreed with Browning's line:

> The sum of all is—yes, my doubt is great,
> My faith's still greater, then my faith's enough.

Other men taught other poets. Chauncey Tinker introduced classes almost as large as those of Phelps' to the thought and art of the age of Samuel Johnson. Stanley Williams, launching what became a great course in American literature, lectured on that Puritanism out of which American thought had sprung, on the Quakerism of John Woolman, on the humane Unitarianism of William Ellery Channing, on Hawthorne's studies of the soul, and on the transcendentalism of Emerson, Thoreau, and Whitman. Teachers of English and American literature did not expound religion as such. But the writings of every century with which they dealt contained the record of the importance of Christianity in Western tradition. At the same time the general courses in history outlined the story of the Christian Church from the fall of Rome through the Reformation. As the decade of the 1930's opened, John M. S. Allison made his course called "The Middle Ages" one of the significant experiences of the large number of men who elected to hear him. Visitors came when he gave his famous lecture on St. Francis of Assisi.

Skepticism as well as faith has its place in the tradition of the West. Skepticism is as old as ancient Greece and in the 1920's was as modern as John Dewey. The names of Hume, Voltaire, Rousseau, Shelley, Marx, Nietzsche recall the challenges of other days to accepted opinion in the search for new enlightenment. Timothy Dwight, at the end of the eighteenth century, had tried to overthrow Hume, Voltaire, and Rousseau by impugning their personal morals. Their reputation survived the attack. Dwight put Paley into the liberal arts curriculum and required every undergraduate to study and recite the Archdeacon's *Natural Theology* and his *Evidences of Christianity*. In the twentieth century the curriculum of the liberal arts included the totality of Western tradition—believers, doubters, Catholics, Protestants, Jews, theists, humanists, naturalists, individualists, socialists.

The history of Western civilization is the record of the failures and the successes of a cluster of great peoples as they strove through time to make life more satisfying and to find meaning in man's earthly journey. A new faith and a new understanding had emerged in the College. The faith was the credo that the free mind brought into contact with the experience, the accumulated knowledge, and the aspirations of the race finds its own way, develops its own strength and creativeness, and acquires the balance necessary if men are to cope with the vicissitudes and hazards of existence. The new understanding was merely a clearer perception of what intelligent men in all ages had known, namely that the present grows out of the past and that the thoughts and institutions of yesterday condition the urgent and on-going search for the truth of tomorrow. So far Yale College had gone since the time when Thomas Clap had required that president, professors, and tutors believe, on pain of dismissal, in the Westminster Confession and accept the Saybrook Platform. In the decade that followed World War I students and faculty began to wonder whether the faith and outlook of the liberal arts could be reconciled with the law of the College that required all undergraduates to attend daily prayers and a preaching service on Sunday.

A variety of circumstances in the 1920's forced the Yale community to give thought to the continuance of compulsory chapel. Outside the University criticism of religion increased

as confidence in science grew. The upsurge of Fundamentalism
and the controversies that resulted disclosed grave weaknesses
in the intellectual armament of the modernist wing of Protestantism. Theology in the old sense of Jonathan Edwards and
Timothy Dwight had all but disappeared. Within the University, student attitudes reflected the temper of the time. Dwight
Hall had lost the campus prestige it enjoyed before the war.
Though most of its presidents received elections to senior societies, the honor usually came in spite of rather than because
of their position in the Association. The problem of chapel
emerged also partly because the student body had burgeoned
after the close of the conflict. Increase in enrollment directly
affected the ancient institution. The undergraduate bodies of
the College and of the new Freshman Year could not crowd
at the same time into Battell. Two shifts appeared in daily
chapel, one for the freshmen and one for the College. Morning
prayers had ceased to function as an institution to solidify a
sense of unity. Instead, the service had become a daily interruption and annoyance. Public criticism—on the part of both
students and faculty—increased. The *News* launched a campaign to end compulsion.

On Washington's Birthday in 1926 Carlos F. Stoddard, who
had recently turned over the chairmanship of the *News* to his
successor, addressed the graduates who had returned for Alumni
Day. He presented to his elders the student attitude of the
time. "We don't get our sense of unity out of chapel," he told
the group. "We don't all meet there now, and if we did have
a building big enough, it would merely be twice as much like
a rabble army and not twice as much like the solidarity of a
family prayers." In recent months some had suggested that a
change in ritual might make it possible to save an institution
more than two centuries old. ". . . you can't bring back the
lost religious atmosphere, if it was ever there," Stoddard went
on, "by any such reorganization of ritual. There is nothing
wrong with the order of events, so to speak. At daily services
the organist plays the same hymns that were heard in places

where people go for the sake of worship. I say the organist plays them because very few people sing them. If you think I'm exaggerating in this, just talk to some of the men who have led these so-called prayer meetings in the last few years. One sure way to turn a man against compulsion is to give him a week as chapel leader. On Sundays the gathering loses whatever religious significance it might hold since the service must not offend any number of faiths. The natural and inevitable result is that while it doesn't offend any faith, neither can it appeal to any faith." Stoddard in dealing with student objections to Sunday chapel might have added that at a time when the motorcar was becoming every man's means of transportation, undergraduates had Sunday interests beyond the boundaries of the campus.

The ex-chairman of the *News* went on to speak specifically for his own class. "Once every Senior Class voted to keep chapel. Not so lately. I remind you that we who have been spokesmen are Seniors, and that our Class is about seven to one against it. We have nothing to gain personally. We *don't* think it would be a good thing for the other fellow now that we are through. We know that it is not a good thing for anybody, and that it's a bad thing for many."[1]

The problem of what to do about chapel came before the General Faculty of the College. The Fellows of the Corporation had appointed a committee made up of stout defenders of an old tradition. But the College Faculty, insisting that the matter lay within its jurisdiction, debated the question without seeking the advice of the committee. Some influential members of the Faculty opposed bitterly the proposal to abolish compulsory attendance at chapel services. Other members argued not only that the institution had become an anachronism but that the inadequate seating capacity of Battell made its continuance impossible. A committee under the chairmanship of Professor Clive Day proposed a compromise that seniors, but not other classes, be excused from the daily service and that the student who did not sign up to attend the Sunday service be required to report for some sort of roll call on that day. Dean Brown attended as College pastor the meeting to take action on the report. He spoke, calling attention to the difficulties of preaching to a captive audience. He concurred in the vote to recommend to the Corporation total abolition of compulsion. The Faculty of Freshman Year made a similar recommendation. On May 8, 1926, the Corporation concurred. That body then drew up for publication a formal statement of policy.

"Yale University," the notice read, "made public today its plans for the future development of the religious life of the institution." The statement noted the similar recommendations from the faculties of Yale College and the Freshman Year. ". . . the Corporation," the announcement continued, "is prepared to make trial of voluntary services. The Corporation recalls that according to the charter of Yale a primary aim for which the University was founded is 'to uphold and propagate the Christian Protestant religion' and that it is incumbent upon the University to see that this purpose is loyally fulfilled. Compulsory chapel will be discontinued at the end of the present year. In its place the University has taken measures to establish a strong undergraduate department of religion; to develop in every way the Church of Christ in Yale University, the official name of the College Church; to maintain and strengthen the various student religious organizations; and to call to the attention of the friends of the University the desirability of a suitable chapel building where voluntary services may be held."[2] In one respect the announcement ran far ahead of events. Twenty years elapsed before the Department of Religion came into being.

A more immediate problem compelled attention. University authorities had condemned the Dwight Hall building even before the war. The reason was not that it had fallen into decay; its builders had erected its walls of stone to stand indefinitely. But after the war the changing Yale architectural scene required a vista for the better view of the Harkness Memorial Tower. In 1928 the old Dwight Hall was cut down like a bit of underbrush beneath a pine. The University made available to the Association two floors in the west entry of Durfee Hall. Work began on the rehabilitation of the Old Library soon after the books it housed had been carted away to the stacks in Sterling. The chaplain consecrated Dwight Memorial Chapel (named for both Dwights) in 1931. The two wings had been built to house the collections of Linonia and Brothers in Unity. The books of Calliope had occupied one of the passageways. Now the staff of the Association occupied one wing while the other became a common room for freshmen. Beside it Dwight Hall maintained a snack bar—useful but an unimpressive substitute for that popular eating place that had occupied the basement of the old building for more than a quarter of a century.

As for chapel the undergraduates had already met the test. On October 4, 1926, at the opening of a new college year the *News* ran a significant editorial. "The challenge to undergraduate Yale," the editor wrote, "is offered today. The first voluntary daily chapel service in the history of Yale will be held this morning at ten-thirty. Yesterday the attendance at the first voluntary Sunday service, at which President Angell delivered the Matriculation Address, was such as to justify no further worry lest Sunday Church drop out of Yale life. The test of daily chapel will be more severe and hence more vital to the best interests of Yale." On the front page appeared the headline, "Fay Campbell [General Secretary of Dwight Hall] Describes Voluntary Daily Services." "Prayers will be held in Battell Chapel daily, except Saturday throughout the University year at 10:30," wrote Campbell. "So far as possible University classes have been discontinued at that time, which should enable all who desire to attend this service to do so. The order of service has been enriched. A new book of responsive readings has been secured . . . and the choir will not only lead the congregational singing but will also provide special music from time to time. A prelude will be played each morning at 10:25 which should help all who attend to enter more quickly into the spirit of the service. This morning Professor [Harry] Jepson will play Jongen's Pensee d'Antomore. It is expected that many of the chaplains will speak briefly. . . . Each chaplain will be free to organize the service as he wishes . . ."

Five years later the daily chapel service was moved to the more congenial Dwight Memorial Chapel. Problems had arisen. There had been experiments as to the best hour. But the institution had survived. Each noon the bells in Harkness Tower reminded the Yale community of prayers.

Having returned to the salt mines after the Christmas vacation, the editor of the *News* in January 1927 cast about for a subject for an editorial. Nothing better offering, he hit upon Dwight Hall. On January 13 the *News* said: "Dwight Hall has and is doing a tremendous service to the less fortunate people of the city through Boys Work and the Hope Mission. It has been a constructive force in the lives of many undergraduates. It has tremendously aided in establishing Chapel on a voluntary basis. But it has not presented to the great majority of undergraduates a worthwhile religious philosophy. This it can and should do."

The editorial spoke much truth. The work of Dwight Hall had been useful but its religion had fallen into confusion. Many causes contributed. That emotional gospel which Henry Drummond and Henry Wright had brought to the campus at the end of the nineteenth century had begun to evaporate, like a morning mist, even before August 1914. In the final phase of wartime idealism the young men of the Association had expressed their religion in doing. They worked for the Student Friendship Fund. They founded the Yale Budget. They caught the vision of the Social Gospel. As the new decade opened, they had high hopes that action would end poverty and social injustice. The Kingdom of God seemed not far in the future.

As for the intellectual content of religion, doing seemed more important than thinking, action more to be desired than a considered philosophy of life. Dean Brown, become pastor of the University Church, preached the new faith. "The final test," he said, "is that of experience. Religion is like a stained glass window in a church. No matter how bright the day may be, you cannot see the beauty of it from the outside. Come in here! Come inside and look at it from within, then you will know. . . . Let religion be judged as other great interests are judged, by its power to contribute to the full development of honored and joyous existence for our common humanity. 'By their fruits ye shall know.' It was the Master of all the higher values in life who proposed this pragmatic test, the test of experience, the ability or the inability of the thing to work out satisfactory results."³ For Dean Brown theory came straight out of William James.

He preached a dangerous doctrine. As the decade of the 1920's ran on, the Kingdom did not come. In spite of the Great Boom poverty did not end. The case of Sacco and Vanzetti provided a commentary on justice. Beyond the borders of the nation the victory in World War I had not translated President Wilson's ideals into social realities. Americans became cynical when men spoke of ideals. The sudden resurgence in Fundamentalism of much of the old biblical literalism disclosed that the modernists scarcely had a theology worthy of the name. Their theological seminaries accepted and pursued biblical scholarship with the result that for many of their instructors the idea of the divinity of Christ lost its old meaning. When the writer of the *News* editorial asked Dwight Hall in January 1927 for a "worthwhile religious philosophy," he gave a tall order. The earnest and well-meaning young men of that organization did not, for the most part, know what religion was all about. The campus devotees of H. L. Mencken doubted that it was about anything of importance.

Dean Brown gave to the University Church its pulpit leadership. He preached normally once a month. He had extraordinary gifts. His sermons moved swiftly in sentences of plain and effective Anglo-Saxon English. He never removed his piercing dark eyes from his congregation even when he read the lesson. The Bible lay open on the desk before him, but he did not look at it. He knew the words. He was indubitably Yale's greatest preacher since the first Timothy Dwight. The preaching of the two men differed, however. Because Dwight thought the subject of primary importance he asked his listeners to use their minds as Sunday after Sunday he worked through the logic behind a particular conclusion in an intricate theology. Brown preached morals. Among other things he commented on the moods and events of the 1920's. He spoke of cynicism: "The word cynic comes from the Greek word which means 'dog,' and the snarling, captious spirit of the cur is characteristic of both animals." He mentioned the irreligion of the times: "The pathetic fact about the poor, godless, irreligious people is that they are half dead and do not know it. They are dead at the top; they are dead at the heart. They are for all the world like blind men groping their way along the street and saying to each other, 'We hear these foolish, superstitious people talking about the beauty of rainbows and sunsets, stained glass windows and rose bushes. How silly they are! There is nothing in it! It is perfectly apparent to us that the whole world is black.' Poor chaps, they are dead in their eyes and the irreligious people are dead in their souls."[4]

Near the middle of the decade the Dean spoke one Sunday of Fundamentalism. "William Jennings Bryan has been telling people that science destroys religion and that scientific men for the most part are godless men. I wonder if he knows what he is talking about. These men of science may not always pronounce the word Shibboleth just as Mr. Bryan pronounces it; they may not always observe the same forms which we are observing here today. But in their single-minded devotion to truth and in their desire to make their intelligence serve the needs of the race, some of them come nearer to the soul of religion than do some of those who give an easy assent to all the creeds. Here was Thomas Huxley saying: 'Science seems to me to teach the great truth embodied in the Christian doctrine of entire surrender to the will of God. Sit down before the fact as a little child. Be prepared to give up if need be every preconceived notion. Follow humbly wherever nature leads or you will not learn anything. I have only gained peace of mind since I resolved at any cost to do just this.' " The Dean, looking out at the congregation, went on. "Is not that about what we mean when we talk about becoming as little children, open-minded, teachable, obedient, that we may enter the kingdom of heaven? Is not that what we mean when we rely on the Spirit of Truth, who is the Holy Spirit, to lead our minds into a deeper knowledge of the truth and our hearts into a richer experience of God's own grace?"[5] The Dean spoke in Battell. When Noah Porter had dedicated that sanctuary, he had, making an obvious reference to the great evolutionist, dealt with the poison "in the brilliant romancing of the scientific lecturer." Just under a half-century later the pastor of the University Church wheeled into action, like a battery of field artillery, paragraphs of this same scientific lecturer to hold off the battalions of the Fundamentalists. The Dean chose his weapons well. But even as he preached, Reinhold Niebuhr, a graduate of the school over which Brown presided, was beginning to ask himself the old questions of theology and was undertaking the slow, hard work of finding new answers appropriate to a new age.

As the decade of the 1920's approached its end, the ideas of Karl Barth began percolating into American religious thought. More important for the Yale campus, however, was the meeting in 1928 of the International Missionary Council at Jerusalem. Representatives of the older churches of the West joined with those of the younger churches that had grown up from seeds planted by missionaries in a conference held significantly in the city so intimately associated with the origin of Christianity. Fay Campbell attended as a representative of the Christian Youth Movement in the United States.

The Jerusalem Conference took the world view that was inevitable when Christians from all five continents met together to consider the mission of the faith they espoused. These men and women discussed the great religions, beside which many of them lived and worked, not as false idolatries but as incomplete expressions of spiritual truth. In a postwar world the delegates saw industrialism moving out from Western Europe and from the United States to affect the lives of men on all continents. The Conference asked the basic question: What has Christianity to offer to men everywhere that will give them strength to meet the conditions of societies in swift and sometimes cataclysmic change? The Archbishop of Canterbury, William Temple, emerged as the most significant figure in the discussions. He took a leading part in preparing the Statement that the Conference adopted and published:

Throughout the world there is a sense of insecurity and instability. Ancient religions are undergoing modification, and in some regions dissolution, as scientific and commercial development alter the current of men's thought. Institutions regarded with age-long veneration are discarded or called in question; well-established standards of moral conduct are brought under criticism; and countries called Christian feel the stress as truly as the peoples of Asia and Africa. On all sides doubt is expressed whether there is any absolute truth or goodness. A new relativism struggles to enthrone itself in human thought. Along with this is found the existence of world-wide suffering and pain, which expresses itself partly in despair of all higher values, partly in a tragically earnest quest of a new basis of life and thought, in the birthpangs of rising nationalism, in the ever keener consciousness of race- and class-oppression . . .

In this world, bewildered and groping for its way, Jesus Christ has drawn to Himself the attention and admiration of mankind as never before. He stands before men as greater than Western civilization, greater than the Christianity that the world has come to know. . . . Our message is Jesus Christ. He is the revelation of what God is and of what man through him may become. In Him we come face to face with the Ultimate Reality of the universe; he makes known to us God as our Father, perfect and infinite in love and righteousness; for in Him we find God incarnate, the final, yet ever-unfolding, revelation of the God in whom we live and move and have our being. We hold that through all that happens, in light and in darkness, God is working, ruling and over-ruling. . . . We re-affirm that God, as Jesus Christ has revealed Him, requires all His children, in all circumstances, at all times, in all human rela-tionships, to live in love and righteousness for his glory . . .[6]

Campbell brought the Statement back to the campus. To the young men of Dwight Hall it spoke with the authority of a great conference that was cosmopolitan in membership but united in faith and in ultimate goals. The Statement had sub-stance and vision. It brought order into the thinking of many a well-meaning but confused young man. The Association, treating it as a kind of Christian Manifesto, made copies avail-able to all who could be interested. A new sense of direction made itself manifest. Dwight Hall began to speak with a more positive voice.

In the difficult years of the 1920's President James Rowland Angell faced squarely the religious problems of the time. He supported the University Church not only by his presence in Sunday chapel when possible but with careful attention to the selection of the clergymen to fill the pulpit. On occasion he responded to requests to address the students on religious matters. He spoke always as a layman and that fact often gave even greater weight to his words, in a time when clergymen, along with religion, came frequently under attack.

In 1926 the President addressed the company of graduates and undergraduates who had assembled to celebrate the fortieth anniversary of Dwight Hall. Appropriately on an occasion that emphasized history he noted the alternations in the past "of periods of interest in religious problems and religious activities with periods of revolt or of complete indifference to religious faith and tradition." He spoke of the low ebb of religion after the American Revolution and at the time of the French Revolution. He commented that in the 1920's Americans had come into another such period. "To be blasé, to have at one's tongue's end all the catch phrases of the nihilistic and blasphemous writers of the day," the President remarked, "is counted good form and as an evidence of intellectual up-to-dateness is regarded as almost as essential as the wearing of the correct cut of clothes, the proper shape of hat, the accepted collar and tie, which taken together are the obvious marks of the socially sophisticated." Angell did not despair. He made no gloomy forecast of the future. "But that man will again and at no distant date, return once more to the perennially invigorating springs of religious faith, I cannot personally doubt."[7]

In October 1926 President Angell preached the Matriculation Sermon. Compulsory chapel had disappeared. For the first time in the history of Yale the President addressed a Sunday service which students were not required to attend. A large number came to hear him. He mentioned the current criticism of religion. Again he noted the even more important indifference toward it that characterized the time. Again he stated his conviction that the temper of the moment would pass. He then made his personal confession of faith:

But the stubborn fact remains that our world presents us with crucial questions touching the meaning and the end of life and the universe, which cannot—at present anyhow—be answered save in terms of faith. Probably few men come to a living religious faith over the road of pure reason. It is rather in response to deep longings of the human spirit, to great revealing human experiences, that such faith is born. It is because the religion of Jesus satisfies those deep and persistent cravings as no other has done, that intelligent men of our time find happiness and peace in allegiance to it. It offers a view of life which satisfies one's instinct for the salvation of humanity and by virtue of this fact appeals deeply to men of noble purpose. In the Christian doctrine of the fatherhood of God and the brotherhood of man, in the teaching of love to one's neighbor, men see the foundations of a moral order in which they can dare to live with confidence and happiness. True it is that the

moral standards which Jesus erected are at the outmost limits of
human power; but any that were less severe would be unworthy of
that which is best in the human soul.[8]

Angell had the orator's gift. He could achieve moving
perorations. His sermon on the historic occasion when voluntary Sunday services began was one of his great efforts. He had
no cheap desire to persuade the general public that Yale had
not abandoned religion. He spoke earnestly to young men
most of whom were groping in a fog. In effect he met the
challenge which the *News* had made to Dwight Hall to provide
a "worthwhile religious philosophy." In a university dedicated
to the search for new truth Angell presented religion as a continuing search for the meaning and end of life, a search, of
necessity, involving the whole personality. In a century of
revolution and violence he pointed to Christian ethics as a
satisfying guide to the good life, a guide whose strength lies
in the almost impossible demands it makes on men. On that
first day of a new era in the history of the Chapel the President
taught a religion appropriate to a great university.

The consequences of the abolition of compulsory chapel had
elements in common with the termination by the General
Assembly of Connecticut of the special privileges of the Congregational Church. In both cases, though in somewhat different senses, the principle of voluntarism prevailed. In Connecticut all churches equally became free and voluntary associations whose members assumed responsibility for their support. By ending compulsion the University put the responsibility for support of religion through attendance upon the
student body and upon the members of the University Church.
The ultimate control of the Church, however, remained in
the hands of the Corporation, where lay the power of appointment of the pastor. That body, moreover, provided for his
salary and residence. Dwight Hall, though not a church, came
closer to the status of the free churches of the United States.

Students managed it with guidance from alumni. Contributions from both students and alumni provided the stipends of
the secretaries and the means to meet other expenses of the
Association. The progression of student generations, however,
gave to Dwight Hall a membership that changed from year to
year and made the organization in this respect quite unlike that
of a parish church.

These different elements in the situation of organized religion in the University provided the background of the de-
liberations of the Corporation when they dealt with the recommendations of two faculties that compulsion be abolished. At
the same time the decline in the 1920's of the prestige of religion in the country at large gave them pause. The public
might consider that the striking down of the ancient requirement of attendance upon religious worship had symbolic
significance. Had Yale gone over to the camp of the infidels?
To counter such a possible interpretation the Corporation took
thought of two symbols that would emphasize the University's
continuing support of religion. First in its statement concerning the change in policy the Corporation advertised discretely
but frankly that it would accept gifts for a new chapel. Second
the Corporation transformed what had become the part-time
office of pastor of the University Church into that of a full-
time pastor and chaplain.

In 1927 Elmore M. McKee became the first chaplain of Yale
University. McKee while still an undergraduate had left the
campus during World War I to accept a commission in the
Sanitary Corps. In this office he did useful work in fighting the
perennial problem of vice in the neighborhood of military
cantonments. He returned to college to get his degree in 1919
and then to serve as a secretary of Dwight Hall. After the completion of his work in theological seminary he took orders in
the Episcopal Church. He was rector of St. Paul's in New
Haven when the University called him to the chaplaincy.

Conscientious, able, and of fine appearance, he took an immediate and lively interest in the affairs of the entire Yale com-

munity. He considered this community his potential parish. His training in natural theology led to his conviction that "every legitimate phase of a university's life leads to worship." He addressed to the Corporation in 1930 in support of a specific proposal an argument whose substance Porter had repeated at the dedication of Battell, which Woolsey had presented with moving eloquence at his inauguration, and which for fifty years undergraduates in Yale College had studied in Paley. "The astronomer at his telescope," said the young chaplain, "or the biologist at his microscope, is asking the question, 'Is there a purpose in the universe and in life, which links together the stars or water-life and the personality making the investigation?' . . . Now the instant a man is conscious of his search for an Order, a Plan, a Purpose beyond himself, he is at the threshold of worship. And when he admits to himself that he has even so much as begun to find a cosmic Purpose, and that he wishes to relate himself to that purpose, then he *is* worshipping. He has begun to become a partner of the Purpose, of Ultimate Reality, of God—though each might name his finding differently . . ."[9]

Inevitably the chaplain interested himself in the forms of the service of worship in the Sunday service in the Chapel. He discovered excellent foundations on which to build. Years before McKee became pastor, the University organist, Harry Jepson, had developed a choir of male voices that gave to Battell music equal in quality to that heard in any English cathedral. McKee's familiarity with Episcopalian forms enabled him to enrich the ritual and to make it more worshipful. The new chaplain himself from time to time occupied the pulpit with dignity and effectiveness.

As he settled into his position, Elmore McKee began to formulate an ambitious project. He set his sights high. Taking his cue from the Corporation's own statement he proposed a new chapel. If, by chance, he read the records of the time when Battell was being planned, he discovered that the second Timothy Dwight, then a professor in the Divinity School, had published in 1871 a strong appeal that the new chapel be placed in the middle of the campus which the authorities planned to surround with buildings. Here, the center of all eyes, it would stand as the symbol of the central interest of the College that had been founded to "support and propagate the Christian Protestant religion." But Presidents Woolsey and Porter had ruled against Dwight. Exercising economy in the use of space, they wedged Battell into the corner of the rising quadrangle. To compensate for its relatively inconspicuous position they gave the sanctuary an impressive porch and above it a clock with chimes to call the hours. They decorated the interior insofar as limited funds would permit, in accordance with the ideas of ecclesiastical magnificence of the time. McKee thought Battell a rather dreary relic of another age that had become inappropriate to a great university. He argued before the President and Fellows for a new chapel.

The Chaplain, however, supported a cause already lost. As far back as 1922 when great benefactions made possible the erection of a significant number of new buildings, there had been talk of a new chapel. In the years that followed, James Gamble Rogers, advisor in architecture to the University, took the suggestion under consideration. Never a man to be content with half measures, Rogers saw in imagination rising on the east side of College Street and facing Sterling Library at the far end of the new Cross Campus, a cathedral in which five thousand persons might gather for worship. Somewhat dismayed, the Yale authorities scaled down the proposed sanctuary to a church that might accommodate a more modest twenty-five hundred. But no eager giver came forward to turn a paper plan into brick and stone.

Meantime the Corporation voted funds to renovate Battell in accordance with plans drawn by Everett Meeks, Dean of the School of Fine Arts. In 1930 the University authorities faced their responsibility of providing proper quarters for the Christian Association after the demolition of Dwight Hall. Casting about, they discovered the quality of that Gothic re-

THE CHAPEL IN AN AGE OF DISILLUSIONMENT

vival structure that had been built in the 1840's to house the books of the College and of the literary societies. The central portion had obviously been inspired by the famous chapel in King's College in Cambridge University. In 1930 builders transformed what in the middle of the nineteenth century had been both reading room and stacks into the beautiful Dwight Chapel. In 1931 Yale had two sanctuaries. A refurbished Battell provided the Sunday services of the University Church. In Dwight Chapel daily prayers were said by those who came to kneel in a spirit of devotion.

Though disappointed that the University was not to have a new and impressive place of worship, McKee considered the proposal secondary to another plan he had in mind. In his first Chaplain's Report he summarized the situation of the University Church and set forth his hopes. The formal organization consisted of a Board of ten undergraduate and six faculty deacons, a clerk, and a treasurer. These with the officers of the Christian Association and a committee of twenty-seven undergraduates who composed the chapel committee together formed the functioning Board of the Church. He hoped to make the church a regular parish—self-supporting, possessed of a Sunday School, and carrying on mission and other religious programs. Looking ahead, he saw the creation "at the heart of a great academic community of an interdenominational Christian parish which shall, in the name of the whole Christian Church, maintain worship, a Christian fellowship, and stimulate Christian thought and action."[10]

McKee thought that the building of such a church required changes in the organization of religion on the campus. He envisioned Dwight Hall as the parish house of the University Church. He thought that the role of the Secretary of the Christian Association should be that of assistant pastor.

When the proposed change came to the attention of Fay Campbell, he expressed the opinion that the traditional principles of Dwight Hall, namely the student initiative that had brought it into being and the student responsibility that had

characterized its work for more than four decades, were of too
great importance to abandon. He considered a prime value of
the Christian Association to be its freedom from any connection with the government of the University and its independence of University support. Campbell, however, offered
to resign if the consensus of opinion favored the proposed plan.

Henry Sloane Coffin, a member of the Corporation and a
graduate who in his years in college and on many occasions
after getting his degree had participated in the activities of the
Association, agreed with Campbell. Coffin did not wish to see
an end put to the status of Dwight Hall as a student-managed
and alumni-guided extracurricular activity. Coffin expressed
his opposition to the Chaplain. McKee had met with his second
disappointment. In 1931 he resigned to accept the pastorate of
a large city church.

In 1932 the Corporation appointed Sidney Lovett, pastor
of a church in Boston, as chaplain of the University. In March,
when the University announced the appointment, the *News*
ran an editorial entitled "Godless Places," written by a young
man, Lyman Spitzer, Jr., who later became a distinguished
theoretical physicist. It ran as follows: "Because students have
refused to accept obsolete doctrines of medieval theology, some
self-righteous reverends see fit to denounce colleges from their
pulpits as Godless places. Others have been dismayed at the
widespread disdain for prayers and worship. Some denounce,
some merely deplore this irreligiousness. Very few realize that
there is a real, deep religion in an American university, that
young men who boastfully claim to have no religion are often
following the most progressive religious minds of the era."

Spitzer affirmed that the college man, really a very young
man, is puzzled and made anxious by a world that "is often
terrifying."

To them prayer is weak mumbling, a confession that they cannot
stand on their own feet. To them the ritual of the Church today

seems filled with century-old fetishes. To them church history seems criminal beyond all other history because the church was, above all other institutions, too small to admit its mistakes, too selfish to lead. Always fighting change, fighting independent thought, fighting science, it lagged behind the great thinkers of the time. To them the moralizing doctrinaires harping on ideals of olden ages are unsympathetic. They have nothing to offer the young man reaching beyond the accomplishments of dead ages. To youth, the good the church has done is not enough to counteract the hostility it inspires for its lack of understanding and sympathy to needs of a new age. So these college men avoid anything that savours of church; they would rather stand alone without any consolation so they can be free to think and to live according to the dictates of their reasoning.

A new chaplain comes among us. What has he to do with religion such as this? Does he come with the consolation of Zoroastrian ritual cloaked in Christian theology? Does he come equipped with ancient superstition disguised in modern forms and methods? Does he come with the God which was good enough for men five centuries ago but not good enough today? Does he come to combat science, to deny the wonders of astronomy, of geology, of evolution? Will he attempt to hand college men the age-old narrow-minded attitude of the church regarding modern discoveries? If he comes with these things, he will have a lonely time at Yale.

But if he comes with a belief in the mental and spiritual ventures of this age, if he makes the mystery of this new world of the twentieth century one bit less terrifying, he will be greatly welcomed. Should he make the existence of men, ridiculous parasites on a dying speck of matter, in infinite space and infinite cold, should he make man's helplessness before the blazing island universes millions of light years away any less dismaying, he will touch the religious heart of Yale.

Reverend Sidney Lovett, 1913, newly-appointed chaplain, comes among men most critical of the Christian church. His task is to adapt the beauties of the life of Jesus and the morals of the Old Testament to the needs of modern ambitious youth. He comes to a "godless place," where enthusiasm, hope, and especially open-mindedness reign supreme. May he prosper here.

In 1956 the chaplain commented publicly on the editorial.

"Well," he said, "after reading the above, remembering the
Yale I knew twenty years earlier and conscious of a new Yale
with which in the interval, I had been largely out of touch,
the Reverend Sidney Lovett was sorely tempted to call up
President Angell and resign his commission. I can still argue
that it would have been better for Yale had I done so, but I
must admit in so doing I would have missed an awful lot of
friendship and joy."[11]

Chapter 14. Religion and Learning, 1757-1957

In 1933 the Church of Christ in Yale University moved into the last quarter of its second century. Yale College, transformed by the residential colleges whose doors opened that year, entered upon a new epoch. The religion of midtwentieth-century Yale was a continuation of developments of nearly two centuries.

The College Church began in controversy. Thomas Clap created a unique institution, a church embedded in a college, to further the Consistent Calvinism of Jonathan Edwards. In Wollebius undergraduates learned the outlines of the Genevan system and the covenant theology basic to the thought of New England Puritanism. Though the College had already broadened its function beyond that of merely training ministers, Clap, and the Corporation behind him, established the supremacy of a particular theology by requiring an oath of tutors, professors, and president.

If Clap represented the older Puritan mind, Ezra Stiles brought to Yale the tolerance of the eighteenth-century Enlightenment. Contending with difficulties created by a long and uncertain rebellion, he saved the College. The first scholar of his day, he supported and enhanced the prestige of learning. Amid the alarms of war and after the conflict through a period of hostility to traditional religion magnified by the French Revolution, Stiles kept alive in his own heart and furthered in the College Church an enquiring and a hopeful faith. When Stiles died, the College, sound in its finances and with a new building program on the way, was prepared to go forward in better times.

Timothy Dwight assumed the presidency in the more stable times that followed the inauguration of the Constitution in 1789. Varied causes—the emphasis of romanticism on feeling as opposed to that of the Enlightenment on reason, the challenge to religion of a virtually unchurched frontier—combined in America to produce an evangelical Protestantism. The effort to win souls called into being the mass emotions of the revival.

Dwight displayed wisdom in expanding the work of the College. A prophet of evangelical Protestantism, he made the College pulpit for two decades the most influential in the nation. Riding the crest of the wave of anti-French feeling at the end of the century, he made effective war on the rationalism of the "religion of Nature." Dwight, who served most of his presidential term as pastor of the College Church, insisted on the primacy of doctrine in religion. In his sermons in the Chapel he unfolded a modified Edwardian theology adapted to the needs of the evangelist. His published system had a wide influence in its day. Dwight took the lead in bringing about in Connecticut the Second Great Awakening. Before his death he saw related developments, the humanitarian and the missionary movements, grow out of evangelical Protestantism. Dwight was an impressive figure in the group of faculty and student members who gathered each month about the communion table. The association led many undergraduates to dedicate their lives to the service of the ministry.

As the century progressed, the cultivation of the arts and sciences in the College became more thorough and more comprehensive. Beginning almost at the turn of the century, key men in the Yale scene began those pilgrimages to European universities that helped to give the College an enlarged participation in the learning of the West. The classroom, as well as the Chapel, made its contribution to religion. In the decades in which the spirit of evangelism dominated the College pulpit, undergraduates, studying William Paley, came into contact with the mood of the Enlightenment, for the Archdeacon marshaled reason to the support of religion. After the 1820's the Scottish common-sense philosophy of Thomas Reid and Dugald Stewart supplemented the arguments of Paley's text-books.

Beginning in the 1820's Eleazar Fitch, Chauncey Goodrich, and—most important of all—Nathaniel W. Taylor used Scottish common sense to reshape Calvinism into the New Haven Theology, a formulation intended, as Dwight's had been, to magnify the power of the evangelist. Taylor modified old doctrines and brought them into harmony with the maturing idealism of American democracy, in particular with its doctrine of the free individual. The New Haven system, first preached in the College Church, radiated outward to liberalize an older Calvinism in New England and the West.

As the event turned out, however, the Taylor system did not become the great and final consummation. At the moment when wide acceptance seemed evidence of triumph Horace Bushnell began affirming that religion cannot be locked up in doctrines and that the emotionalism of the contrived and parochial revival fell far short of what religious experience should be. Urging, as Emerson at the time was doing, the validity of intuition, the former Yale tutor emphasized the power of the Divine Spirit when it illuminates the inner life and moves in the will of a man. At the same time, the Hartford theologian took a hopeful view of the achievements of reason as expressed in the rising sciences. Bushnell's thought, so controversial in the middle decades, pointed to the New Theology of the end of the century.

At a time when the Hartford clergyman enjoyed among Yale undergraduates a greater popularity than any other visiting preacher, President Woolsey held fast to religious positions close to those of Nathaniel W. Taylor. But the fact that he invited Bushnell to the Chapel pulpit demonstrated his spirit of tolerance. Woolsey sorrowfully noted the decay of old beliefs and the rise of secularism. In the 1860's he defended the essential positions of the religion traditional in the College and, pointing out the inadequacies of secularism, warned against its sophistries.

At Yale, James Dwight Dana, geologist, who taught the course in cosmogony, stood out as a transitional figure, blending in his thought the older attitude toward the Bible and a new determination to harmonize religion with science. While Dana was lecturing in cosmogony President Noah Porter became one of the early artisans of the New Theology. Published sermons and books on ethics and philosophy that had wide use in American colleges made him one of the most influential philosophers of his time and enabled him to impress his ideas about Christianity on his generation. Though he rejected Huxley, he accepted, in the manner of Dana, evolution as a concept in theology. He spoke of the law of love destined to be one of the most important ideas in the discourse of the social gospel at the turn of the century. Finally Porter anticipated William James in the pragmatic defense of religious faith. Porter, like Dana, was a transitional figure, a man who looked backward to the old faith and forward to a new theology.

The second Timothy Dwight abandoned completely the Calvinist system. In the tradition of Bushnell he preached the primacy of the inner life. In his time the new theology, with its acceptance of the scholarship of science and of the historical criticism of the Bible, became central to the preaching in the College Church, and Benjamin Bacon, New Testament scholar, became its pastor. Theology, however, played little part in the faith of the campus that centered in Dwight Hall. In this religion an uncritical study of the Bible fostered a pietistic emphasis on feeling. Henry B. Wright, a mystic who had a genius for personal evangelism, was its dominant figure.

World War I opened an age of violence and anxiety. But

the conflict came at a time when a major shift in American thought was already under way. The penetration of the atom had begun around the turn of the century. Einstein's theory of relativity had provided a new outlook on the cosmos. The discoveries of nuclear physics and Einstein's revision of Euclid's mathematics disturbed what had been the certainties of the old Newtonian universe. The majestic new triumphs of reason in the exploration of nature, coming on top of Darwin's epoch-making evolutionary hypothesis, gave to natural science a prestige among educated men surpassing even that which it enjoyed in the eighteenth-century Enlightenment.

At the same time Charles Pierce, William James, and John Dewey, in the creation out of evolution of the philosophy of pragmatism, reoriented American thinking about society. They abandoned the comfortable absolutisms of the nineteenth century. They insisted upon the importance of relativism and of empiricism in a universe in which the very master pattern of creation is unfinished. They taught that the truth of an idea can be determined only by its consequences. Dewey added that in a chancy world we have only intelligence on which to depend, and ideas must be the instruments with which we seek to make improvements. Pragmatism, as the event turned out, was both prelude and stimulus to that vastly significant development of the twentieth century, the social sciences.

In the time of the first Timothy Dwight the undergraduates of Yale College derived their ideas about society from Jedidiah Morse's *American Geography,* Joseph Priestley's *Lectures on History,* Vattel's *Law of Nations,* Montesquieu's *Spirit of Laws,* and William Paley's *Moral and Political Philosophy.* After 1900 and particularly after World War I, history and the social sciences underwent a swift development in the emerging university. In America, economics, human geography, anthropology, sociology, political science, and social psychology, pushing forward in their contiguous and often overlapping domains, set off the twentieth from any previous century. All aspects of society—business enterprise, government, the family, organized

religion—came under the scrutiny and underwent the analyses
of investigators. Psychology dealt with the person moving
within an enveloping culture. As the century passed its meridi-
an, men assumed that, though progress had been great, the
development of the social sciences had but begun.

In this new world of the natural and the social sciences the
liberal arts, in spite of growth and change, did not alter their
ancient essential character. They still sought to discover the
nature of the universe, its purpose and meaning, and man's
destiny in it. They still tried to find out the characteristics of
the good life for society and for the individual. But the sum of
knowledge had grown to a vast magnitude. Transformation
in civilization visibly followed the accumulation of this knowledge. More and more men put their hope for a better world
in the use of reason. Secularism provided the major outlook of
educated Americans in the middle decades of the century.

But the liberal arts, conserving, criticizing, and developing
the tradition of the West, could not ignore religion. From before the beginning of recorded history man had been preoccupied with religion. At Yale the study of religion appeared
again and again in the disciplines of the liberal arts. Anthropologists at Yale amassed in the Human Relations Area Files
a vast body of knowledge about religions (and all other important aspects of culture) drawn from scores of subliterate
and many literate societies. The Files, organized to make information easily and quickly accessible, became an aid to research of prime importance. Instruction in the social sciences,
using a positivistic approach, dealt with religion as an omni-
present aspect of culture. The Department of Religion, including both Christian and Jewish scholars, explored and taught
the Judaic-Christian heritage of the West.

The study of literature and the fine arts evolved in the
twentieth century as vigorously as that of the sciences. Inevitably the arts and the literature of ancient and modern Europe
reflect the hopes and aspirations, the values and the faith of
Western man as he has moved through three millennia.

Dante, Michelangelo, and Milton are only a few of those who remind us how impossible it is to escape religion in the fields of literature and art. These also, of course, reflect the conquests, the exploitations, the hates, and the doubts of other centuries. The twentieth-century University fostered the study of literature and the arts not only that its students might know the heritage of the past and learn to appreciate the beautiful but that they might come to understand the possibilities of the human spirit.

History could no more avoid dealing with religion than could anthropology or art. Twentieth-century Yale historians explored many aspects of the Judeo-Christian tradition so important for the West—excavations bringing to light at Dura-Europos in the Middle East a shrine of Mithra and near it an early Christian baptistry; the editing of the Dead Sea Scrolls of St. Mark's monastery; an analysis of the symbols of Judaism in the Greco-Roman period; the expression of medieval Christianity in the early Gothic of Notre Dame of Noyon and in the abbey of St. Denis; the revolt of Martin Luther; the exploration of the Christian symbolism of the Spanish renaissance built into the churches of Mexico; the studies of men who affected the development of Christianity in the United States and of the relation of Christianity to American ideals and values. This partial list suggests the range.

Nor was investigation limited to Judaism and Christianity. Since 1844, when Edward Elbridge Salisbury published *Memoirs of the History of Buddhism,* Yale had been pre-eminent in Indic and Buddhistic studies—language, history, and art. A notable event in a distinguished record occurred in 1950. In that year the Dalai Lama of Tibet had specially printed as a gift to the Sterling Library the one hundred volumes of the Lhasa edition of the Kanjur, the scriptures of the Lamaist form of Buddhism. An ancient and aloof mountain people in a fine gesture shared their best with the great Republic of the New World.

An event in 1951 reminded a twentieth-century generation that criticism and controversy were also part of the religious tradition at Yale. President Clap, when he seceded from the First Church and founded an independent congregation in the College, raised up enemies who would neither forgive nor forget. Their running attack, aided by a student revolt, forced him finally out of office. Moreover, the ill will engendered by Clap's policies and actions smoldered in Connecticut for more than a quarter of a century until Stiles' statesmanship put out the fires by bringing about a new and firm understanding with the state.

In 1828 a sermon in which Nathaniel W. Taylor detailed the liberal affirmations of the New Haven Theology he had done so much to formulate roused into action a large company of preachers of a conservative Calvinism. Benet Tyler, clergyman, of the Class of 1804, led the campaign against Yale's Professor of Didactic Theology. When the protagonists of orthodoxy failed to compel the Corporation to dismiss Taylor, they founded at East Windsor the Theological Institute of Connecticut, to conserve and propagate the truth as the conservatives saw it. The strength and duration of this attack on the manner of dealing with theology at Yale is suggested by the fact that Tyler held for twenty-three years the post of president of the institution founded to combat the errors that passed for religion in New Haven.

In 1951 William F. Buckley, Jr., who as an undergraduate had been Chairman of the *News,* published a book called *God and Man at Yale.* The young man addressed his message to the graduates of the University. Buckley, a Roman Catholic who held strong views on religious and economic matters, argued that the method of dealing with religion in the scholarship and teaching of Yale College was "anti-Christian." Instructors, he said in effect, must not merely lead students in a search for truth; instructors must declare the truth as set forth in orthodox formulations of religious faith. In a spirited conclusion Buckley, who was soon to associate himself with the work of

Senator Joseph McCarthy of Wisconsin, warned his fellow
alumni of "Yale's intellectual drive toward agnosticism and
collectivism."[1] He declared that the alumni should require an
erring faculty to teach sound doctrine in economics and in
religion. Although the book caused some momentary flurry,
in contrast with the prolonged contentions of other days the
controversy it stirred up was short-lived and soon forgotten.

In 1953, two years after the appearance of the Buckley book,
Edmund W. Sinnott, botanist and geneticist, published *Two
Roads to Truth*. In it he amplified a position he had taken in
1947 when he had addressed a company of scientists gathered
to celebrate the centennial of the Sheffield Scientific School of
which Sinnott was the Director. In the speech and in the later
book Sinnott addressed himself to the same problem that had
caused Benjamin Silliman concern, namely the relations of
science and religion. "These two great roads to truth," said
Sinnott, "—the way of science, confident in reason, and the
way of faith, depending on the insights of the spirit—do not
follow the same course. Sometimes they lie not far apart, but
oftener they seem to move in very different directions."
Horace Bushnell said much the same thing in his famous
lectures in 1848 in New Haven, Cambridge, and Andover.
He urged, as did Sinnott, that men put confidence in the intuitions of the spirit. And both men reached the same conclusions regarding science and religion. "As time goes on,"
said Sinnott, ". . . as religion gives up its primitive dogmatisms
and as a deeper understanding of the universe tempers the
naïve materialism of primitive science, these two avenues seem
less divergent and to be leading toward the same destination."
Along with Silliman's concern for science and religion and
with Bushnell's preoccupation with the life of the spirit, the
religious tradition at Yale had emphasized from the beginning
the reality of the problem of evil. Sinnott dealt also with this
in the book that reflected so often the thinking and the diffi-

culties of earlier generations at Yale. "Let us not delude ourselves," said the Director of the Scientific School in 1953,
"into an easy optimism that science must inevitably support
religion or that there is now no conflict between them. Something too much of this there long has been with those who seek
an easy faith. Man is a creature of both mind and spirit, and
destined to be the battleground between them." The situation
does not call for pessimism. "We should not regret these differences between the disciplines of reason and of spirit but
rather rejoice in them. They are the two halves that make man
whole. From tension between them character is born. Perhaps
in us is being fought out a skirmish in the great battle of the
universe. Man, half ape and half angel, half matter and half
spirit, has a place within each world. Herein lies his glory, his
tragedy, and the possibility for him of tremendous things. . . .
Science and religion, ministering so diversely to the life of
man, will necessarily follow different roads but they still can
powerfully reinforce one another. Surely they should enlarge
their boundaries together."[2] At Yale, well before the Church
reached the end of its second century, the boundaries of religion were enlarging along with those of science.

In the expanded parish of the University the Church carried
on quietly but effectively. As always, faculty families and some
from the town joined with undergraduates and with students
in the graduate schools to make up the membership and the
congregation. The Secretary of Dwight Hall became an associate pastor, thus interlocking the work of the Christian Association with that of the Church. An assistant pastor organized
and led a Sunday School for children. A succession of visiting
clergymen brought to Battell each his own message from the
Christian faith. The pastor and associate pastor, however, conducted the service each Sunday and themselves preached from
time to time. In this way they maintained the continuity that
characterizes a living church. Normally once a year the Church
brought to Yale a clergyman or layman outstanding for his
contributions to the religious life of the century to conduct a

mission. Here were considered the outlook and the faith of religion together with their potential meanings for the good life.

The passing years after 1928 accumulated evidence that the abolition of compulsory chapel had brought strength rather than weakness to the Church. Battell became a place where worship through music, ritual, and prayers took precedence over preaching, important and distinguished as the latter was. Battell served on Sundays. On five days each week the Harkness chimes called those who cared to come to a noonday service in Dwight Chapel. Noah Porter, refusing in the 1870's to accede to an undergraduate request that compulsion be abolished, did not believe that voluntary weekday services could succeed. Their continuance, after 1928, with only an interruption in time of war, suggests that the Church had achieved a maturity in the twentieth-century University it never reached in the days of the old College.

A third sanctuary, Branford Chapel, a retreat for meditation and prayer, was consecrated in Harkness Tower. At the same time Marquand Chapel in the Divinity School held prayers on weekdays and special services in periods such as Advent and Lent. The existence of four chapels, each dedicated to a special purpose, did not signify that a revival of the type fostered by the elder Dwight had swept through the Yale community. Great numbers of busy undergraduates and members of the faculty passed them by. But they stood in the midst of the University, places where those who chose to make the effort could find enlargement of the life of the spirit. The open doors of the four chapels symbolized the approach to religion of the twentieth-century Yale Church. "Religion," said Sidney Lovett one Sunday in Battell, "is not a metaphysic; religion is a way of life."

Notes

CHAPTER I

1. The addresses are quoted in George P. Fisher, *A Discourse Commemorative of the History of the Church of Christ in Yale College during the First Century of Its Existence, Preached in the College Chapel, November 22, 1857* (1858), pp. 49–50. Fisher was a first-class historian. Both his address and his voluminous appendices contain a wealth of information.

CHAPTER 2

1. Thomas Clap published in the form of pamphlets four writings in 1745. Two dealt with a controversy with Jonathan Edwards growing out of a misunderstanding on Clap's part of the theological significance of some of Edwards' publications. Another dealt with what Clap considered the menace to the standing order arising from the preaching of Whitefield. A fourth set forth the reasons for the expulsion of Brainerd.

2. Diary in the Yale Library. Printed as an appendix in George P. Fisher, *A Discourse Commemorating the History of the Church of Christ in Yale College,* 1858.

3. John Wollebius, *The Abridgement of Christian Divinity* (1660), pp. 14, 83, 86, 169, 231.

4. Thomas Clap, *The Religious Constitution of Colleges, Especially Yale College,* 1754.

5. Pamphlet in the Yale Library.

CHAPTER 3

1. Quoted in E. Edwards Beardsley, *The History of the Episcopal Church in Connecticut* (1865), p. 255.

2. Quoted in Beardsley, p. 260.

3. Franklin B. Dexter, ed., *The Literary Diary of Ezra Stiles* (New York, 1901), *2,* 279.

4. Timothy Dwight, *A Discourse on Some Events in the Last Century,* 1801. Pamphlet in the Yale Library.

5. Dexter, *Diary, 2,* 351.

6. Ibid., p. 492.

7. Ibid., p. 423.

8. Ibid., *3,* 531.

9. Ibid., p. 123.

10. Quoted in Francis Parsons, *Six Men of Yale* (New Haven, 1939), p. 46.

11. Dexter, *Diary, 3,* 326.

12. Manuscript in the Yale Library.

13. Dexter, *Diary, 3,* 386–7.

CHAPTER 4

1. Timothy Dwight, *Sermons* (1828), *1*, 394–5.
2. Timothy Dwight, *Dwight's Travels in New England and New York* (1822), *4*, 173 f.
3. Theodore Dwight, Jr., *President Dwight's Decisions of Questions Discussed by the Senior Class in Yale College in 1813 and 1814* (1833), pp. 84, 88.
4. William Child. Quoted in William L. Kingsley, *Yale College, a Sketch of Its History* (N.Y. 1879), *1*, 273–4.
5. Lyman Beecher, *Autobiography* (1864–65), p. 44.
6. Quoted in George P. Fisher, *Life of Benjamin Silliman* (1866), *1*, 115.
7. Letter of Daniel Mulford, written in Jan. 1806, in the Yale Library.
8. *Travels, 4*, 465, 468.
9. *Sermons, 1*, 49–50.
10. Ibid., pp. 341 f.
11. *The Duty of Americans, at the Present Crisis, illustrated in a Discourse Preached on the Fourth of July, 1798 . . . at the request of the citizens of New Haven*, 1798 (pamphlet).
12. Quoted in George P. Fisher, *Life of Benjamin Silliman* (1866), *1*, 83.
13. *Sermons, 2*, 199.
14. Records of the Moral Society, in the Yale Library.
15. *Sermons, 2*, 417.
16. Beecher, *Autobiography, 1*, 46.
17. E. W. Dwight, *Memoir of Henry Obookiah* (New York [n.d.]), pp. 26–7.
18. Ibid., p. 31.
19. *Travels, 4*, 323–32.

CHAPTER 5

1. Timothy Dwight, *Memories of Yale Life and Men* (New York, 1903), p. 34.
2. *Autobiography, 1*, 384.
3. John Mitchell, *Scenes and Characters in College* (1847), p. 202.
4. Ibid., p. 106.
5. *Microscope*, No. 14.
6. Ibid., No. 37.
7. *The Religious Intelligencer, 12*, No. 33 (Jan. 12, 1828); No. 34 (Jan. 19, 1828).
8. Mitchell, *Scenes and Characters*, pp. 158–64.
9. Ibid., pp. 191–3.

CHAPTER 7

1. William Paley, *Works*, 1849; *Moral and Political Philosophy*, pp. 9, 24, 35, 134.
2. *Works; Evidences of Christianity*, pp. 68 f.

3. *Works; Natural Theology*, p. 102, III.

4. Benjamin Silliman, *Consistency of the Discoveries of Modern Geology with the Sacred History of the Creation and the Deluge; Being a Supplement to the Second American from the Fourth English Edition of Bakewell's Geology* (1833), pp. 5, 49, 78.

5. November 20, 1824.

6. *Addresses at the Inauguration of President Woolsey, October 21, 1846* (pamphlet).

7. Ibid.

CHAPTER 8

1. *The Yale Literary Magazine* (April 1857), p. 247.

2. *Addresses at the Inauguration of Theodore Woolsey*, p. 59.

3. Daniel Coit Gilman, in *The Yale Literary Magazine* (Nov. 1851), pp. 48–9.

4. Ibid. (April 1852), p. 206.

5. T. D. Woolsey Manuscripts, Yale Library.

6. The Minute Books are in the Yale Library.

7. Manuscript diary of Seabury Ford, Book V, p. 32; Book VI, p. 84, in the Yale Library.

8. Dwight, *Memories of Yale Life and Men*, pp. 77–8.

9. Eleazar T. Fitch, *Sermons Practical and Descriptive Preached in the Pulpit of Yale College* (1871), pp. 329–30.

10. *Yale Tomahawk* (Nov. 1849), p. 1.

11. Jeremiah Day, *A Sermon Delivered in Boston, September 17, 1823* (pamphlet).

12. The Sketch Book of the Band, with these and other biographies, is in the Yale Library.

13. Woolsey Manuscripts.

14. Oct. 1851, pp. 31–2.

15. *Lit* (Nov. 1851), p. 47.

16. Ibid. (Oct. 1851), p. 36.

17. George P. Fisher, *Thoughts Proper to the Present Crisis*, 1861 (pamphlet).

18. Quoted in Mary Bushnell Cheney, *Life and Letters of Horace Bushnell* (1880), pp. 485–7.

CHAPTER 9

1. Charles W. Beets, in *Harper's New Monthly Magazine* (Oct. 1871), quoted in Charles Schuchert and Clara M. LeVene, *O. C. Marsh, Pioneer in Paleontology* (New Haven, 1940), p. 104.

2. *The New Englander, 70* (Jan. 1871), 157–8.

3. *Addresses at the Farewell Dinner to Herbert Spencer . . .* (pamphlet).

4. James D. Dana, *The Genesis of the Heavens and the Earth and All the Most of Them* (1890), pp. 7, 62, 67–9.

5. Quoted in Harris E. Starr, *William Graham Sumner* (New York, 1925), pp. 167–8.

6. Timothy Dwight, *Yale College—The New Era* (1871), pp. 84–5.

7. Noah Porter, *Fifteen Years in the College Chapel* (1888), pp. 19–20.

8. Ibid., pp. 49–50, 55.

9. Starr, *Sumner,* pp. 346–7.

10. Ibid., p. 360. The original communication is in the Yale Library.

11. Henry A. Beers, *The Ways of Yale in the Consulship of Plancus* (New York, ed. of 1910), p. 382.

CHAPTER 10

1. *The Yale Record, 4* (1875–76), 272.

2. *Fifteen Years in the College Chapel,* 44–5.

3. *Record, 4,* 439.

4. *Two Centuries of Christian Activity at Yale* (1901), p. 169.

5. Horace Bushnell, *God in Christ* (1877), pp. 314, 353–4.

6. Theodore Woolsey, *Religion of the Present and of the Future* (1871), pp. 388, 401.

7. *Fifteen Years in the College Chapel,* pp. 249–56.

8. Ibid., pp. 408–9.

9. *Memories of Yale Life and Men,* pp. 471–3.

10. Timothy Dwight, *Thoughts for and of the Inner Life* (1899), p. 164.

CHAPTER 11

1. *The Ways of Yale,* p. 10.

2. Ibid., pp. 11–12.

3. Henry Drummond, *Natural Law in the Spiritual World* (1884), pp. ii, 309.

4. William Lyon Phelps, *Autobiography with Letters* (New York and London, 1939), pp. 200–1.

5. Benjamin Bacon, *Jesus and Paul* (New York, 1921), p. 250.

6. Arthur Twining Hadley, *Baccalaureate Addresses and Other Talks on Kindred Themes* (New York, 1907), p. 89.

7. George Stewart, Jr., *The Life of Henry B. Wright* (New York, 1925), p. vii.

8. Ibid., pp. 222 f.

9. The letters of Coffin, Mendell, Sherrill, and Noyes are in the Angell Papers in Woodbridge Hall, Yale University.

CHAPTER 12

1. Sidney Lovett, *Association Address, Ninth Annual Conference of the National Association of College and University Chaplains,* Vassar College, April 10, 1956.

2. Charles Reynolds Brown, *Yale Talks* (New Haven, 1919), pp. 155–6.

3. George H. Nettleton, *Yale in the World War* (New Haven, 1925), *1,* 285.

4. Oct. 27, 1933, in Angell Papers, in Woodbridge Hall.

5. *Association Address.*
6. Benjamin Bacon, *Non-resistance, Christian or Pagan?* (New Haven, 1918), pp. 5, 25, 27.

CHAPTER 13

1. *Yale Alumni Weekly,* 35 (1926), 589–90.
2. Corporation Records, in Woodbridge Hall, Yale University.
3. Ralph H. Gabriel, ed., *Christianity and Modern Thought* (New Haven, 1924), p. 16.
4. Charles Reynolds Brown, *What Is Your Name?* (New Haven, 1924), pp. 80, 126.
5. Ibid., pp. 82–3.
6. Jerusalem Meeting I.M.C., 1928, *The Christian Message,* 1 (1928), 401–2.
7. Angell Papers, in Woodbridge Hall, Yale University.
8. *Yale Daily News,* Oct. 4, 1926.
9. Corporation Records.
10. Angell Papers.
11. Lovett, *Association Address.*

CHAPTER 14

1. William F. Buckley, Jr., *God and Man at Yale: the Superstitions of Academic Freedom* (Chicago, 1951), p. 114.
2. Edmund W. Sinnott, *Two Roads to Truth* (New York, 1953), pp. 203, 234 f.

Index

scholar, 198; Dwight Hall Bible classes, 204, 208, 210; fundamentalism and biblical literalism, 222; Yale courses in biblical literature, 223; Charles R. Brown reads Scripture, 232; and pietism at turn of 20th century, 248. *See also* Biblical criticism

Biblical criticism: Silliman interprets Genesis, 114–15; Dana interprets Bible in terms of cosmogony, 157–8; D. F. Straus on Jesus as myth, 163; Benjamin Bacon on Jesus and Paul, 198; abandonment of criticism in Dwight Hall Bible classes, 204, 208, 210; Christology in the *1920's*, 231; lack of criticism and pietism at turn of 20th century, 248

Black, Hugh, 178

Blount, Charles, 69

Board of Foreign Missions of the Presbyterian Church, 200

Borden, William, 202

Boston Tea Party, 35, 73

Bracebridge Hall, 107

Brainerd, David, 16

Branford Chapel, 255

Brick Row, 79, 92, 96, 98

Brothers in Unity: founded, 22; originally secret, 72; persists along with newer fraternities and societies, 129; rivalry with other debating societies, 148–9; library, 187, 229; practice of oratory, 187

Brown, Charles Reynolds: at "Wednesday at Five" meeting, 204; patriotic sermon, World War I, 214–15; breaks with pacifists, 217; repents of intolerance toward pacifists, 219; opposes compulsory chapel, 228; as preacher, characteristics of his thought, 231–3

Brown, John, 150

Brown University, 126, 142

Bryan, William Jennings, 222, 232

Buchman, Frank N. D., 205–6

Buckley, William F., Jr., 252–3

Buddha, 218 f.

Buddhism, 251

Bully, office of, 73, 88, 94

Burgoyne, Gen. John, 38

Bushnell, David, 80

Bushnell, Horace: leads student rebellion, 84; influenced by Coleridge, 122; fa-

vorite chapel preacher, 126–7; founds Beethoven Society, 146; preaches a transcendental theology, 147, 173–4, 247, 253; memorial address at Commencement, *1865,* 151

Byers Hall, 191

Caesar, 194; Timothy Dwight (first), as "Caesar," 44, 79

Calhoun, John C., 101

Calliope: founded, 88; persists beside newer fraternities and societies, 129; membership made up of students from the South, 148–50; encourages oratory, 187; library of, 229

Calvin, John, 81. *See also* Calvinism

Calvinism: Sabbath as symbol, 1–2; of Thomas Clap, 10; in 18th-century Connecticut churches, 13; Edwards modifies, 14; Old Lights and New Lights, 16; fosters constitutionalism, 18; doctrines presented by Wollebius, 22–5; and Ezra Stiles, 39; modified by (first) Timothy Dwight, 56; basic to Dwight's thought, 81; in early 19th-century Yale, 83; doctrine of conversion in early 19th century, 86–7; emphasis on duty, 103; criticism of doctrine of determinism, 121; as modified in the New Haven Theology, 133–7, 247; of President Woolsey, 175–6; Mark Twain's rejection of, 192; in Thomas Clap's Yale, 245, 252; and the problem of evil, 253

Cambridge University, 7, 101, 109, 187, 241; King's College Chapel, 241

Camp, Walter, 187–8, 198

Campbell, Charles, 219–20

Campbell, E. Fay, 216, 219 ff., 233–5, 241–2

Capone, Al, 222

Carleton College, 145

Carlyle, Thomas, 224

Carr, Eugene A., 152

Cartwright, Peter, 75

Catholicism: in New France, 6–7, 29–30; Wollebius on, 24; Stiles and Catholics in Rochambeau's army, 47; (first) Timothy Dwight on, 48, 70; and Spanish missions on frontier, 58; and John R. Mott, 199; fund raising in World War I, 220; Ku Klux Klan

century, 222, 234; as part of tradition of Western civilization, 224–5

Sketch Book, 129

Smith, Adam, 109

Smith, Charles H., 171–2

Smollett, Tobias George, 7

Snowbound, 9

Social Gospel, 184–5, 195, 202–3, 207, 230, 248

Social sciences. *See* Science, social

Socialism, 194–5

Sociology, 156, 163, 164–7, 249 f.

Socrates, 67

Sophocles, 64

Sparks, Jared, 102

Speer, Robert E., 200, 206

Spencer, Herbert, 154–5, 163 f., 165–7, 179 ff.

Spirit of Laws, 47, 249

Spitzer, Lyman, Jr., 242–3

Stagg, Alonzo, 202

Stamp Act, 34, 51, 65–6

Standing Order of Connecticut, 2, 10, 12, 15, 33–4, 56, 59, 85–6, 87

Stanford University, 215

Stewart, Dugald, 135, 247

Stewart, George, Jr., 203, 205

Stewart, Gilbert, 81

Stiles, Ezra: as Hebrew scholar, 21; as scholar, 21, 45–8, 100, 108, 148, 245; attitude toward deism, 30, 51–2; tolerance, 30, 39, 47–8, 51–3, 245; president of Yale, 38–53; plan for a university, 38; as chapel preacher, 41–3, 50–1, 97, 137; and (first) Timothy Dwight, 43–4, 48–9; as administrator, 45, 49, 99, 158, 252; and B. Franklin, 51–2, 65; J. L. Kingsley and, 102; death, 54; and J. Meigs, 54, 61–2

Stoeckel, Gustav, 147

Stowe, Harriet Beecher, 86, 149

Straus, D. F., 163

Stuart, Moses, 62

Student Friendship Fund, 220, 230

Student life: in Clap's time, 11–12, 14, 16 f., 18–20, 30–1; in Stiles' time, 49–51; in time of (first) Timothy Dwight, 62–3, 71–9; in Day's time, 83–5, 87–90, 94–6; *1828–60,* 126–30, 132, 134, 139, 142–50; in last third of 19th century, 187–9; in opening years of 20th cen-

tury, 207–11; after World War I, 220, 226–8

Student Volunteer Movement, 199

Sumner, William Graham, 159–60, 162, 165–7, 175, 181, 183, 185–6, 196 f., 206, 223, 250

Tacitus, 102

Tales of a Traveler, 107

Taney, Roger B., 150

Taylor, Nathaniel William, 132–7, 144, 149, 161, 173, 247, 252

Taylor, Zachary, 117

Temple, William, Archbishop of Canterbury, 234–5

Tennyson, Alfred, 224

Test oath of orthodoxy, 26–7, 28, 30, 39, 46–7, 100

Thales, 67

Theater, in America, 64

Theological Institute of Connecticut, 252

Theology: doctrine of conversion, 14, 87; of Clap, 22–5, 29, 245; of Wollebius, 22–5; of (first) Timothy Dwight, 56, 61, 80–2, 246; natural theology, 110, 113, 122, 180, 239; of Woolsey, 122–4, 175; and science, 114–16, 122–4, 155–6, 175, 193, 254; New Haven Theology, 133–7, 173, 247, 252; of Bushnell, 147, 173–6, 247; of Porter, 162–3, 130; of Drummond, 193; of Rauschenbusch, 197; of (second) Timothy Dwight, 200; in *1920's,* 226; of C. R. Brown, 231–3; of McKee, 239; of Sinnott, 254

Theology of an Evolutionist, 178

Thomas, Norman, 207, 216

Thoreau, Henry David, 138, 224

Thoughts of and for the Inner Life, 185

Thurston, John L., 201

Tinker, Chauncey B., 224

Tolstoi, Leo, 218

Tomlinson, Gideon, 99

Townshend Acts, 34

Transcendentalism, 103, 122–4, 133, 138, 173, 224

Treatise on the Gods, 222

Treaty of Paris, 29

Trinity Church of New Haven, 17

Triumph of Infidelity, 48–9

Trumbull, John (painter), 81, 120